双语名著无障碍阅读丛书

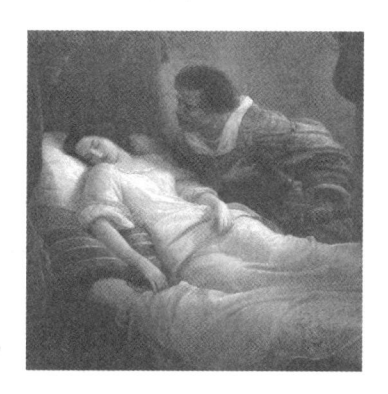

经典集锦

奥赛罗

Othello

[英国] 莎士比亚 著
朱生豪 译

中国出版集团
中译出版社

图书在版编目(CIP)数据

奥赛罗:英汉对照 / (英)莎士比亚著;朱生豪译. —北京:中译出版社,2017.6(2019.4 重印)

(双语名著无障碍阅读丛书)

ISBN 978-7-5001-5277-4

Ⅰ.①奥… Ⅱ.①莎… ②朱… Ⅲ.①英语－汉语－对照读物 ②悲剧－剧本－英国－中世纪 Ⅳ.①H319.4: I

中国版本图书馆CIP数据核字(2017)第108694号

出版发行 / 中译出版社
地　　址 / 北京市西城区车公庄大街甲4号物华大厦6层
电　　话 / (010) 68359827；68359303（发行部）；53601537（编辑部）
邮　　编 / 100044
传　　真 / (010) 68357870
电子邮箱 / book@ctph.com.cn
网　　址 / http://www.ctph.com.cn

总 策 划 / 张高里　贾兵伟
策划编辑 / 胡晓凯
责任编辑 / 胡晓凯　范祥镇
封面设计 / 潘　峰
排　　版 / 北京竹页文化传媒有限公司
印　　刷 / 保定市中画美凯印刷有限公司
经　　销 / 新华书店

规　　格 / 710毫米×1000毫米　1/16
印　　张 / 17.75
字　　数 / 278千字
版　　次 / 2017年6月第一版
印　　次 / 2019年4月第二次

ISBN 978-7-5001-5277-4　定价：25.00元

版权所有　侵权必究

中 译 出 版 社

出版前言

多年以来，中译出版社有限公司（原中国对外翻译出版有限公司）凭借国内一流的翻译和出版实力及资源，精心策划、出版了大批双语读物，在海内外读者中和业界内产生了良好、深远的影响，形成了自己鲜明的出版特色。

二十世纪八九十年代出版的英汉（汉英）对照"一百丛书"，声名远扬，成为一套最权威、最有特色且又实用的双语读物，影响了一代又一代英语学习者和中华传统文化研究者、爱好者；还有"英若诚名剧译丛""中华传统文化精粹丛书""美丽英文书系"，这些优秀的双语读物，有的畅销，有的常销不衰反复再版，有的被选为大学英语阅读教材，受到广大读者的喜爱，获得了良好的社会效益和经济效益。

"双语名著无障碍阅读丛书"是中译专门为中学生和英语学习者精心打造的又一品牌，是一个新的双语读物系列，具有以下特点：

选题创新——该系列图书是国内第一套为中小学生量身打造的双语名著读物，所选篇目均为教育部颁布的语文新课标必读书目，或为中学生以及同等文化水平的社会读者喜闻乐见的世界名著,重新编译为英汉(汉英)对照的双语读本。这些书既给青少年读者提供了成长过程中不可或缺的精神食粮,又让他们领略到原著的精髓和魅力,对他们更好地学习英文大有裨益;同时,丛书中入选的《论语》《茶馆》《家》等汉英对照读物,亦是热爱中国传统文化的中外读者所共知的经典名篇,能使读者充分享受阅读经典的无限乐趣。

无障碍阅读——中学生阅读世界文学名著的原著会遇到很多生词和文化难点。针对这一情况,我们给每一本读物原文中的较难词汇和不易理解之处都加上了注释,在内文的版式设计上也采取英汉(或汉英)对照方式,扫清了学生阅读时的障碍。

优良品质——中译双语读物多年来在读者中享有良好口碑,这得益于作者和出版者对于图书质量的不懈追求。"双语名著无障碍阅读丛书"继承了中译双语读物的优良传统——精选的篇目、优秀的译文、方便实用的注解,秉承着对每一个读者负责的精神,竭力打造精品图书。

愿这套丛书成为广大读者的良师益友,愿读者在英语学习和传统文化学习两方面都取得新的突破。

目录 CONTENTS

DRAMATIS PERSONAE
剧中人物 ……………………………………… 003

SCENE
地点 …………………………………………… 003

ACT I
第一幕

Scene I.　Venice. A street.
第一场　威尼斯　街道 …………………… 007

Scene II.　Another street.
第二场　另一街道 ………………………… 021

Scene III.　A council chamber.
第三场　议事厅 …………………………… 031

目录
CONTENTS

ACT II
第二幕

Scene I.　A seaport in Cyprus. An open place near the quay.
第一场　塞浦路斯岛海口一市镇
　　　　码头附近的广场 ·················· 063

 Scene II.　A street.
第二场　街道 ·························· 087

Scene III.　A hall in the castle.
第三场　城堡中的厅堂 ·················· 089

ACT III
第三幕

Scene I.　Before the castle.
第一场　城堡前 ························ 119

Scene II.　A room in the castle.
第二场　城堡中的一室 ·················· 125

Scene III.　The garden of the castle.
第三场　城堡中的花园 ·················· 127

目录
CONTENTS

Scene IV.　Before the castle.
第四场　城堡前 ················ 165

ACT IV
第四幕

Scene I.　Cyprus. Before the castle.
第一场　塞浦路斯　城堡前 ················ 183

Scene II.　A room in the castle.
第二场　城堡中的一室 ················ 205

Scene III.　Another room in the castle.
第三场　城堡中的另一室 ················ 225

ACT V
第五幕

Scene I.　Cyprus. A street.
第一场　塞浦路斯　街道 ················ 235

Scene II.　A bedchamber in the castle.
第二场　城堡中的卧室 ················ 247

William Shakespeare

DRAMATIS PERSONAE

Othello, the Moor, general of the Venetian forces
Desdemona, wife to Othello
Iago, a villan, ensign to Othello
Emilia, wife to Othello, lady-in-waiting to Desdemona
Cassio, an Honourable lieutenant, lieutenant to Othello
Duke of Venice
Brabantio, Venetian Senator, father of Desdemona
Gratiano, nobleman of Venice, brother of Brabantio
Lodovico, nobleman of Venice, kinsman of Brabantio
Roderigo, a gull'd Gentleman, rejected suitor of Desdemona
Bianca, mistress Of Cassio
Montano, a Cypriot official
A Clown in service to Othello
Senators, Sailors, Messengers, Officers, Gentlemen, Musicians and Attendants

SCENE

Act I. at Venice; Others at a seaport in Cyprus

剧中人物

威尼斯公爵
勃拉班修　　　　元老
格拉蒂亚诺　　　勃拉班修之弟
洛多维科　　　　勃拉班修的亲戚
奥赛罗　　　　　摩尔族贵裔，供职威尼斯政府
卡西奥　　　　　奥赛罗的副将
伊阿古　　　　　奥赛罗的旗官
罗德利哥　　　　威尼斯绅士
蒙塔诺　　　　　塞浦路斯总督，奥赛罗的前任者
小丑　　　　　　奥赛罗的仆人
苔丝狄蒙娜　　　勃拉班修之女，奥赛罗之妻
埃米莉亚　　　　伊阿古之妻
比安卡　　　　　卡西奥的情妇

元老，水手，吏役，绅士，使者，乐工，传令官，侍从等

地　点

第一幕在威尼斯；其余各幕在塞浦路斯岛一海口

ACT I

第一幕

Scene I. Venice. A street.

Enter Roderigo and Iago.

Rod. Tush, never tell me! I take it much unkindly
That thou, Iago, who hast had my purse
As if the **strings**① were thine, shouldst know of this.

Iago. 'Sblood, but you will not hear me.
If ever I did dream of such a matter,
Abhor② me.

Rod. Thou told'st me, thou didst hold him in thy hate.

Iago. Despise me, if I do not. Three great ones of the city,
In personal suit to make me his **lieutenant**③,
Off-capp'd to him; and by the faith of man,
I know my price, I am worth no worse a place.
But he, as loving his own pride and purposes,
Evades④ them, with a bumbast circumstance
Horribly stuff'd with **epithets**⑤ of war,
And in conclusion,
Nonsuits⑥ my mediators. For "certes," says he,
"I have already chose my officer."
And what was he?

第一场　威尼斯　街道

① string[striŋ] *n.* 线，带，细绳

② abhor [əb'hɔ:] *v.* （厌恶地）回避

③ lieutenant [lef'tenənt; lu:'t-] *n.* 副职官员

④ evade [i'veid] *v.* （巧妙地）逃脱，逃避

⑤ epithet ['epiθet] *n.* 表达方式，措辞

⑥ nonsuit [,nɔn'sju:t] *v.* （法院）驳回（原告、诉讼案）

罗德利哥及伊阿古上。

罗德利哥　嘿！别对我说，伊阿古；我把我的钱袋交给你支配，让你随意花用，你却做了他们的同谋，这太不够朋友啦。

伊阿古　他妈的！你总不肯听我说下去。要是我做梦会想到这种事情，你不要把我当作人。

罗德利哥　你告诉我你一向对他怀恨的。

伊阿古　要是我不恨他，你从此别理我。这城里的三个当道要人亲自向他打招呼，举荐我做他的副将；凭良心说，我知道我自己的价值，难道我就做不得一个副将？可是他眼睛里只有自己没有别人，对于他们的请求，都用一套充满了军事上口头禅的空话回绝了；因为，他说："我已经选定我的将佐了。"他选中的是个什么人呢？哼，一个算学大家，一个叫作迈克尔·卡西奥的佛罗伦萨人，一个几乎因为娶了娇妻而误了终身的家伙；他从来不曾在战场上领过一队兵，对于布阵作战的知识，简直比不上一个老守空闺的女人知道得更多；即使懂得一些书本上的理论，那些身穿宽袍的元老大

ACT I

        Forsooth①, a great **arithmetician**②,
        One Michael Cassio, a Florentine
        A fellow almost damn'd in a fair wife,
        That never set a **squadron**③ in the field,
        Nor the division of a battle knows
        More than a spinster. Unless the bookish theoric:
        Wherein the toged **consuls**④ can propose
        As masterly as he. Mere **prattle**⑤ without practice
        Is all his soldiership. But he, sir, had the election;
        And I, of whom his eyes had seen the proof
        At Rhodes, at Cyprus and on other grounds,
        Christian and **heathen**⑥, must be belee'd and calm'd
        By debitor and creditor. This counter-caster,
        He in good time must his lieutenant be,
        And I — God bless the mark! — his Moorship's Ancient.
Rod.   By heaven, I rather would have been his hangman.
Iago.   Why, there's no remedy. 'tis the curse of service,
        Preferment goes by letter and affection,
        And not by old gradation, where each second
        Stood heir to the first. Now sir, be judge yourself,
        Whether I in any just term am **affined**⑦
        To love the Moor?
Rod.   I would not follow him then.
Iago.   O sir, content you.
        I follow him to serve my turn upon him:
        We cannot all be masters, nor all masters
        Cannot be truly follow'd. You shall mark
        Many a **duteous**⑧ and knee-crooking **knave**⑨,
        That doting on his own **obsequious**⑩ bondage
        Wears out his time, much like his master's ass,

① forsooth [fɔ'su:θ] *ad.* [古语] 的确，确实，真的，无疑 [现多用于反语，含讽刺意味]
② arithmetician [ə,riθmə'tiʃən] *n.* 算术家；精通算术的人
③ squadron ['skwɔdrən] *n.* 一队
④ consul ['kɔnsəl] *n.* （古罗马的）两执政官之一
⑤ prattle ['prætl] *v.* 空谈

⑥ heathen ['hi:ðən] *a.* 异教徒的，异教信仰的

⑦ affined [ə'faind] *a.* （法律上或道德上）有义务（约束）的

⑧ duteous ['dju:tjəs] *a.* 尽职的，守本分的，恭顺的
⑨ knave [neiv] *n.* [古语] 童仆，男仆；出身或地位卑贱的人
⑩ obsequious [əb'si:kwiəs] *a.* 谄媚的，奉承的，巴结的

人们讲起来也会比他更头头是道；只有空谈，毫无实际，这就是他的全部的军人资格。可是，老兄，他居然得到了任命；我在罗兹岛、塞浦路斯岛，以及其他基督徒和异教徒的国土之上，立过多少的军功，都是他亲眼看见的，现在却必须低首下心，受一个市侩的指挥。这位掌柜居然做起他的副将来，而我呢——上帝恕我这样说——却只在这位黑将军的麾下充一名旗官。

罗德利哥 天哪，我宁愿做他的刽子手。

伊阿古 这也是没有办法呀。说来真叫人恼恨，军队里的升迁可以全然不管古来的定法，按照各人的阶级依次递补，只要谁的脚力大，能够得到上官的欢心，就可以越级蹿升。现在，老兄，请你替我评一评，我究竟为了什么得要跟这摩尔人要好。

罗德利哥 假如是我，我就不愿跟随他。

伊阿古 啊，老兄，你放心吧；我之所以跟随他，不过是要利用他达到我自己的目的。我们不能每个人都是主人，每个主人也不是都有忠心的仆人。有一辈天生的奴才，他们卑躬屈膝，拼命讨主人的好，甘心受主人的鞭策，像一头驴子似的，为了一些粮草而出卖他们的一生，等到年纪老了，主人就把他们撵走；这种老实的奴才是应该抽一顿鞭子的。还

>   For nought but provender, and when he's old, cashier'd.
>   Whip me such honest knaves. Others there are
>   Who trimm'd in forms and **visages**① of duty,
>   Keep yet their hearts attending on themselves,
>   And throwing but shows of service on their lords
>   Do well thrive by them; and when they have lined their coats
>   Do themselves **homage**②. These fellows have some soul,
>   And such a one do I **profess**③ myself. For sir,
>   It is as sure as you are Roderigo,
>   Were I the Moor, I would not be Iago.
>   In following him, I follow but myself;
>   Heaven is my judge, not I for love and duty,
>   But seeming so, for my peculiar end.
>   For when my outward action doth demonstrate
>   The native act and figure of my heart
>   In complement extern, 'tis not long after
>   But I will wear my heart upon my sleeve
>   For **daws**④ to peck at: I am not what I am.
> **Rod.** What a full fortune does the thick-lips owe,
>   If he can carry 't thus?
> **Iago.** Call up her father,
>   Rouse him, make after him, poison his delight,
>   Proclaim him in the streets, incense her kinsmen,
>   And though he in a fertile climate dwell,
>   Plague him with flies; though that his joy be joy,
>   Yet throw such changes of vexation on 't,
>   As it may lose some color.
> **Rod.** Here is her father's house; I'll call aloud.
> **Iago.** Do, with like **timorous**⑤ accent and dire yell,
>   As when, by night and **negligence**⑥, the fire

第一幕

① visage ['vizidʒ] n. 面貌，外表

② homage ['hɔmidʒ] n. 尊敬，敬意

③ profess [prəu'fes] v. 承认

有一种人，他们表面上尽管装出一副鞠躬如也的样子，骨子里却是为他们自己打算；看上去好像替主人做事，实际却在靠着主人发展自己的势力，等捞足了油水，就可以知道他所尊敬的其实是他本人；这种人还有几分头脑，我自己就属于这一类。因为，老兄，正像你是罗德利哥，不是别人一样，我要是做了那摩尔人，我就不会是伊阿古。虽说跟随他，其实还是跟随自己。上天是我的公证人，我这样对他赔着小心，既不是为了感情，又不是为了义务，只是为了自己的利益，才装出这一副假脸。要是我表面上的行动果然出于内心的自然流露，那么不久我就要掏出我的心来，让乌鸦们乱啄了。世人所知道的我，并不是实在的我。

④ daw [dɔ:] n.【鸟类】寒鸦，鹅哥

罗德利哥　要是那厚嘴唇的家伙也有这一手，那他干什么都会顺利哩！

伊阿古　叫起她的父亲来；不要放过他，打断他的兴致，在各处街道上宣布他的罪恶；激怒她的亲族。让他虽然住在气候宜人的地方，也免不了受蚊蝇的滋扰，虽然享受着盛大的欢乐，也免不了受烦恼的缠绕。

罗德利哥　这儿就是她父亲的家里；我要高声叫喊。

伊阿古　很好，你嚷起来吧，就像在一座人口众多的城里，因为晚间失慎而起火的时候，人们用那种惊骇

⑤ timorous ['timərəs] a. 胆小的，畏怯的，易受惊的

⑥ negligence ['neglidʒəns] n. 疏忽，玩忽；玩忽行为

ACT I

        Is spied in populous cities.
Rod.   What, ho, Brabantio! Signior Brabantio, ho!
Iago.   Awake! What, ho, Brabantio! Thieves! Thieves!
        Look to your house, your daughter, and your bags!
        Thieves! Thieves!
        Brabantio appears above, at a window.
Bra.   What is the reason of this terrible summons?
        What is the matter there?
Rod.   Signior, is all your family within?
Iago.   Are your doors lock'd?
Bra.   Why? Wherefore ask you this?
Iago.   Sir, you're robb'd, for shame, put on your **gown**①;
        Your heart is burst, you have lost half your soul;
        Even now, now, very now, an old black **ram**②
        Is tupping your white **ewe**③. Arise, arise,
        Awake the snorting citizens with the bell,
        Or else the devil will make a **grandsire**④ of you.
        Arise, I say!
Bra.   What, have you lost your wits?
Rod.   Most **reverend**⑤ signior, do you know my voice?
Bra.   Not I. What are you?
Rod.   My name is Roderigo.
Bra.   The worser welcome.
        I have charged thee not to haunt about my doors:
        In honest plainness thou hast heard me say,
        My daughter is not for thee. And now, in madness,
        Being full of supper and distempering **draughts**⑥,
        Upon malicious bravery, dost thou come
        To start my quiet.
Rod.   Sir, sir, sir—

惶恐的声音呼喊一样。

罗德利哥　喂,喂,勃拉班修!勃拉班修先生,喂!

伊阿古　醒来!喂,喂,勃拉班修!捉贼!捉贼!捉贼!留心你的屋子,你的女儿和你的钱袋!捉贼!捉贼!

　　　　　　勃拉班修自上方窗口上。

勃拉班修　大惊小怪地叫什么呀?出了什么事?

罗德利哥　先生,您家里的人没有缺少吗?

伊阿古　您的门都锁上了吗?

勃拉班修　咦,你们为什么这样问我?

伊阿古　哼!先生,有人偷了您的东西去啦,还不赶快披上您的袍子!您的心碎了,您的灵魂已经丢掉半个;就在这时候,就在这一刻工夫,一头老黑羊在跟您的白母羊交尾哩。起来,起来!打钟惊醒那些鼾睡的市民,否则魔鬼要让您抱孙子啦。喂,起来!

勃拉班修　什么!你发疯了吗?

罗德利哥　老先生,您听得出我的声音吗?

勃拉班修　我听不出,你是谁?

罗德利哥　我的名字是罗德利哥。

勃拉班修　讨厌!我叫你不要在我的门前走动;我已经老老实实明明白白对你说,我的女儿是不能嫁给你的;现在你吃饱了饭,喝醉了酒,疯疯癫癫,不怀好意,又要来扰乱我的安静了。

罗德利哥　先生,先生,先生!

① gown [gaun] *n.* 宽大的长外衣

② ram [ræm] *n.* 公羊

③ ewe [ju:] *n.* 母(绵)羊

④ grandsire ['grænd,saiə] *n.* [古语](外)祖父

⑤ reverend ['revərənd] *a.* 应受尊敬的,可尊敬的

⑥ draught [drɑ:ft; dræft] *n.* [口语]从桶中汲取的一份啤酒;散装啤酒

Bra. But thou must needs be sure,

My spirit and my place have in them power

To make this bitter to thee.

Rod. Patience, good sir.

Bra. What tell'st thou me of robbing?

This is Venice; My house is not a **grange**①.

Rod. Most grave Brabantio,

In simple and pure soul, I come to you.

Iago. Zounds, sir, you are one of those that will not serve God, if the devil bid you. Because we come to do you service, and you think we are **ruffians**②, you'll have your daughter covered with a Barbary horse; you'll have your nephews neigh to you; you'll have **coursers**③ for cousins, and gennets for germans.

Bra. What **profane**④ wretch art thou?

Iago. I am one, sir, that comes to tell you, your daughter and the Moor are now making the beast with two backs.

Bra. Thou are a villain.

Iago. You are a senator.

Bra. This thou shalt answer; I know thee, Roderigo.

Rod. Sir, I will answer anything. But I **beseech**⑤ you,

If 't be your pleasure and most wise **consent**⑥,

As partly I find it is, that your fair daughter,

At this odd even and dull watch o' the night,

Transported with no worse nor better guard,

But with a knave of common hire, a **gondolier**⑦,

To the gross clasps of a **lascivious**⑧ Moor:

If this be known to you, and your allowance,

We then have done you bold and **saucy**⑨ wrongs.

But if you know not this, my manners tell me,

We have your wrong **rebuke**⑩. Do not believe

① grange [greindʒ] *n.* 田庄，农庄

② ruffian ['rʌfiən] *n.* 流氓，无赖，恶棍

③ courser ['kɔ:sə] *n.* [诗歌用语] 骏马，战马

④ profane [prəu'fein] *a.* 平凡的；鄙俗的

⑤ beseech [bi'si:tʃ] *v.* 哀求，恳求

⑥ consent [kən'sent] *n.* 同意

⑦ gondolier [,gɔndə'liə] *n.* 威尼斯小划船船夫

⑧ lascivious [lə'siviəs] *a.* 好色的

⑨ saucy ['sɔ:si] *a.* 无礼的

⑩ rebuke [ri'bju:k] *n.* 斥责，训斥

勃拉班修 可是你必须明白，我不是一个好说话的人，要是你惹我发火，凭着我的地位，只要略微拿出一点力量来，你就要叫苦不迭了。

罗德利哥 好先生，不要生气。

勃拉班修 说什么有贼没有贼？这儿是威尼斯；我的屋子不是一座独家的田庄。

罗德利哥 最尊严的勃拉班修，我是一片诚心来通知您。

伊阿古 嘿，先生，您也是那种因为魔鬼叫他敬奉上帝，而把上帝丢在一旁的人。您把我们当作了坏人，所以把我们的好心看成了恶意，宁愿让您的女儿给一头黑马骑了，替您生下一些马子马孙，攀一些马亲马眷。

勃拉班修 你是个什么混账东西，敢这样胡说八道？

伊阿古 先生，我是一个特意来告诉您一个消息的人，令爱现在正在跟那摩尔人干那件禽兽一样的勾当哩。

勃拉班修 你是个混蛋！

伊阿古 您是一位——元老呢。

勃拉班修 你留点儿神吧；罗德利哥，我认识你。

罗德利哥 先生，我愿意负一切责任；可是请您允许我说一句话。要是令爱因为得到您的明智的同意，所以才会在这样更深人静的午夜，让一个公爵的奴才，一个下贱的船夫，把她载到一个贪淫的摩尔人的粗野的怀抱里——要是您对于这件事情不但知道，而且默许——照我看来，您至少已经给她一部分的同意——那么我们的确太放肆太冒昧了；可是假如您果真不知道这件事，那么从礼貌上说起来，您也不应该对我们恶声相向。难道我会这样一点不懂规矩，敢来戏侮像您这样一位年

ACT I

        That from the sense of all civility,
        I thus would play and **trifle with**① your reverence.
        Your daughter, if you have not given her leave,
        I say again, hath made a gross revolt,
        Tying her duty, beauty, wit and fortunes
        In an **extravagant**② and wheeling stranger
        Of here, and everywhere: straight satisfy yourself.
        If she be in her chamber or your house,
        Let loose on me the justice of the State
        For thus deluding you.
Bra.   Strike on the tinder, ho!
        Give me a **taper**③! call up all my people!
        This accident is not unlike my dream,
        Belief of it oppresses me already.
        Light, I say, light!
        Exit.
Iago.   Farewell, for I must leave you.
        It seems not meet, nor wholesome to my place,
        To be produced as if I stay, I shall
        Against the Moor. For I do know the state,
        However this may gall him with some check,
        Cannot with safety cast him. For he's **embark'd**④
        With such loud reason to the Cyprus wars,
        Which even now stands in act, that for their souls,
        Another of his **fathom**⑤ they have none,
        To lead their business. In which regard,
        Though I do hate him as I do hell pains,
        Yet for necessity of present life,
        I must show out a flag and sign of love,
        Which is indeed but sign, that you shall surely find him,

① trifle with 玩弄

② extravagant [ik'strævəgənt] a. [古语]游荡的，漫游的，闲逛的；流浪的

③ taper ['teipə] n. (细长)小蜡烛

④ embark [em'bɑ:k] v. 开始工作

⑤ fathom ['fæðəm] n. 洞察力，理解力

尊的长者吗？我再说一句，要是令爱没有得到您的许可，就把她的责任、美貌、智慧和财产，全部委弃在一个到处为家、漂泊流浪的异邦人的身上，那么她的确已经干下了一件重大的逆行了。您可以立刻去调查一个明白。要是她好好儿地在她的房间里或是在您的屋子里，那么我是欺骗了您，您可以按照国法惩办我。

勃拉班修　喂，点起火来！给我一支蜡烛！把我的仆人全都叫起来！这件事情很像我的噩梦，它的极大的可能性已经重压在我的心头上了。喂，拿火来！拿火来！（自上方下）

伊阿古　再会，我要少陪了；要是我不去，我就不得不与这摩尔人当面对质，那不但不大相宜，而且在我的地位上也有很多不便；因为我知道无论他将要因此而受到什么谴责，政府方面现在还不能就冒险将他免职，他就要出发指挥那正在进行中的塞浦路斯的战事了，这是他们必须宽宥他的一个重大的理由，因为没有第二个人有像他那样的才能，可以担当这一个重任。所以虽然我恨他像恨地狱里的刑罚一样，可是为了事实上的必要，我不得不和他假意周旋，那也不过是表面上的敷衍而已。你等他们出来找人的时候，只要领他们到市政厅去，一定可以找到他；我也在那边跟他在一起。再见。（下）

勃拉班修率众仆持火炬自下方上。

ACT I

Lead to the Sagittary, the raised search:

And there will I be with him. So farewell.

Exit.

Enter, below, Brabantio, in his nightgown, and Servants with torches.

Bra. It is too true an evil. Gone she is,

And what's to come of my despised time,

Is nought but bitterness. Now Roderigo,

Where didst thou see her? Oh unhappy girl!

With the Moor, say'st thou? Who would be a father?

How didst thou know 'twas she? Oh she deceives me

Past thought: what said she to you? Get more tapers:

Raise all my **kindred**①. Are they married think you?

Rod. Truly I think they are.

Bra. Oh Heaven! How got she out? Oh treason of the blood!

Fathers, from hence trust not your daughters' minds

By what you see them act. Is there not charms,

By which the property of youth, and maidhood

May be abused? Have you not read, Roderigo,

Of some such thing?

Rod. Yes, sir, I have indeed.

Bra. Call up my brother. Oh would you had had her!

Some one way, some another. Do you know

Where we may **apprehend**② her and the Moor?

Rod. I think I can discover him, if you please

To get good guard and go along with me.

Bra. Pray you lead on. At every house I'll call,

I may command at most: get weapons, ho!

And raise some special officers of night.

On, good Roderigo, I'll deserve your pains.

Exeunt.

第一幕

勃拉班修 真有这样的祸事！她去了；只有悲哀怨恨伴着我这衰朽的余年！罗德利哥，你在什么地方看见她的？——啊，不幸的孩子！——你说跟那摩尔人在一起吗？——谁还愿意做一个父亲！——你怎么知道是她？——唉，想不到她会这样欺骗我！——她对你怎么说？——再拿些蜡烛来！唤醒我的所有的亲族！——你想他们有没有结婚？

罗德利哥 说老实话，我想他们已经结了婚啦。

勃拉班修 天啊！她怎么出去的？啊，血肉的叛逆！做父亲的人啊，从此以后，你们千万留心你们女儿的行动，不要信任她们的心思。世上有没有一种引诱青年少女失去贞操的魔术？罗德利哥，你有没有在书上读到过这一类的事情？

罗德利哥 是的，先生，我的确读到过。

勃拉班修 叫起我的兄弟来！唉，我后悔不让你娶了她去！你们快去给我分头找寻！你知道我们可以在什么地方把她和那摩尔人一起捉到？

罗德利哥 我想我可以找到他的踪迹，要是您愿意多派几个得力的人手跟我前去。

勃拉班修 请你带路。我要到每一个人家去搜寻；大部分的人家都在我的势力之下。喂，多带一些武器！叫起几个巡夜的警吏！去，好罗德利哥，我一定重谢你的辛苦。（同下）

① kindred ['kindrid] *n.* [总称] 亲属，亲戚

② apprehend [ˌæpri'hend] *v.* 逮捕，捕捉

Scene II. Another street.

Enter Othello, Iago and Attendants with torches.

Iago. Though in the trade of war I have **slain**① men,
Yet do I hold it very stuff o' the conscience
To do no **contrived**② murther: I lack **iniquity**③
Sometimes to do me service. Nine or ten times
I had thought to have yerk'd him here under the ribs.

Othello. 'Tis better as it is.

Iago. Nay but he **prated**④,
And spoke such **scurvy**⑤ and provoking terms
Against your honor,
That with the little godliness I have,
I did full hard forbear him. But I pray you, sir,
Are you fast married? Be assured of this,
That the Magnifico is much beloved,
And hath in his effect a voice potential
As double as the Duke's. He will divorce you,
Or put upon you, what restraint and grievance,
The law, with all his might to enforce it on,
Will give him cable.

第二场　另一街道

① slay [slei] v. 杀死
② contrive [kən'traiv] v. 策划
③ iniquity [i'nikwəti] n. 罪恶

④ prate [preit] v. 唠叨
⑤ scurvy ['skə:vi] a. 卑鄙的，无耻的，下流的

　　　　　　奥赛罗，伊阿古及侍从等持火炬上。
伊阿古　虽然我在战场上杀过不少的人，可是总觉得有意杀人是违反良心的；缺少作恶的本能，往往使我不能做我所要做的事。好多次我想要把我的剑从他的肋骨下面刺进去。
奥赛罗　还是随他说去吧。
伊阿古　可是他唠里唠叨地说了许多破坏您的名誉的难听话，虽然像我这样一个荒唐的家伙，也实在忍不住我的怒气。可是请问主帅，你们有没有完成婚礼？您要注意，这位元老是很得人心的，他的潜势力比公爵还要大上一倍；他会拆散你们的姻缘，尽量运用法律的力量来给您种种压制和迫害。

ACT I

Othello. Let him do his **spite**①.
    My services, which I have done the Signiory,
    Shall out-tongue his complaints. 'tis yet to know,
    Which when I know, that boasting is an honor,
    I shall **promulgate**②. I fetch my life and being,
    From men of royal siege, and my **demerits**③
    May speak unbonneted to as proud a fortune
    As this that I have reach'd. For know Iago,
    But that I love the gentle Desdemona,
    I would not my unhoused free condition
    Put into **circumscription**④ and confine,
    For the sea's worth. But look, what lights come yond?
Iago. Those are the raised father and his friends.
    You were best go in.
Othello. Not I; I must be found.
    My parts, my title, and my perfect soul
    Shall manifest me rightly. Is it they?
Iago. By Janus, I think no.
Enter Cassio, with torches.
Othello. The servants of the Duke? And my Lieutenant?
    The goodness of the night upon you, friends.
    What is the news?
Cassio. The Duke does greet you, general,
    And he requires your haste-post-haste appearance,
    Even on the instant.
Othello. What is the matter, think you?
Cassio. Something from Cyprus, as I may divine:
    It is a business of some heat. The galleys
    Have sent a dozen sequent messengers
    This very night at one another's heels:

① spite [spait] *n.* 恶意，歹意

② promulgate ['prɔməlgeit] *v.* 公布，宣布

③ demerit [di:'merit] *n.* 缺点，短处

④ circumscription [ˌsə:kəm'skripʃən] *n.* 立界，划界

奥赛罗 随他怎样发泄他的愤恨吧；我对贵族们所立的功劳，就可以驳倒他的控诉。世人还没有知道——要是夸口是一件荣耀的事，我就到处宣布——我是高贵的祖先的后裔，我有充分的资格，享受我目前所得到的值得骄傲的幸运。告诉你吧，伊阿古，倘不是我真心爱恋温柔的苔丝狄蒙娜，即使给我大海中所有的珍宝，我也不愿意放弃我的无拘无束的自由生活，来俯就家室的羁缚的。可是瞧！那边举着火把走来的是些什么人？

伊阿古 她的父亲带着他的亲友来找您了；您还是进去躲一躲吧。

奥赛罗 不，我要让他们看见我；我的地位和我的清白的人格可以替我表明一切。是不是他们？

伊阿古 两面神在上，我想不是。

　　　　卡西奥及若干吏役持火炬上。

奥赛罗 原来是公爵手下的人，还有我的副将。晚安，各位朋友！有什么消息？

卡西奥 主帅，公爵向您致意，请您立刻就过去。

奥赛罗 你知道是为了什么事？

卡西奥 照我猜想起来，大概是塞浦路斯方面的事情，看样子很是紧急。就在这一个晚上，战船上已经连续派了十二个使者赶来告急；许多元老都从睡梦中

And many of the Consuls, raised and met,

Are at the Duke's already. You have been hotly call'd for,

When being not at your **lodging**① to be found,

The Senate hath sent about three several quests,

To search you out.

Othello. 'Tis well I am found by you:

I will but spend a word here in the house,

And go with you.

Exit.

Cassio. Ancient, what makes he here?

Iago. Faith, he tonight hath boarded a land **carack**②;

If it prove lawful prize, he's made for ever.

Cassio. I do not understand.

Iago. He's married.

Cassio. To who?

Re-enter Othello.

Iago. Marry to — Come Captain, will you go?

Othello. Have with you.

Cassio. Here comes another troop to seek for you.

Iago. It is Brabantio. General, be advised,

He comes to bad intent.

Enter Brabantio, Roderigo, and Officers with torches and weapons.

Othello. Holla! stand there!

Rod. Signior, it is the Moor.

Bra. **Down with**③ him, thief!

They draw on both sides.

Iago. You, Roderigo? Come sir, I am for you.

Othello. Keep up your bright swords, for the **dew**④ will **rust**⑤ them.

Good signior, you shall more command with years,

Than with your weapons.

① lodging ['lɔdʒiŋ] n.（临时）住处;（临时性）寓所

② carack ['kærək] n.【航海学】古代大战船

③ down with 打倒

④ dew [dju:; du:] n. 露水
⑤ rust [rʌst] v. 生锈

被人叫了起来，在公爵府里集合了。他们正在到处找您；因为您不在家里，所以元老院派了三队人出来分头寻访。

奥赛罗 幸而我给你找到了。让我到这儿屋子里说一句话，就来跟你同去。（下）

卡西奥 他到这儿来有什么事？

伊阿古 不瞒你说，他今天夜里登上了一艘陆地上的大船；要是能够证明那是一件合法的战利品，他可以从此成家立业了。

卡西奥 我不懂你的话。

伊阿古 他结了婚啦。

卡西奥 跟谁结婚？

奥赛罗重上。

伊阿古 呃，跟——来，主帅，我们走吧。

奥赛罗 好，我跟你走。

卡西奥 又有一队人来找您了。

伊阿古 那是勃拉班修。主帅，请您留心点儿；他来是不怀好意的。

勃拉班修，罗德利哥及吏役等持火炬武器上。

奥赛罗 喂！站住！

罗德利哥 先生，这就是那摩尔人。

勃拉班修 杀死他，这贼！（双方拔剑）

伊阿古 你，罗德利哥！来，我们来比个高下。

奥赛罗 收起你们明晃晃的剑，它们沾了露水会生锈的。老先生，像您这么年高德劭的人，有什么话不可以命令我们，何必动起武来呢？

Bra. O thou foul thief, where hast thou stow'd my daughter?
　　　　Damn'd as thou art, thou hast **enchanted**① her,
　　　　For I'll refer me to all things of sense,
　　　　If she in chains of magic were not bound,
　　　　Whether a maid so tender, fair and happy,
　　　　So opposite to marriage that she **shunn'd**②
　　　　The wealthy curled darlings of our nation,
　　　　Would ever have, to incur a general mock,
　　　　Run from her guardage to the **sooty**③ bosom,
　　　　Of such a thing as thou: to fear, not to delight?
　　　　Judge me the world, if 'tis not gross in sense,
　　　　That thou hast practiced on her with foul charms,
　　　　Abused her delicate youth with drugs or minerals,
　　　　That weaken motion. I'll have 't disputed on;
　　　　'Tis probable, and **palpable**④ to thinking;
　　　　I therefore apprehend and do attach thee
　　　　For an abuser of the world, a practicer
　　　　Of arts **inhibited**⑤ and out of warrant;
　　　　Lay hold upon him, if he do resist,
　　　　Subdue⑥ him at his peril.

Othello. Hold your hands,
　　　　Both you of my inclining and the rest.
　　　　Were it my cue to fight, I should have known it
　　　　Without a **prompter**⑦. Where will you that I go
　　　　To answer this your charge?

Bra. To prison, till fit time
　　　　Of law and course of direct session
　　　　Call thee to answer.

Othello. What if I do obey?
　　　　How may the Duke be therewith satisfied,

① enchant [in'tʃɑ:nt; en-] v. 用妖术（或法术）迷惑

② shun [ʃʌn] v. 避开

③ sooty ['su:ti] a. 炭黑色的

④ palpable ['pælpəbl] a. 明显可知的

⑤ inhibit [in'hibit] v. 抑制，约束

⑥ subdue [səb'dju:] v. 征服

⑦ prompter ['prɔmptə] n. 敦促者

勃拉班修 啊，你这恶贼！你把我的女儿藏到什么地方去了？你不想想你自己是个什么东西，胆敢用妖法蛊惑她；我们只要凭着情理判断，像她这样一个年轻貌美娇生惯养的姑娘，多少我们国里有财有势的俊秀子弟她都看不上眼，倘不是中了魔，怎么会不怕人家的笑话，背着尊亲投奔到你这个丑恶的黑鬼的怀里？——吓都把她吓坏了，还有什么乐趣可言。世人可以替我评一评，是不是显而易见你用邪恶的符咒欺诱她的娇弱的心灵，用药饵丹方迷惑她的知觉；我要叫他们评论评论，这种事情是不是很可能的。所以我现在逮捕你；妨害风化，行使邪术，便是你的罪名。抓住他；要是他敢反抗，你们就用武力制伏他。

奥赛罗 帮助我的，反对我的，大家放下你们的手！我要是想打架，我自己会知道应该在什么时候动手。您要我到什么地方去答复您的控诉？

勃拉班修 到监牢里去，等法庭上传唤你的时候你再开口。

奥赛罗 要是我听从您的话去了，那么怎么答复公爵呢？他的使者就在我的身边，因为有紧急的公事，

ACT I

           Whose messengers are here about my side,
           Upon some present business of the State
           To bring me to him.
1st Officer.   'Tis true, most worthy Signior;
           The Duke's in Council, and your noble self,
           I am sure, is sent for.
Bra.   How? The Duke in **council**[①]?
           In this time of the night? Bring him away;
           Mine's not an idle cause. The Duke himself,
           Or any of my brothers of the State,
           Cannot but feel this wrong as 'twere their own:
           For if such actions may have passage free,
           Bond-slaves and **pagans**[②] shall our **statesmen**[③] be.
           Exeunt.

① council ['kaunsəl] *n.* 会议

② pagan ['peigən] *n.* 异教徒
③ statesman ['steitsmən] *n.* 政治家

等候着带我去见他。

吏役 真的，大人；公爵正在举行会议，我相信他已经派人请您去了。

勃拉班修 怎么！公爵在举行会议！在这样夜深的时候！把他带去。我的事情也不是一件等闲小事；公爵和我的同僚们听见了这个消息，一定会感到这种侮辱简直就像加在他们自己身上一般。要是这样的行为可以置之不问，奴隶和异教徒都要来主持我们的国政了。（同下）

Scene III. A council chamber.

The Duke and Senators sitting at a table. Officers attending.

Duke.   There is no composition in these news,
   That gives them credit.

1st Senator.   Indeed they are **disproportion'd**①;
   My letters say a hundred and seven galleys.

Duke.   And mine, a hundred and forty.

2nd Senator.   And mine, two hundred.
   But though they jump not on a just account,
   As in these cases where the aim reports,
   'Tis off with difference yet do they all confirm
   A Turkish fleet, and **bearing up to**② Cyprus.

Duke.   Nay, it is possible enough to judgement:
   I do not so secure me in the error,
   But the main article I do approve
   In fearful sense.

Sailor.   [*Within.*] What hoa! what, hoa! what, hoa!

1st Officer.   A messenger from the galleys.
   Enter Sailor.

Duke.   Now, what's the business?

第三场　议事厅

① disproportion [dɪsprə'pɔːʃən]
v. 使不成比例

② bear up to 向……接近

公爵及众元老围桌而坐；吏役等随侍。

公爵　这些消息彼此分歧，令人难以置信。
元老甲　它们真是参差不一；我的信上说是共有船只一百零七艘。
公爵　我的信上说是一百四十艘。
元老乙　我的信上又说是二百艘。可是它们所报的数目虽然各自不同，因为根据估计所得的结果，难免多少有些出入，不过它们都证实确有一支土耳其舰队在向塞浦路斯岛进发。
公爵　嗯，这种事情推想起来很有可能；即使消息不尽正确，大体上总是有根据的，我们倒不能不担着几分心事。
水手　（在内）喂！喂！喂！有人吗？
吏役　一个从船上来的使者。
　　　——水手上。
公爵　什么事？

ACT I

Sailor. The Turkish preparation makes for Rhodes,
    So was I bid report here to the State
    By Signior Angelo.
Duke. How say you by this change?
1st Senator. This cannot be
    By no **assay**① of reason. 'Tis a **pageant**②
    To keep us in false gaze, when we consider
    The importancy of Cyprus to the Turk,
    And let ourselves again but understand,
    That as it more concerns the Turk than Rhodes,
    So may he with more **facile**③ question bear it,
    For that it stands not in such warlike brace,
    But altogether lacks the abilities
    That Rhodes is dress'd in. If we make thought of this,
    We must not think the Turk is so unskillful
    To leave that latest, which concerns him first,
    Neglecting an attempt of ease and gain,
    To wake and wage a danger profitless.
Duke. Nay, in all confidence, he's not for Rhodes.
1st Officer. Here is more news.

Enter a Messenger.

Messenger. The Ottomites, reverend and gracious,
    Steering with due course toward the isle of Rhodes,
    Have there injointed them with an after fleet.
1st Senator. Ay, so I thought. How many, as you guess?
Messenger. Of thirty sail; and now they do re-stem
    Their backward course, bearing with frank appearance
    Their purposes toward Cyprus. Signior Montano,
    Your trusty and most **valiant**④ **servitor**⑤,
    With his free duty recommends you thus,

① assay [ə'sei] *n.* 检查
② pageant ['pædʒənt] *n.* 夸耀；虚饰

③ facile ['fæsail] *a.* 易做到的

④ valiant ['væljənt] *a.* 英勇的
⑤ servitor ['sə:vitə] *n.* (男)侍从，仆人

水手 安杰洛大人叫我来此禀告殿下，土耳其人调集舰队，正在向罗兹进发。

公爵 你们对于这一个变动有什么意见？

元老甲 照常识判断起来，这是不会有的事；它无非是转移我们目标的一种诡计。我们只要想一想塞浦路斯对于土耳其人的重要性，远在罗兹岛以上，而且攻击塞浦路斯岛，也比攻击罗兹岛容易得多，因为它的防备比较空虚，不像罗兹岛那样戒备严密；我们只要想到这一点，就可以断定土耳其人绝不会那样愚笨，甘心舍本逐末，避轻就重，进行一场无益的冒险。

公爵 嗯，他们的目标绝不是罗兹岛，这是可以断定的。

吏役 又有消息来了。

　　　　一使者上。

使者 向罗兹岛前进的土耳其人，已经和后来的另外一支舰队会合了。

元老甲 嗯，果然符合我的预料。照你猜想起来，一共有多少船只？

使者 三十艘模样；它们现在已经回过头来，显然是要开向塞浦路斯岛去的。蒙塔诺大人，您的忠实英勇的仆人，叫我来向您报告这一个消息。

ACT I

And prays you to believe him.
Duke. 'Tis certain then for Cyprus.
Marcus Luccicos, is not he in town?
1st Senator. He's now in Florence.
Duke. Write from us, to him, post-post-haste **dispatch**①.
1st Senator. Here comes Brabantio and the valiant Moor.

Enter Brabantio, Othello, Iago, Roderigo and Officers.

Duke. Valiant Othello, we must straight employ you,
Against the general enemy Ottoman.
[*To Brabantio.*] I did not see you: welcome, gentle signior;
We lack'd your **counsel**② and your help tonight.
Bra. So did I yours. Good your grace, pardon me.
Neither my place nor aught I heard of business
Hath raised me from my bed, nor doth the general care
Take hold on me; for my particular grief
Is of so **flood-gate**③ and o'erbearing nature,
That it **engluts**④ and swallows other sorrows,
And it is still itself.
Duke. Why? What's the matter?
Bra. My daughter: oh my daughter!
All. Dead?
Bra. Ay, to me.
She is abused, stol'n from me and corrupted
By spells and medicines, bought of **mountebanks**⑤;
For nature, so **preposterously**⑥ to err,
Being not deficient, blind, or lame of sense,
Sans witchcraft could not.
Duke. Whoe'er he be, that in this foul proceeding
Hath thus **beguiled**⑦ your daughter of herself,
And you of her, the bloody Book of Law

① dispatch [dis'pætʃ] n.（尤指公文）快信，快件，急件

② counsel ['kaunsəl] n. 商议

③ flood-gate ['flʌdgeit] n. 大量

④ englut [in'glʌt] v. [古语、诗歌]（一口）吞下

⑤ mountebank ['mauntibæŋk] n. 江湖骗子

⑥ preposterous [pri'pɔstərəs] a. 反常的

⑦ beguile [bi'gail] v. 欺骗，诱骗

公爵 那么一定是到塞浦路斯岛去了的了。马库斯·勒西科斯不在威尼斯吗？

元老甲 他现在到佛罗伦萨去了。

公爵 替我写一封十万火急的信给他。

元老甲 勃拉班修和那勇敢的摩尔人来了。

　　　　勃拉班修、奥赛罗、伊阿古、罗德利哥及吏役等上。

公爵 英勇的奥赛罗，我们必须立刻派你出去向我们的公敌土耳其人作战。（向勃拉班修）我没有看见你；欢迎，先生，我们今晚正需要你的指教和帮助呢。

勃拉班修 我也同样需要您的指教和帮助。殿下，请您原谅，我并不是因为职责所在，也不是因为听到了什么国家大事而从床上惊起；国家的安危不能引起我的注意，因为我的个人的悲哀是那么压倒一切，把其余的忧虑一起吞没了。

公爵 啊，为了什么事？

勃拉班修 我的女儿！啊，我的女儿！

公爵、众元老 死了吗？

勃拉班修 嗯，她对于我是死了。她已经被人污辱，人家把她从我的地方拐走，用江湖骗子的符咒药物引诱她堕落；因为一个没有残疾、眼睛明亮、理智健全的人，倘不是中了魔法的蛊惑，绝不会犯这样荒唐的错误的。

公爵 用这种邪恶的手段引诱你的女儿，使她丧失自己的本性，使你丧失了她的，无论他是什么人，你都可以根据无情的法律，照你自己的解释给他应得的严刑；即使他是我的儿子，你也可以照样控诉他。

ACT I

>You shall yourself read in the bitter letter,
>After your own sense: yea, though our proper son
>Stood in your action.

Bra. Humbly I thank your grace.
>Here is the man, this Moor, whom now, it seems,
>Your special **mandate**① for the state affairs
>Hath hither brought.

All. We are very sorry for 't.

Duke. [*To Othello.*] What in your own part can you say to this?

Bra. Nothing, but this is so.

Othello. Most potent, grave, and reverend signiors,
>My very noble and approved good masters,
>That I have ta'en away this old man's daughter,
>It is most true; true I have married her;
>The very head and front of my offending,
>Hath this extent, no more. Rude am I in my speech,
>And little blest with the soft phrase of peace;
>For since these arms of mine, had seven years' pith,
>Till now some nine moons wasted, they have used
>Their dearest action in the tented field,
>And little of this great world can I speak,
>More than **pertains to**② feats of broil and battle;
>And therefore little shall I grace my cause,
>In speaking for myself. Yet, by your gracious patience,
>I will a round **unvarnish'd**③ tale deliver,
>Of my whole course of love: what drugs, what charms,
>What **conjuration**④, and what mighty magic,
>For such proceeding I am charged withal,
>I won his daughter.

Bra. A **maiden**⑤ never bold,

第一幕

① mandate ['mændeit] *n.* 命令

勃拉班修 感谢殿下。罪人就在这儿,就是这个摩尔人;好像您有重要的公事召他来的。

公爵、众元老 那我们真是抱憾得很。

公爵 (向奥赛罗)你自己对于这件事有什么话要分辩?

勃拉班修 没有,事情就是这样。

奥赛罗 威严无比,德高望重的各位大人,我的尊贵的贤良的主人们,我把这位老人家的女儿带走了,这是完全真实的,我已经和她结了婚,这也是真的;我的最大的罪状仅止于此,别的就不是我所知道的了。我的言语是粗鲁的,一点不懂得那些温文尔雅的辞令;因为自从我这双手臂长了七年的膂力以后,直到最近这九个月时间在无所事事中蹉跎过去以前,它们一直都在战场上发挥它们的本领;对于这一个广大的世界,我除了冲锋陷阵以外,几乎一无所知,所以我也不能用什么动人的字句替我自己辩护。可是你们要是愿意耐心听我说下去,我可以向你们讲述一段质朴无文的,关于我的恋爱的全部经过的故事;告诉你们我用什么药物、什么符咒、什么驱神役鬼的手段、什么神奇玄妙的魔法,骗到了他的女儿,因为这是他所控诉我的罪名。

② pertain to 涉及

③ unvarnished [ʌn'vɑ:niʃt] *a.* 未加修饰的

④ conjuration [ˌkɔndʒuə'reiʃən] *n.* 魔法

⑤ maiden ['meidən] *n.* (未婚的)青年女子

勃拉班修 一个素来胆小的女孩子,她的生性是那么幽

· 037 ·

ACT I

        Of spirit so still and quiet, that her motion
        Blush'd at herself; and she, in spite of nature,
        Of years, of country, credit, everything,
        To fall in love with what she fear'd to look on;
        It is judgement maim'd and most imperfect,
        That will confess perfection so could err
        Against all rules of nature, and must be driven
        To find out practices of **cunning**① hell
        Why this should be. I therefore vouch again,
        That with some mixtures powerful o'er the blood,
        Or with some **dram**② conjured to this effect,
        He wrought upon her.

Duke.   To **vouch**③ this is no proof,
        Without more wider and more **overt**④ test
        Than these thin habits and poor likelihoods
        Of modem seeming do prefer against him.

1st Senator.   But, Othello, speak.
        Did you by indirect, and forced courses
        Subdue⑤ and poison this young maid's affections?
        Or came it by request, and such fair question
        As soul to soul affordeth?

Othello.   I do beseech you,
        Send for the lady to the Sagittary,
        And let her speak of me before her father.
        If you do find me foul in her report,
        The trust, the office I do hold of you,
        Not only take away, but let your sentence
        Even fall upon my life.

Duke.   Fetch Desdemona hither.

Othello.   Ancient, conduct them; you best know the place.

① cunning ['kʌniŋ] a. 狡猾的

② dram [dræm] n.（酒）少许

③ vouch [vautʃ] v. 证实

④ overt ['əuvə:t; əu'və:t] a. 明显的，公开的

⑤ subdue [səb'dju:] v. 使服从

娴贞静，甚至于心里略为动了一点感情，就会满脸羞愧；像她这样的性格，像她这样的年龄，竟会不顾国族的畛域，把名誉和一切作为牺牲，去跟一个她瞧着都会感到害怕的人发生恋爱！假如有人竟会宣称，像她这样的好姑娘会做出这样有悖常理的事，这个人的头脑肯定是出了毛病。一定要细细查究，看到底是用了什么诡计才会发生这样的事。我断定他一定曾经用烈性的药饵或是邪术炼成的毒剂麻醉了她的血液。

公爵　没有更确实显明的证据，单单凭着这些表面上的猜测和莫须有的武断，是不能使人信服的。

元老甲　奥赛罗，你说，你有没有用不正当的诡计诱惑这一位年轻的女郎，或是用强暴的手段逼迫她服从你；还是正大光明地对她披肝沥胆，达到你的求爱的目的？

奥赛罗　请你们差一个人到马人旅馆去接这位小姐来，让她当着她的父亲的面告诉你们我是怎么一个人。要是你们根据她的报告，认为我是有罪的，你们不但可以撤销你们对我的信任，解除你们给我的职权，还可以把我判处死刑。

公爵　去把苔丝狄蒙娜带来。
奥赛罗　旗官，你领他们去；你知道她在什么地方。（伊

ACT I

Exeunt Iago and Attendants.

And till she come, as truly as to heaven,
I do confess the vices of my blood,
So justly to your grave ears, I'll present
How I did thrive in this fair lady's love,
And she in mine.

Duke. Say it, Othello.

Othello. Her father loved me, oft invited me,
Still question'd me the story of my life,
From year to year: the battles, **sieges**①, fortunes,
That I have pass'd.
I ran it through, even from my boyish days,
To the very moment that he bade me tell it.
Wherein I spake of most disastrous chances:
Of moving accidents by flood and field,
Of **hair-breadth**② 'scapes i' the **imminent**③ deadly breach,
Of being taken by the **insolent**④ foe,
And sold to slavery, of my **redemption**⑤ thence,
And portance in my travels' history.
Wherein of **antres**⑥ vast and deserts idle,
Rough quarries, rocks, and hills whose heads touch heaven,
It was my hint to speak. Such was the process,
And of the **Cannibals**⑦ that each other eat,
The Anthropophagi, and men whose heads
Do grow beneath their shoulders. These things to hear
Would Desdemona seriously incline;
But still the house affairs would draw her hence,
Which ever as she could with haste dispatch,
She'ld come again, and with a greedy ear
Devour⑧ up my discourse; which I observing,

阿古及侍从等下）当她没有到来以前，我要像对天忏悔我的血肉的罪恶一样，把我怎样得到这位美人的爱情和她怎样得到我的爱情的经过情形，忠实地向各位陈诉。

公爵 说吧，奥赛罗。

奥赛罗 她的父亲很看重我，常常请我到他家里，每次谈话的时候，总是问起我过去生命中的历史，要我讲述我所经历的各次战争、围城和意外的遭遇；我就把我的一生事实，从我的童年时代起，直到他叫我讲述的时候为止，原原本本地说了出来。我说起最可怕的灾祸，海上陆上惊人的奇遇，间不容发的脱险，在傲慢的敌人手中被俘为奴和遇赎脱身的经过，以及旅途中的种种见闻；那些广大的岩窟，荒凉的沙漠，突兀的崖嶂，巍峨的峰岭，以及彼此相食的野蛮部落和肩下生头的化外异民，都是我的谈话的题目。苔丝狄蒙娜对于这种故事，总是出神倾听；有时为了家庭中的事务，她不能不离座而起，可是她总是尽力把事情赶紧办好，再回来孜孜不倦地把我所讲的每一个字都听了进去。我注意到她这种情形，有一天在一个适当的时间，从她的嘴里逗出了她的真诚的心愿：她希望我能够把我一生的经历，对她做一次详细的复述，因为她平日所听到的，只是一鳞半爪，残缺不全的片段。我答应了她的要求；当我讲到我在少年时代所遭逢的不幸的打击的时候，她往往忍不住掉下泪来。我的故事讲完以后，她用无数的叹息酬劳我；她发誓说，那是非常奇异而悲惨的；她希望她没有听到这段故事，可是又

① siege [siːdʒ] n. 包围

② hair-breadth ['hɛəbredθ] a. 间不容发的

③ imminent ['iminənt] a. 即将发生的

④ insolent ['insələnt] a. 傲慢的

⑤ redemption [ri'dempʃən] n. 赎回

⑥ antre ['æntə] n. [古语、诗歌用语] 洞窟

⑦ cannibal ['kænibəl] n. 食人肉的人，食人生番

⑧ devour [di'vauə] v. 饥饿地、贪婪地、狼吞虎咽地吃

Took once a **pliant**① hour, and found good means
To draw from her a prayer of earnest heart,
That I would all my **pilgrimage**② **dilate**③,
Whereof by parcels she had something heard,
But not intentively. I did consent,
And often did beguile her of her tears,
When I did speak of some distressful stroke
That my youth suffer'd: My story being done,
 She gave me for my pains a world of sighs;
 She swore in faith 'twas strange: 'twas passing strange,
'twas pitiful, 'twas wondrous pitiful.
She wish'd she had not heard it, yet she wish'd
That heaven had made her such a man. She thank'd me,
And bade me, if I had a friend that loved her,
I should but teach him how to tell my story,
And that would woo her. Upon this hint I spake,
She loved me for the dangers I had pass'd,
And I loved her that she did pity them.
This only is the witchcraft I have used.
Here comes the Lady; let her witness it.
Enter Desdemona, Iago, and Attendants.

Duke. I think this tale would win my daughter too,
Good Brabantio,
Take up this **mangled**④ matter at the best:
Men do their broken weapons rather use
Than their bare hands.

Bra. I pray you hear her speak.
If she confess that she was half the wooer,
Destruction on my head, if my bad blame
Light on the man. Come hither gentle Mistress.

① pliant ['plaiənt] *a.* 灵活的
② pilgrimage ['pilgrimidʒ] *n.* 远游，人生经历
③ dilate [dai'leit] *v.* [古语] 详述

希望上天为她造下这样一个男子。她向我道谢，对我说，要是我有一个朋友爱上了她，我只要教他怎样讲述我的故事，就可以得到她的爱情。我听了这一个暗示，才向她吐露我的求婚的诚意。她为了我所经历的种种患难而爱我，我为了她对我所抱的同情而爱她；这就是我的唯一的妖术。她来了，让她为我证明吧。

苔丝狄蒙娜，伊阿古及侍从等上。

公爵 像这样的故事，我想我的女儿听了也会着迷的。勃拉班修，木已成舟，不必懊恼了。刀剑虽破，比起手无寸铁来，总是略胜一筹。

④ mangle ['mæŋgl] *v.*（因大错而）毁损，损坏，弄糟

勃拉班修 请殿下听她说；要是她承认她本来也有爱慕他的意思，而我却还要归咎于他，那就让我不得好死吧。过来，好姑娘，你看这在座的济济众人之间，谁是你所最应该服从的？

ACT I

    Do you perceive in all this noble company?
    Where most you owe obedience?
Desde. My noble father,
    I do perceive here a divided duty.
    To you I am bound for life and education;
    My life and education both do learn me,
    How to respect you. You are the lord of duty,
    I am **hitherto**① your daughter. But here's my husband,
    And so much duty as my mother show'd
    To you, preferring you before her father,
    So much I challenge that I may profess
    Due to the Moor, my lord.
Bra. God be with you! I have done.
    Please it your Grace, on to the state affairs;
    I had rather to adopt a child than get it.
    Come **hither**② Moor.
    I here do give thee that with all my heart,
    Which, but thou hast already, with all my heart
    I would keep from thee. For your sake, jewel,
    I am glad at soul, I have no other child;
    For thy escape would teach me tyranny,
    To hang **clogs**③ on them. I have done, my lord.
Duke. Let me speak like yourself, and lay a sentence,
    Which, as a grise or step, may help these lovers.
    When remedies are past, the griefs are ended
    By seeing the worst, which late on hopes depended.
    To mourn a **mischief**④ that is past and gone,
    Is the next way to draw new mischief on.
    What cannot be preserved when Fortune takes,
    Patience her injury a **mockery**⑤ makes.

① hitherto [ˌhiðə'tu:] ad. 到目前为止，迄今

② hither ['hiðə] ad. 向这里

③ clog [klɔg] n.（尤指绑在动物腿上以阻碍其行动的）重物

④ mischief ['mistʃif] n.（人为的）损害；祸害

⑤ mockery ['mɔkəri] n. 嘲笑，讥笑

苔丝狄蒙娜 我的尊贵的父亲，我在这里所看到的，是我的分歧的义务：对您说起来，我深荷您的生养教育的大恩，您给我的教养使我明白我应该怎样敬重您；您是我的家长和严君，我直到现在都是您的女儿。可是这儿是我的丈夫，正像我的母亲对您克尽一个妻子的义务，把您看得比她的父亲更重一样，我也应该有权利向这位摩尔人，我的夫主，尽我应尽的名分。

勃拉班修 上帝和你同在！我没有话说了。殿下，请您继续处理国家的要务吧，我宁愿抚养一个义子，也不愿自己生男育女。过来，摩尔人。我现在用我的全副诚心，把她给了你；倘不是你早已得到了她，我一定不会让她到你手里。为了你的缘故，宝贝，我很高兴我没别的儿女，否则你的私奔将要使我变成一个虐待儿女的暴君，替他们手脚加上镣铐。我没有话说了，殿下。

公爵 让我设身处地，说几句话给你听听，也许可以帮助这一对恋人，使他们能够得到你的欢心。

　　眼看希望幻灭，厄运临头，
　　无可挽回，何必满腹牢愁？
　　为了既成的灾祸而痛苦，
　　徒然招惹出更多的灾祸。
　　既不能和命运争强斗胜，
　　还是付之一笑，安心耐忍。

ACT I

    The robb'd that smiles steals something from the thief;
    He robs himself that spends a **bootless**① grief.
Bra. So let the Turk of Cyprus us beguile;
    We lose it not so long as we can smile.
    He bears the sentence well, that nothing bears
    But the free comfort which from thence he hears;
    But he bears both the sentence and the sorrow,
    That, to pay grief, must of poor patience borrow.
    These sentences, to sugar or to gall,
    Being strong on both sides, are **equivocal**②.
    But words are words; I never yet did hear
    That the bruised heart was pierced through the ear.
    I humbly beseech you, proceed to the affairs of state.
Duke. The Turk with a most mighty preparation makes for Cyprus. Othello, the **fortitude**③ of the place is best known to you; and though we have there a substitute of most allowed sufficiency, yet opinion, a sovereign mistress of effects, throws a more safer voice on you. You must therefore be content to **slubber**④ the **gloss**⑤ of your new fortunes, with this more stubborn, and **boisterous**⑥ **expedition**⑦.
Othello. The Tyrant Custom, most grave Senators,
    Hath made the **flinty**⑧ and steel couch of war
    My thrice-driven bed of down. I do agnize
    A natural and prompt **alacrity**⑨,
    I find in hardness and do undertake
    These present wars against the Ottomites.
    Most humbly therefore bending to your state,
    I crave fit disposition for my wife,
    Due reference of place and exhibition,
    With such accommodation and besort
    As levels with her **breeding**⑩.

① bootless ['bu:tlis] *a.* 无益的

② equivocal [i'kwivəkəl] *a.* 含糊的，不确定的

③ fortitude ['fɔ:titju:d] *n.* [废语] 坚固

④ slubber ['slʌbə] *v.* 弄脏
⑤ gloss [glɔs] *n.* （表面的）光泽
⑥ boisterous ['bɔistərəs] *a.* （大海、风浪、天气等）狂暴的
⑦ expedition [,ekspi'diʃən] *n.* 远征
⑧ flinty ['flinti] *n.* 极坚硬的
⑨ alacrity [ə'lækrəti] *n.* 乐意，欣然
⑩ breeding ['bri:diŋ] *n.* 身份

聪明人遭盗窃毫不介意；
痛哭流涕反而伤害自己。

勃拉班修 让敌人夺去我们的海岛，
我们同样可以付之一笑。
那感激法官仁慈的囚犯，
他可以忘却刑罚的苦难；
倘然他怨恨那判决太重，
他就要忍受加倍的惨痛。
种种譬解虽能给人慰藉，
它们也会格外添人悲戚；
可是空言毕竟无补实际，
几曾有一句话深入心底？
请殿下继续进行原来的公事吧。

公爵 土耳其人正在向塞浦路斯大举进犯；奥赛罗，那岛上的实力你是知道得十分清楚的；虽然我们派在那边代理总督职务的是一个公认为很有能力的人，可是大家的意思，都觉得由你去负责镇守，才可以万无一失；所以说只得打扰你的新婚的快乐，辛苦你去跑这一趟了。

奥赛罗 各位尊严的元老们，习惯的暴力已经使我把冷酷无情的战场当作我的温软的眠床，对于艰难困苦，我总是挺身而赴。我愿意接受你们的命令，去和土耳其人作战；可是我要请求你们给我的妻子一个适当的安置，按照她的身份，供给她一切日常的需要。

ACT I

Duke. If you please,
    Be 't at her father's.
Bra. I'll not have it so.
Othello. Nor I.
Desde. Nor would I there reside,
    To put my father in impatient thoughts
    By being in his eye. Most gracious Duke,
    To my unfolding lend your prosperous ear,
    And let me find a charter in your voice
    To assist my simpleness.
Duke. What would you, Desdemona?
Desde. That I did love the Moor to live with him,
    My downright violence and storm of fortunes,
    May trumpet to the world. My heart's subdued
    Even to the very quality of my lord.
    I saw Othello's **visage**[①] in his mind,
    And to his honors and his valiant parts,
    Did I my soul and fortunes **consecrate**[②].
    So that, dear lords, if I be left behind,
    A moth of peace, and he go to the war,
    The rites for which I love him are bereft me,
    And I a heavy **interim**[③] shall support
    By his dear absence. Let me go with him.
Othello. Let her have your voices.
    Vouch with me, Heaven, I therefore beg it not
    To please the **palate**[④] of my appetite,
    Nor to comply with heat — the young affects
    In me **defunct**[⑤] — and proper satisfaction.
    But to be free and **bounteous**[⑥] to her mind:
    And heaven defend your good souls, that you think

第一幕

公爵　你要是同意的话,可以让她住在她父亲的家里。

勃拉班修　我不愿意容留她。

奥赛罗　我也不能同意。

苔丝狄蒙娜　我也不愿住在父亲的家里,让他每天看见我生气。最仁慈的公爵,愿您俯听我的陈请,让我的卑微的衷忱得到您的谅解和赞助。

公爵　你有什么请求,苔丝狄蒙娜?

苔丝狄蒙娜　我大胆的行动可以代我向世人宣告,我因为爱这摩尔人,所以愿意和他过共同的生活;我的心灵完全为他的高贵的德行所征服;在他崇高的精神里,我看见他奇伟的仪表;我已经把我的灵魂和命运一起呈献给他了。所以,各位大人,要是他一个人迢迢出征,把我遗留在和平的后方,像醉生梦死的蜉蝣一样,我将要因为不能朝夕侍奉他,而在镂心刻骨的离情别绪中度日如年了。让我跟他去吧。

奥赛罗　请你们允许了她吧。上天为我作证,我向你们这样请求,并不是为了满足我自己的欲望,因为青春的热情在我已成过去了:我的唯一的动机,只是不忍使她失望。请你们千万不要抱着那样的思想,以为她跟我在一起,会使我懈怠了你们所托付给我的重大的使命。不,要是插翅的爱神的风流解数,可以蒙蔽了我的灵明的理智,使我因为贪恋欢娱而

① visage ['vizidʒ] *n.* 脸,面容

② consecrate ['kɔnsi,kreit] *v.* 奉献

③ interim ['intərim] *n.* 其间

④ palate ['pælit] *n.* 爱好,趣味

⑤ defunct [di'fʌŋkt] *a.* 不再存在的

⑥ bounteous ['bauntiəs] *a.* 慷慨的,大方的

· 049 ·

ACT I

   I will your serious and great business **scant**①
   For she is with me. No, when light-wing'd toys
   Of feather'd Cupid, **seel**② with wanton dullness
   My **speculative**③ and officed instruments,
   That my **disports**④ corrupt and taint my business,
   Let housewives make a **skillet**⑤ of my helm,
   And all **indign**⑥ and base adversities,
   Make head against my estimation.
Duke. Be it as you shall privately determine,
   Either for her stay or going: the affair cries haste,
   And speed must answer 't: you must hence tonight.
Desde. Tonight, my lord?
Duke. This night.
Othello. With all my heart.
Duke. At nine i' the morning here we'll meet again.
   Othello, leave some officer behind,
   And he shall our commission bring to you,
   With such things else of quality and respect
   As doth import you.
Othello. So please your grace, my Ancient;
   A man he is of honesty and trust.
   To his **conveyance**⑦ I assign my wife,
   With what else needful your good grace shall think
   To be sent after me.
Duke. Let it be so.
   Good night to everyone. And noble Signior,
   If virtue no delighted beauty lack,
   Your son-in-law is far more fair than black.
1st Senator. Adieu, brave Moor, use Desdemona well.
Bra. Look to her, Moor, if thou hast eyes to see;

① scant [skænt] *v.* 减少，克扣
② seel [si:l] *v.* [古语] 闭上（眼睛）；弄瞎……的眼睛
③ speculative ['spekjulətiv] *a.* 思索的
④ disport [dis'pɔ:t] *n.* 娱乐，玩乐
⑤ skillet ['skilit] *n.* 煮锅
⑥ indign [in'dain] *a.* 耻辱的，不光彩的

⑦ conveyance [kən'veiəns] *n.* 运输，运送

误了正事，那么让主妇们把我的战盔当作水罐，让一切的污名都丛集于我的一身吧！

公爵 她的去留行止，可以由你们自己去决定。事情很是紧急，你必须立刻出发。

元老甲 今天晚上你就得动身。
奥赛罗 很好。
公爵 明天早上九点钟，我们还要在这儿聚会一次。奥赛罗，请你留下一个将佐在这儿；你的委任状由他转交给你，要是我们随后还有什么决定，可以叫他把我们的训令传达给你。

奥赛罗 殿下，我的旗官是一个很适当的人物，他的为人是忠实而可靠的；我还要请他负责护送我的妻子，要是此外还有什么必须寄给我的物件，也请殿下一起交给他。

公爵 很好。各位晚安！（向勃拉班修）尊贵的先生，倘然以才德取人，不凭容貌，你这位贤东床难道比不上翩翩年少？

元老甲 再会，勇敢的摩尔人！好好看顾苔丝狄蒙娜。
勃拉班修 留心看着她，摩尔人，不要视而不见；她已

ACT I

She has deceived her father, and may thee.
Exeunt Duke, Senators and Officers.

Othello. My life upon her faith. Honest Iago,
My Desdemona must I leave to thee.
I **prithee**①, let thy wife attend on her,
And bring them after in the best advantage.
Come, Desdemona. I have but an hour
Of love, of worldly matters and direction,
To spend with thee. We must obey the time.
Exeunt Othello and Desdemona.

Rod. Iago.
Iago. What say'st thou, noble heart?
Rod. What will I do, thinkest thou?
Iago. Why, go to bed and sleep.
Rod. I will **incontinently**② drown myself.
Iago. If thou dost, I shall never love thee after.
Why thou silly gentleman!
Rod. It is silliness to live, when to live is torment, and then have we a prescription to die, when death is our physician.
Iago. O villainous! I have looked upon the world for four times seven years, and since I could distinguish **betwixt**③ a benefit and an injury: I never found man that knew how to love himself. Ere I would say, I would drown myself for the love of a **guinea hen**④, I would change my humanity with a **baboon**⑤.
Rod. What should I do? I confess it is my shame to be so fond, but it is not in my virtue to amend it.
Iago. Virtue? A fig! 'Tis in ourselves that we are thus or thus. Our bodies are gardens, to the which our wills are gardeners; so that if we will plant **nettles**⑥ or sow **lettuce**⑦, set **hyssop**⑧ and weed up **thyme**⑨, supply it with one gender of herbs or distract it with many, either to have it sterile

① prithee ['priði:] int. [古语] 请；请求您

② incontinently [in'kɔntinəntli] ad. 不能自制地

③ betwixt [bi'twikst] prep. 在中间

④ guinea hen 雌（珍）珠鸡

⑤ baboon [bə'bu:n] n. 狒狒

⑥ nettle ['netl] n. 荨麻

⑦ lettuce ['letis] n. 莴苣

⑧ hyssop ['hisəp] n. 牛膝草

⑨ thyme [taim] n. 百里香

经愚弄了她的父亲。她也会把你欺骗。（公爵，众元老，吏役等同下）

奥赛罗 我用生命保证她的忠诚！正直的伊阿古，我必须把我的苔丝狄蒙娜托付给你，请你叫你的妻子当心照料她；看什么时候有方便，就烦你护送她们启程。来，苔丝狄蒙娜，我只有一小时的工夫和你诉说衷情，料理庶事了。我们必须服从环境的支配。（奥赛罗、苔丝狄蒙娜同下）

罗德利哥 伊阿古！

伊阿古 你怎么说，好人儿？

罗德利哥 你想我该怎么办？

伊阿古 上床睡觉去吧。

罗德利哥 我立刻就投水去。

伊阿古 好，要是你投了水，我从此不喜欢你了。嘿，你这傻大少爷！

罗德利哥 要是活着这样受苦，傻瓜才愿意活下去；一死可以了却烦恼，还是死了的好。

伊阿古 啊，该死！我在这世上也经历过四七二十八个年头了，自从我能够辨别利害以来，我从来不曾看见过什么人知道怎样爱惜他自己。要是我也会为了爱上一个雌儿的缘故而投水自杀，我宁愿变成一只猴子。

罗德利哥 我该怎么办？我承认这样痴心是一件丢脸的事，可是我没有力量把它补救过来呀。

伊阿古 力量！废话！我们要这样那样，只有靠我们自己。我们的身体就像一座园圃，我们的意志是这园圃里的园丁；不论我们插荨麻，种莴苣，栽下牛膝草，拔起百里香，或者单独培植一种草木，或者把全园种得万卉纷披，让它荒废不治也好，把它辛勤

with idleness or **manured**① with industry, why the power and **corrigible**② authority of this lies in our wills. If the balance of our lives had not one scale of reason to poise another of sensuality, the blood and baseness of our natures would conduct us to most preposterous conclusions. But we have reason to cool our raging motions, our carnal stings, our unbitted lusts; whereof I take this, that you call love, to be a sect or scion.

Rod. It cannot be.

Iago. It is merely a lust of the blood and a permission of the will. Come, be a man: drown thyself? Drown cats and blind puppies. I have professed me thy friend, and I confess me knit to thy deserving with cables of **perdurable**③ toughness; I could never better stead thee than now. Put money in thy purse; follow thou the wars; defeat thy favor with an usurped beard. I say put money in thy purse. It cannot be that Desdemona should long continue her love to the Moor — put money in thy purse — nor he his to her. It was a violent **commencement**④, and thou shalt see an answerable **sequestration**⑤, put but money in thy purse. These Moors are changeable in their wills: fill thy purse with money. The food that to him now is as **luscious**⑥ as locusts, shall be to him shortly, as **acerb**⑦ as the coloquintida. She must change for youth; when she is sated with his body, she will find the error of her choice. She must have change, she must; therefore put money in thy purse. If thou wilt needs damn thyself, do it a more delicate way than drowning. Make all the money thou canst. If **sanctimony**⑧ and a frail vow betwixt an erring barbarian and a supersubtle Venetian be not too hard for my wits and all the tribe of hell, thou shalt enjoy her: therefore **make money**⑨. A pox of drowning thyself! It is clean out of the way. Seek

① manure [məˈnjuə] v. 耕种，施肥于
② corrigible [ˈkɔːridʒəbl] a. 可改正的

③ perdurable [pəˈdjurəbl] a. 非常耐久的

④ commencement [kəˈmensmənt] n. 开始（时间）；发端
⑤ sequestration [ˌsiːkweˈstreiʃən] n. 隐退
⑥ luscious [ˈlʌʃəs] a. 甜的，香甜的
⑦ acerb [əˈsəːb] a. 酸涩的

⑧ sanctimony [ˈsæŋktiˌməuni] n. 假装圣洁
⑨ make money 赚钱；发财

耕垦也好，那权力都在于我们的意志。要是在我们的生命之中，理智和情欲不能保持平衡，我们血肉的邪心就会引导我们到一个荒唐的结局；可是我们有的是理智，可以冲淡我们汹涌的热情，肉体的刺激和奔放的淫欲；我认为你所称为"爱情"的，也不过是那样一种东西。

罗德利哥 不，那不是。

伊阿古 那不过是在意志的默许之下一阵情欲的冲动而已。算了，做一个汉子。投水自杀！捉几头大猫小狗投在水里吧！我曾经声明我是你的朋友，我承认我对你的友谊是用不可摧折的坚韧的缆索连接起来的；现在正是我应该为你出力的时候。把银钱放在你的钱袋里；跟他们出征去；装上一脸假胡子，遮住你的本来面目；我说，把银钱放在你的钱袋里。苔丝狄蒙娜爱那摩尔人绝不会长久——把银钱放在你的钱袋里——他也不会长久爱她。她一开始就把他爱得这样热烈，他们感情的破裂一定也是很突然的；你只要把银钱放在你的钱袋里。这些摩尔人很容易变心——把你的钱袋装满了钱——现在他吃起来像蝗虫一样美味的食物，不久便要变得像苦苹果一样涩口了。她必须换一个年轻的男子；当他的肉体使她餍足了以后，她就会觉悟她的选择的错误。她必须换换口味，她必须换；所以把银钱放在你的钱袋里。要是你一定要寻死，也得想一个比投水巧妙一点的死法。尽你的力量搜括一些钱。要是凭着我的计谋和魔鬼们的奸诈，破坏这一个鲁莽的蛮子和这一个狡猾的威尼斯女人之间的脆弱的盟誓，还不算是一件难事，那么你一定可以享受她；所以快去设法弄些钱来吧。投水自杀！什么话！那根本就不用提；你宁

ACT I

thou rather to be hanged in **compassing**① thy joy, than to be drowned and go without her.

Rod. Wilt thou be fast to my hopes, if I depend on the issue?

Iago. Thou art sure of me: go, make money. I have told thee often, and I retell thee again and again, I hate the Moor. My cause is **hearted**②; thine hath no less reason. Let us be **conjunctive**③ in our revenge against him. If thou canst **cuckold**④ him, thou dost thyself a pleasure, and me a sport. There are many events in the womb of time, which will be delivered. Traverse, go, provide thy money. We will have more of this tomorrow. Adieu.

Rod. Where shall we meet i' the morning?

Iago. At my lodging.

Rod. I'll be with thee **betimes**⑤.

Iago. Go to, farewell. Do you hear, Roderigo?

Rod. What say you?

Iago. No more of drowning, do you hear?

Rod. I am changed; I'll go sell all my land.

Exit.

Iago. Thus do I ever make my fool my purse,
For I mine own gain'd knowledge should profane
If I would time **expend**⑥ with such a snipe
But for my sport and profit. I hate the Moor,
And it is thought abroad that 'twixt my sheets
He has done my office. I know not if 't be true,
But I for mere suspicion in that kind,
Will do as if for surety. He holds me well,
The better shall my purpose work on him.
Cassio's a proper man. Let me see now,
To get his place, and to plume up my will
In double knavery. How, how? Let's see.

① compass ['kʌmpəs] v. 图谋

② hearted ['hɑːtid] a. 放在心上的，铭记在心的

③ conjunctive [kən'dʒʌŋktiv] a. 联合的

④ cuckold ['kʌkəld] v. 使戴绿帽，与……的妻子通奸

⑤ betimes [bi'taimz] ad. 早，很早；及时，准时

⑥ expend [ik'spend] v. 花费（金钱、时间、精力等）

　　可因为追求你的快乐而被人吊死，总不要在没有一亲她的香泽以前投水自杀。

罗德利哥　要是我期待着这样的结果，你一定会尽力帮助我达到我的愿望吗？

伊阿古　你可以完全信任我。去，弄一些钱来。我常常对你说，一次一次反复告诉你，我恨那摩尔人；我的怨毒蓄积在心头，你也对他抱着同样深刻的仇恨，让我们同心合力向他复仇；要是你能够替他戴上一顶绿头巾，你固然是如愿以偿，我也可以拍掌称快。无数人事的变化孕育在时间的胚胎里，我们等着看吧。去，预备好你的钱。我们明天再谈这件事情。再见。

罗德利哥　明天早上我们在什么地方会面？

伊阿古　就在我的寓所里吧。

罗德利哥　我一早就来看你。

伊阿古　好，再会。你听见吗，罗德利哥？

罗德利哥　你说什么？

伊阿古　别再提起投水的话了，你听见没有？

罗德利哥　我已经变了一个人。我要去把我的田地一起变卖。（罗德利哥下）

伊阿古　好，再会！多往你的钱袋里放些钱。我总是这样让这种傻瓜掏出钱来给我花用；因为倘不是为了替自己解解闷，打算占些便宜，那我浪费时间跟这样一个呆子周旋，那才冤枉哩。我恨那摩尔人；有人说他和我的妻子私通，我不知道这句话是真是假；可是在这种事情上，即使不过是嫌疑，我也要把它当作实有其事一样看待。他对我很有好感，这样可以使我对他实行我的计策的时候格外方便一些。卡西奥是一个俊美的男子；让我想想看：夺到他的位置，实现我的一举两得的阴谋；怎么办？怎

After some time, to abuse Othello's ears,
That he is too familiar with his wife.
He hath a person and a smooth dispose
To be suspected-framed to make women false.
The Moor is of a free and open nature,
That thinks men honest that but seem to be so,
And will as tenderly be led by the nose
As asses are.
I have 't. It is engender'd. Hell and night
Must bring this monstrous birth to the world's light.
Exit.

么办?让我看:等过了一些时候,在奥赛罗的耳边捏造一些鬼话,说他跟他的妻子看上去太亲热了;他长得漂亮,性情又温和,天生一种媚惑妇人的魔力,像他这种人是很容易引起疑心的。那摩尔人是一个坦白爽直的人,他看见人家在表面上装出一副忠厚诚实的样子,就以为一定是个好人;我可以把他像一头驴子一般牵着鼻子跑。有了!我的计策已经产生。地狱和黑夜酝酿成这空前的罪恶,它必须向世界显露它的面目。(下)

ACT II

第二幕

Scene I. A seaport in Cyprus. An open place near the quay①.

Enter Montano and two Gentlemen.

Mont. What from the **cape**② can you discern at sea?

1st Gentleman. Nothing at all. It is a high, wrought flood;
 I cannot 'twixt the heaven and the main,
 Descry③ a sail.

Mont. Methinks, the wind hath spoke aloud at land;
 A fuller blast ne' er shook our **battlements**④.
 If it hath ruffian'd so upon the sea,
 What ribs of oak, when mountains melt on them,
 Can hold the mortise? What shall we hear of this?

2nd Gentleman. A **segregation**⑤ of the Turkish fleet.
 For do but stand upon the foaming shore,
 The chidden **billow**⑥ seems to **pelt**⑦ the clouds;
 The wind-shaked surge, with high and monstrous main,
 Seems to cast water on the burning bear,
 And quench the guards of the ever-fixed pole.
 I never did like **molestation**⑧ view
 On the enchafed flood.

第一场　塞浦路斯岛海口一市镇码头附近的广场

① quay [kiː] *n.* 码头

② cape [keip] *n.* 岬，（海）角

③ descry [di'skrai] *v.* 望见，看到

④ battlement ['bætlmənt] *n.* [常作复数]（城堡要塞顶上的）雉

⑤ segregation [ˌsegri'geiʃən] *n.* 分开

⑥ billow ['biləu] *n.* 巨浪

⑦ pelt [pelt] *v.* 重重地拍打

⑧ molestation [ˌməule'steiʃən] *n.* 打扰

蒙塔诺及二绅士上。

蒙塔诺　你从那海岬望出去，看见海里有什么船只没有？

甲绅　一点望不见。波浪很高，在海天之间，我看不见一片船帆。

蒙塔诺　风在陆地上吹得很厉害；从来不曾有这么大的暴风打击过我们的雉堞。要是它在海上也这么猖狂，哪一艘橡树造成的船身支持得住山一样的巨涛迎头倒下？我们将要从这场风暴中间听到什么消息呢？

乙绅　土耳其的舰队一定要被风浪冲散了。你只要站在白沫飞溅的海岸上，就可以看见咆哮的汹涛直冲云霄，被狂风卷起的怒浪奔腾山立，好像要把海水浇向光明的大熊星上，熄灭那照耀北极的亘古不移的斗宿一样。我从来没有见过这样可怕的惊涛骇浪。

ACT II

Mont.   If that the Turkish fleet
   Be not enshelter'd and **embay'd**①, they are drown'd;
   to bear it out.
   Enter a third Gentleman.
3rd Gentleman.   News, lads! our wars are done.
   The desperate tempest hath so bang'd the Turks,
   That their **designment**② halts. A noble ship of Venice,
   Hath seen a grievous wreck and sufferance
   On most part of their fleet.
Mont.   How? Is this true?
3rd Gentleman.   The ship is here put in.
   A Veronesa, Michael Cassio,
   Lieutenant to the warlike Moor, Othello,
   Is come on shore; the Moor himself at sea,
   And is in full commission here for Cyprus.
Mont.   I am glad on 't; 'tis a worthy Governor.
3rd Gentleman.   But this same Cassio, though he speak of comfort,
   Touching the Turkish loss, yet he looks sadly
   And prays the Moor be safe; for they were parted
   With foul and violent tempest.
Mont.   Pray heavens he be,
   For I have served him, and the man commands
   Like a full soldier. Let's to the seaside,
   As well to see the vessel that's come in
   As to throw out our eyes for brave Othello,
   Even till we make the main and the aerial blue,
   An **indistinct**③ regard.
3rd Gentleman.   Come, let's do so,
   For every minute is **expectancy**④
   Of more arrivance.

① embay [im'bei] v. 把（船）驶进港湾（以保护或避难）

② designment [di'zainmənt] n. 打算

蒙塔诺 要是土耳其舰队没有避进港里，它们一定沉没了；这样的风浪是抵御不了的。

另一绅士上。

丙绅 报告消息！小伙子们！咱们的战事已经结束了。土耳其人遭受这场暴风浪的突击，不得不放弃他们进攻的计划。一艘从威尼斯来的大船一路上看见他们的船只或沉或破，大部分零落不堪。

蒙塔诺 啊！这是真的吗？

丙绅 这一艘船已经在这儿进港，是一艘维罗纳造的船；迈克尔·卡西奥，那勇武的摩尔人奥赛罗的副将，已经上岸来了；那摩尔人自己还在海上，他是奉到全权委任，到塞浦路斯这儿来的。

蒙塔诺 我很高兴，这是一位很有才能的总督。

丙绅 可是这个卡西奥说起土耳其的损失，虽然兴高采烈，同时却满脸愁容，祈祷着那摩尔人的安全，因为他们是在险恶的大风浪中彼此失散的。

蒙塔诺 但愿他平安无恙；因为我曾经在他手下做过事，知道他在治军用兵这方面，的确是一个大将之才。来，让我们到海边去！一方面看看新到的船舶，一方面把我们的眼睛遥望到海天相接的远处，盼候着勇敢的奥赛罗。

丙绅 来，我们去吧；因为每一分钟都会有更多的人到来。

③ indistinct [ˌindis'tiŋkt] a. 相连的

④ expectancy [ik'spektənsi] n.（被）期待

ACT II

Enter Cassio.

Cassio. Thanks, you the valiant of this warlike Isle,
　　That so approve the Moor! O, let the heavens
　　Give him defense against the elements,
　　For I have lost him on a dangerous sea.

Mont. Is he well shipp'd?

Cassio. His **bark**① is stoutly timber'd, and his **pilot**②
　　Of very expert and approved allowance;
　　Therefore my hopes, not **surfeited**③ to death,
　　Stand in bold cure.

[*Within.*] A sail, a sail, a sail!

Enter a fourth Gentleman.

Cassio. What noise?

4th Gentleman. The town is empty; on the brow o' the sea
　　Stand ranks of people, and they cry, "A sail!"

Cassio. My hopes do shape him for the governor.

Guns heard.

2nd Gentleman. They do discharge their shot of courtesy,
　　Our friends at least.

Cassio. I pray you, sir, go forth,
　　And give us truth who 'tis that is arrived.

2nd Gentleman. I shall.

Exit.

Mont. But, good lieutenant, is your general wived?

Cassio. Most fortunately: he hath achieved a maid
　　That paragons description and wild fame,
　　One that excels the quirks of blazoning pens,
　　And in the essential **vesture**④ of creation,
　　Does tire the ingener.

Enter the second Gentleman.

卡西奥上。

卡西奥 谢谢,你们这座尚武的岛上的各位壮士,因为你们这样褒奖这位摩尔人。啊!但愿上天帮助他战胜风浪,因为我是在险恶的波涛之中和他失散的。

蒙塔诺 他的船靠得住吗?

卡西奥 船身很是坚固,舵师是一个很有经验的人,所以我还抱着很大的希望。(内呼声:"一条船!一条船!一条船!")

一使者上。

卡西奥 什么声音?

使者 全城的人都出来了;海边站满了人,他们在嚷:"一条船!一条船!"

卡西奥 我希望那就是我们新任的总督。(炮声)

乙绅 他们在放礼炮了;即使不是总督,至少也是我们的朋友。

卡西奥 先生,请你去看一看,回来告诉我们究竟是什么人来了。

乙绅 我就去。(下)

蒙塔诺 可是,副将,你们主帅有没有结过婚?

卡西奥 他的婚姻是再幸福不过的。他娶到了一位女郎,她的美貌才德,胜过一切的形容和盛大的名誉;笔墨的赞美不能写尽她的好处,没有一句适当的言语可以充分表现出她的天赋的优美。

乙绅重上。

---

① bark [bɑːk] *n.* 船
② pilot ['pailət] *n.* 舵手,领航员
③ surfeit ['səːfit] *v.* 使过度沉溺于
④ vesture ['vestʃə] *n.* 覆盖物

ACT II

        How now? Who has put in?

2nd Gentleman.   'Tis one Iago, ancient to the general.

Cassio.   He has had most favorable and happy speed:
        Tempests themselves, high seas, and **howling**① winds,
        The gutter'd rocks, and **congregated**② sands,
        Traitors ensteep'd to clog the guiltless **keel**③,
        As having sense of beauty, do omit
        Their mortal natures, letting go safely by
        The divine Desdemona.

Mont.   What is she?

Cassio.   She that I spake of, our great captain's captain,
        Left in the conduct of the bold Iago,
        Whose footing here anticipates our thoughts
        A se'nnight's speed. Great Jove, Othello guard,
        And swell his sail with thine own powerful breath,
        That he may bless this bay with his tall ship,
        Make love's quick pants in Desdemona's arms,
        Give renew'd fire to our extincted spirits,
        And bring all Cyprus comfort.
        Enter Desdemona, Emilia, Iago, Roderigo and Attendants.
        O, behold,
        The riches of the ship is come on shore:
        Ye men of Cyprus, let her have your knees.
        Hall to thee, lady? And the grace of heaven,
        Before, behind thee, and on every hand,
        Enwheel thee round!

Desde.   I thank you, valiant Cassio.
        What **tidings**④ can you tell me of my lord?

Cassio.   He is not yet arrived, nor know I aught
        But that he's well and will be shortly here.

① howling ['hauliŋ] *a.* 嗥叫的

② congregate ['kɔŋgri‚geit] *v.* 使聚集

③ keel [ki:l] *n.*（船、艇等的）龙骨

卡西奥 啊！谁到来了？

乙绅 是元帅麾下的一个旗官，名叫伊阿古。

卡西奥 他倒一帆风顺地到了。汹涌的怒涛，咆哮的狂风，埋伏在海底的礁石沙碛，似乎也懂得爱惜美人，收敛了它们凶恶的本性，让神圣的苔丝狄蒙娜安然通过。

蒙塔诺 她是谁？

卡西奥 就是我刚才说起的，我们大帅的主帅。勇敢的伊阿古护送她到这儿来，想不到他们路上走得这么快，比我们的预期还早七天。伟大的乔武¹啊，保佑奥赛罗，吹一口你的大力的气息在他的船帆上，让他高大的桅樯在这儿海港里显现它的雄姿，让他跳动着一颗恋人的心投进了苔丝狄蒙娜的怀里，重新燃起我们奄奄欲绝的精神，使整个塞浦路斯充满了兴奋吧！

　　　　苔丝狄蒙娜、埃米莉亚、伊阿古、罗德利哥及侍从等上。

卡西奥 啊！瞧，船上的珍宝到岸上来了，塞浦路斯人啊，向她下跪吧。祝福你，夫人！愿神灵在你的周遭呵护你！

苔丝狄蒙娜 谢谢您，英勇的卡西奥。你知道我的丈夫有什么消息吗？

卡西奥 他还没有到来；我只知道他是平安的，大概不久就会到来。

④ tidings ['taidiŋz] *n.* 消息，音讯

---

1 乔武（Jove）是罗马神话中主神朱庇特（Jupiter）的别称。

ACT II

Desde. O, but I fear: How lost you company?

Cassio. The great contention of the sea and skies
    Parted our fellowship. But, hark! A sail!

[*Within.*] A sail, a sail!

    Gun heard.

2nd Gentleman. They give their greeting to the **citadel**①;
    This likewise is a friend.

Cassio. See for the news.

    Exit Gentleman.

    Good ancient, you are welcome.
    [*To Emilia.*]
    Welcome, mistress.
    Let it not gall your patience, good Iago,
    That I extend my manners; 'tis my breeding
    That gives me this bold show of courtesy.

    Kisses her.

Iago. Sir, would she give you so much of her lips,
    As of her tongue she oft bestows on me,
    You'ld have enough.

Desde. Alas, she has no speech.

Iago. In faith, too much;
    I find it still when I have list to sleep.
    Marry, before your ladyship I grant,
    She puts her tongue a little in her heart
    And **chides**② with thinking.

Emilia. You have little cause to say so.

Iago. Come on, come on. You are pictures out of doors,
    Bells in your **parlors**③, wild-cats in your kitchens,
    Saints in your injuries, devils being offended,
    Players in your **housewifery**④, and housewives in your beds.

苔丝狄蒙娜 啊!可是我怕——你们怎么会分散的?

卡西奥 天风和海水的猛烈的激战,使我们彼此失散。可是听!有船来了。(内呼声:"一条船!一条船!"炮声)

① citadel ['sitədəl] *n.* 城堡,要塞

乙绅 他们向我们城上放礼炮了;到来的也是我们的朋友。

卡西奥 你去探看探看。(乙绅下,向伊阿古)老总,欢迎!(向埃米莉亚)欢迎!嫂子!请你不要恼怒,好伊阿古,我总得有个礼貌,按我的教养,就得来这么一个放肆的见面礼。(吻埃米莉亚)

伊阿古 老兄,要是她向你掀动她的嘴唇,也像她向我掀动她的舌头一样,那你就要叫苦不迭了。

苔丝狄蒙娜 唉!她又不会多嘴。

伊阿古 真的,她太会多嘴了;每次我想睡觉的时候,总是被她吵得不得安宁。不过,在您夫人的面前,我还要说一句,她有些话是放在心里说的,人家瞧她不开口,她却在心里骂人。

② chide [tʃaid] *v.* 责骂

埃米莉亚 你没有理由这样冤枉我。

伊阿古 得啦,得啦,你们跑出门来像图画,走进房去像响铃;到了灶下像野猫;设计害人的时候,面子上装得像一个圣徒;人家冒犯了你们,你们便活像夜叉;叫你们管家,你们只会一味胡闹,一上床却又十足像个忙碌的主妇。

③ parlor ['pɑːlə] *n.* 客厅

④ housewifery ['hauswifəri; 'hʌzifri] *n.* 家务;家政

ACT II

Desde. O, **fie**① upon thee, slanderer.

Iago. Nay, it is true, or else I am a Turk:

You rise to play, and go to bed to work.

Emilia. You shall not write my praise.

Iago. No, let me not.

Desde. What wouldst thou write of me, if thou shouldst praise me?

Iago. Oh, gentle lady, do not put me to 't,

For I am nothing if not critical.

Desde. Come on, **assay**②. There's one gone to the harbor?

Iago. Ay, madam.

Desde. I am not merry: but I do beguile

The thing I am by seeming otherwise.

Come, how wouldst thou praise me?

Iago. I am about it, but indeed my invention

Comes from my **pate**③ as **birdlime**④ does from frize;

It plucks out brains and all. But my Muse labors,

And thus she is deliver'd.

If she be fair and wise, fairness and wit,

The one's for use, the other useth it.

Desde. Well praised! How if she be black and witty?

Iago. If she be black, and thereto have a wit,

She'll find a white that shall her blackness fit.

Desde. Worse and worse.

Emilia. How if fair and foolish?

Iago. She never yet was foolish that was fair,

For even her folly help'd her to an heir.

Desde. These are old **fond**⑤ paradoxes to make fools laugh i' the **alehouse**⑥.

What miserable praise hast thou for her that's foul and foolish?

Iago. There's none so foul and foolish **thereunto**⑦,

But does foul pranks which fair and wise ones do.

① fie [fai] *int.* 真丢脸！呸！

② assay [ə'sei] *v.* 试验

③ pate [peit] *n.* 头，脑袋

④ birdlime ['bə:dlaim] *n.* 粘鸟胶

⑤ fond [fɔnd] *a.* [主方言] 愚蠢的

⑥ alehouse ['eilhaus] *n.* 酒馆

⑦ thereunto [,ðɛər'ʌntu:] *ad.* [废语] 此外，另外

苔丝狄蒙娜 啊，啐！你这乱造谣言的家伙！

伊阿古 不，我说的话几千真万确，
你们起来游戏，上床工作。

埃米莉亚 我再也不要你写赞美我的诗句。

伊阿古 对，可别叫我写。

苔丝狄蒙娜 要是叫你赞美我，你要怎么写法呢？

伊阿古 啊，好夫人，别叫我做这件事，因为我的脾气是要吹毛求疵的。

苔丝狄蒙娜 不，试试看。有人到港口去了吗？

伊阿古 是，夫人。

苔丝狄蒙娜 我虽然心里愁闷，姑且强作欢容。来，你怎么赞美我？

伊阿古 我正在想着呢；可是我的诗情粘在我的脑壳里，用力一挤就会把脑浆一起挤出的。我的诗神难产了。好了，有了：
她要是既漂亮又智慧，
就不会误用她的娇美。

苔丝狄蒙娜 赞美得好！要是她虽黑丑而聪明呢？

伊阿古 她要是虽黑丑却聪明，
包她找到一位俊郎君。

苔丝狄蒙娜 不成话。

埃米莉亚 要是美貌而愚笨呢？

伊阿古 美女人绝不是笨冬瓜，
蠢煞也会抱个小娃娃。

苔丝狄蒙娜 这些都是在酒店里骗傻瓜们笑笑的古老的歪诗。还有一种又丑又笨的女人，你也能够勉强赞美她两句吗？

伊阿古 别嫌她心肠笨相貌丑，
女人的戏法一样拿手。

ACT II

Desde. O heavy ignorance! Thou praisest the worst best. But what praise couldst thou bestow on a **deserving**① woman indeed? One that in the authority of her merit, did justly put on the vouch of very malice itself?

Iago. She that was ever fair and never proud,
Had tongue at will and yet was never loud,
Never lack'd gold and yet went never gay,
Fled from her wish and yet said now I may;
She that, being anger'd, her revenge being nigh,
Bade her wrong stay and her displeasure fly;
She that in wisdom never was so frail,
To change the **cod's**② head for the **salmon's**③ tail;
She that could think and ne'er disclose her mind,
See suitors following and not look behind;
She was a wight, if ever such wight were.

Desde. To do what?

Iago. To **suckle**④ fools and chronicle small beer.

Desde. Oh most lame and **impotent**⑤ conclusion! Do not learn of him, Emilia, though he be thy husband. How say you, Cassio? Is he not a most profane and liberal counselor?

Cassio. He speaks home, madam. You may relish him more in the soldier than in the scholar.

Iago. [*Aside.*] He takes her by the palm; ay, well said, whisper. With as little a web as this will I **ensnare**⑥ as great a fly as Cassio. Ay, smile upon her, do; I will **gyve**⑦ thee in thine own courtship. You say true; 'tis so, indeed. If such tricks as these strip you out of your lieutenantry, it had been better you had not kissed your three fingers so oft, which now again you are most apt to play the sir in. Very good. Well kissed an excellent

① deserving [di'zə:viŋ] *a.* 该赞扬的

② cod [kɔd] *n.* 鳕鱼
③ salmon ['sæmən] *n.* 鲑鱼

④ suckle ['sʌkl] *v.* 给……喂奶
⑤ impotent ['impətənt] *a.* 无力的

⑥ ensnare [in'snɛə] *v.* 使落入陷阱
⑦ gyve [dʒaiv] *v.* [古语、诗歌用语] 使加足械；使上脚镣

苔丝狄蒙娜 啊，岂有此理！你把最好的赞美给了最坏的女人。可是对于一个贤惠的女人——连十足的坏蛋也只得由衷赞美的好女人——你又怎么赞美她呢？

伊阿古 她生得美，却不骄傲，
能说会道，却不吵闹；
有的是钱，但不妖娆；
心想不得，亦不强求；
受了恶气，虽可报仇；
却自平气，打消烦恼；
明白事理，端庄稳重，
虽食鳕鱼头，不思鲑鱼尾；¹
脑筋灵活，嘴却很牢，
有人盯梢，也不扭头；
要是真有这样的小娇娘——

苔丝狄蒙娜 要她干什么呢？

伊阿古 奶傻孩子，记油盐账。

苔丝狄蒙娜 啊，这可真是最蹩脚、最没劲的收尾！埃米莉亚，不要听他的话，虽然他是你的丈夫。您怎么说，卡西奥？他是不是一个胡说八道的家伙？

卡西奥 他说得很实在，夫人。您要是把他当作一个军人，不把他当作一个文士，您就不会嫌他出言粗俗了。

伊阿古 （旁白）他捏着她的手心。嗯，交头接耳，好得很。我只要张起这么一个小小的网，就可以捉住像卡西奥这样一只大苍蝇。嗯，对她微笑，很好；我要叫你跌翻在你自己的礼貌中间。——您说得对，正是正是。——要是这种鬼殷勤会葬送你的前程，您还是不要老是吻着你的三个指头，表示你的绅士风度吧。很好；吻得不错！绝妙的礼貌！正是

---

1 鳕鱼头比喻傻瓜；全句意为：嫁了傻瓜也并不另找漂亮的相好。

ACT II

courtesy: 'tis so indeed. Yet again your fingers to your lips? Would they were **clyster-pipes**① for your sake! [*Trumpet within.*]

The Moor. I know his trumpet.

Cassio. 'Tis truly so.

Desde. Let's meet him and receive him.

Cassio. Lo, where he comes!

Enter Othello and Attendants.

Othello. O my fair warrior!

Desde. My dear Othello!

Othello. It gives me wonder, great as my content
To see you here before me. Oh my soul's joy:
If after every tempest come such calms,
May the winds blow till they have waken'd death:
And let the laboring bark climb hills of seas
Olympus-high, and duck again as low,
As hell's from heaven. If it were now to die,
'Twere now to be most happy; For I fear
My soul hath her content so absolute,
That not another comfort like to this,
Succeeds in unknown fate.

Desde. The heavens forbid
But that our loves and comforts should increase,
Even as our days do grow.

Othello. Amen to that, sweet powers!
I cannot speak enough of this content;
It stops me here; it is too much of joy.
And this, and this, the greatest **discords**② be, [*kisses her*]
That e'er our hearts shall make.

Iago. Oh you are well tuned now:
But I'll set down the pegs that make this music,

① clyster pipe 灌肠管

正是。又把你的手指放到你的嘴唇上去了吗？对你来说手指头变作肠管才好呢是不是。（喇叭声）主帅来了！我听得出他的喇叭声音。

卡西奥 真的是他。

苔丝狄蒙娜 让我们去迎接他。

卡西奥 瞧！他来了。

　　　　奥赛罗及侍从等上。

奥赛罗 啊，我的娇美的战士！

苔丝狄蒙娜 我的亲爱的奥赛罗！

奥赛罗 看见你比我先到这里，真使我又惊又喜。啊，我的心爱的人！要是每一次暴风雨之后，都有这样的和煦的阳光，那么尽管让狂风肆意地吹，把死亡都吹醒了吧！让那辛苦挣扎的船舶爬上一座座如山的高浪，就像从高高的天上堕下幽深的地狱一般，一泻千丈地跌下来吧！要是我现在死去，那才是最幸福的；因为我怕我的灵魂已经尝到了无上的欢乐，此生此世，再也不会有同样令人欣喜的事情了。

苔丝狄蒙娜 但愿上天眷顾，让我们的爱情和欢乐与日俱增！

奥赛罗 阿门，慈悲的神明！我不能充分说出我的心头的快乐；太多的欢喜窒住了我的呼吸。（吻苔丝狄蒙娜）一个——再来一个——这便是两颗心儿间最大的冲突了。

② discord ['diskɔ:d; dis'kɔ:d] n.（想法、意见、事物等之间的）不一致

伊阿古 （旁白）啊，你们现在是琴瑟调和，看我不动声色，叫你们弦断柱裂。

ACT II

              As honest as I am.

Othello. Come, let us to the castle.

              News friends: our wars are done, the Turks are drown'd.

              How does my old acquaintance of this Isle?

              Honey, you shall be well desired in Cyprus;

              I have found great love amongst them. Oh my sweet,

              I **prattle**① out of fashion, and I dote

              In mine own comforts. I prithee, good Iago,

              Go to the Bay and disembark my **coffers**②.

              Bring thou the Master to the citadel;

              He is a good one, and his worthiness

              Does challenge much respect. Come, Desdemona,

              Once more well met at Cyprus.

              Exeunt all but Iago and Roderigo.

Iago. Do thou meet me presently at the harbor. Come hither, if thou be'st valiant, as they say base men being in love have then a nobility in their natures more than is native to them, list me. The lieutenant tonight watches on the Court of Guard. First, I must tell thee this: Desdemona is directly in love with him.

Rod. With him? Why, 'tis not possible.

Iago. Lay thy finger thus, and let thy soul be instructed. Mark me with what violence she first loved the Moor, but for bragging and telling her fantastical lies. To love him still for prating, let not thy discreet heart think it. Her eye must be fed. And what delight shall she have to look on the devil? When the blood is made dull with the act of sport, there should be a game to inflame it and to give **satiety**③ a fresh appetite. Loveliness in favor, sympathy in years, manners, and beauties: all which the Moor is **defective**④ in. Now for want of these required conveniences, her delicate tenderness will find itself abused, begin to heave the **gorge**⑤, disrelish and abhor the Moor; very nature will instruct her in it and

第二幕

奥赛罗　来，让我们到城堡里去。好消息，朋友们；我们的战事已经结束，土耳其人全都淹死了。我的岛上的旧友，您好？爱人，你在塞浦路斯将要受到众人的宠爱，我觉得他们都是非常热情的。啊，亲爱的，我太高兴了，所以会说出这样忘形的话来。好伊阿古，请你到港口去一趟，把我的箱子搬到岸上。带那船长到城堡里来；他是一个很好的家伙，他的才能非常叫人钦佩。来，苔丝狄蒙娜。（除伊阿古、罗德利哥外均下）

伊阿古　你马上就到港口来会我。过来。人家说，爱情可以刺激懦夫，使他鼓起本来所没有的勇气；要是你果然有胆量，请听我说。副将今晚在卫舍守夜。第一我必须告诉你，苔丝狄蒙娜是直接跟他发生恋爱的。

罗德利哥　跟他发生恋爱！那是不会有的事。

伊阿古　闭住你的嘴，好好听我说。你看她当初不过因为这摩尔人向她吹了些法螺，撒下了一些漫天的大谎，她就爱得他那么热烈；难道她会继续爱他，只是为了他的吹牛的本领吗？你是个聪明人，不要以为世上会有这样的事。她的视觉必须得到满足；她能够从魔鬼脸上感到什么佳趣？情欲在一阵兴奋过了以后而渐生厌倦的时候，必须换一换新鲜的口味，方才可以把它重新刺激起来，或者是容貌的漂亮，或者是年龄的相称，或者是举止的风雅，这些都是这摩尔人所欠缺的；她因为在这些必要的方面

① prattle ['prætl] v. 像小孩似的颠三倒四地讲话
② coffer ['kɔfə] n.（存放金钱或贵重物品的）箱子

③ satiety [sə'taiəti; 'seiʃiəti] n. 饱足，满足
④ defective [di'fektiv] a. 有缺陷的
⑤ gorge [gɔ:dʒ] n. 怨恨

ACT II

compel her to some second choice. Now sir, this granted as it is a most pregnant and unforced position, who stands so eminently in the degree of this fortune as Cassio does: a knave very **voluble**①; no further **conscionable**② than in putting on the mere form of civil and humane **seeming**③, for the better compass of his salt and most hidden loose affection? Why none, why none: a slipper and subtle knave, a finder of occasions, that has an eye can stamp and **counterfeit**④ advantages, though true advantage never present itself. A devilish knave: besides, the knave is handsome, young and hath all those requisites in him that folly and green minds look after. A **pestilent**⑤ complete knave, and the woman hath found him already.

Rod. I cannot believe that in her; she's full of most blessed condition.

Iago. Blessed fig's end, The wine she drinks is made of grapes. If she had been blessed, she would never have loved the Moor: Blessed pudding! Didst thou not see her paddle with the palm of his hand? Didst not mark that?

Rod. Yes, that I did; but that was but courtesy.

Iago. **Lechery**⑥, by this hand; an index and obscure prologue to the history of lust and foul thoughts. They met so near with their lips that their breaths embraced together. **Villainous**⑦ thoughts, Roderigo! When these **mutualities**⑧ so marshal the way, hard at hand comes the master and main exercise, the incorporate conclusion. Pish, But sir, be you ruled by me. I have brought you from Venice. Watch you tonight; for the command, I'll lay 't upon you. Cassio knows you not. I'll not be far from you. Do you find some occasion to anger Cassio, either by speaking too loud, or tainting his discipline, or from what other course you please, which the time shall more favorably minister.

Rod. Well.

Iago. Sir, he is rash and very sudden in **choler**⑨: and haply may strike at you, provoke him, that he may; for even out of that will I cause these of

① voluble ['vɔljubl] *a.* 健谈的，有口才的
② conscionable ['kɔnʃənəbl] *a.* 凭良心的；正直的
③ seeming ['si:miŋ] *n.* 外观，外貌
④ counterfeit ['kauntəfit] *v.* 伪造，仿造
⑤ pestilent ['pestilənt] *a.* 致命的

⑥ lechery ['letʃəri] *n.* 淫荡之举
⑦ villainous ['vilənəs] *a.* 邪恶的
⑧ mutuality ['mju:tʃu'æləti] *n.* 亲密

⑨ choler ['kɔlə] *n.* 怒气

不能得到满足，一定会觉得她的青春娇艳所托非人，而开始对这摩尔人由失望而憎恨，由憎恨而厌恶，她的天性就会迫令她再做第二次的选择。这种情形是很自然而可能的：要是承认了这一点，试问哪一个人比卡西奥更有享受这一种福分的便利？一个很会讲话的家伙，为了达到他的秘密的淫邪的欲望，他会恬不为意地装出一副殷勤文雅的外表。哼，谁也比不上他；一个狡猾阴险的家伙，惯会乘机取利，无孔不入；一个鬼一样的家伙！而且，这家伙又漂亮，又年轻，凡是可以使无知的妇女醉心的条件，他无一不备；一个十足害人的家伙，这女人已经把他勾上了。

罗德利哥　我不能相信，她是一位圣洁的女郎。

伊阿古　他妈的圣洁！她喝的酒也是用葡萄酿成的；她要是圣洁，她就不会爱这摩尔人了。哼，圣洁！你没有看见她捏他的手心吗？你没有看见吗？

罗德利哥　是的，我看见的；可是那不过是礼貌罢了。

伊阿古　我举手为誓，这明明是奸淫！这一段意味深长的楔子，就包括无限淫情欲念的交流。他们的嘴唇那么贴近，他们的呼吸简直互相拥抱了。该死的思想，罗德利哥！这种表面上的亲热一开了端，主要的好戏就会跟着上场，肉体的结合是必然的结论。呸！可是，老兄，你听我说。我特意把你从威尼斯带来，今晚你代我值班守夜；卡西奥是不认识你的；我就在离你不远的地方看着你；你见了卡西奥就找一些借口向他挑衅，或者高声辱骂，或者毁谤他的军誉，或者随你的意思用其他无论什么比较适当的方法。

罗德利哥　好。

伊阿古　他是个性情暴躁、易于发怒的人，也许会向你

Cyprus to mutiny. Whose qualification shall come into no true taste again but by the **displanting**① of Cassio. So shall you have a shorter journey to your desires by the means I shall then have to prefer them, and the **impediment**② most profitably removed, without the which there were no expectation of our prosperity.

Rod. I will do this, if I can bring it to any opportunity.

Iago. I warrant thee. Meet me by and by at the Citadel. I must fetch his necessaries ashore. Farewell.

Rod. Adieu.

Exit.

Iago. That Cassio loves her, I do well believe it;
That she loves him, 'tis apt and of great credit.
The Moor, howbeit that I endure him not,
Is of a constant, loving, noble nature,
And I dare think he'll prove to Desdemona
A most dear husband. Now I do love her too,
Not out of absolute lust, though **peradventure**③
I stand accountant for as great a sin,
But partly led to diet my revenge,
For that I do suspect the lusty Moor
Hath leap'd into my seat; the thought whereof,
Doth like a poisonous mineral **gnaw**④ my inwards,
And nothing can or shall content my soul
Till I am even'd with him, wife for wife.
Or failing so, yet that I put the Moor
At least into a jealousy so strong
That judgement cannot cure. Which thing to do,
If this poor trash of Venice, whom I trace
For his quick hunting, stand the putting on,
I'll have our Michael Cassio **on the hip**⑤,

① displant [ˌdɪsˈplɑːnt] v. 把……逐出家园

② impediment [ɪmˈpedɪmənt] n. 阻碍

③ peradventure [ˌpərədˈventʃə; ˈpəːrædˌv-] a. [古语] 可能

④ gnaw [nɔː] v. 咬

⑤ on the hip [古语] 处于不利地位

动武；即使他不动武，你也要激动他和你打起架来；因为借着这一个理由，我就可以在塞浦路斯人中间煽起一场暴动，假如要平息他们的愤怒，除了把卡西奥解职以外没有其他方法。这样你就可以在我的设计协助之下，早日达到你的愿望，你的阻碍也可以从此除去，否则我们的事情是绝无成功之望的。

罗德利哥 我愿意这样干，要是我能够找到下手的机会。

伊阿古 那我可以向你保证。等会儿在城门口见我。我现在必须去替他们把应用物件搬上岸来。再会。

罗德利哥 再会。（下）

伊阿古 卡西奥爱她，这一点我是可以充分相信的；她爱卡西奥，这也是一件很自然而可能的事。这摩尔人我虽然气他不过，却有一副坚定仁爱正直的性格；我相信他会对苔丝狄蒙娜做一个最多情的丈夫。讲到我自己，我也是爱她的，并不完全出于情欲的冲动——虽然也许我也犯着这样的罪名——可是一半是为要报复我的仇恨，因为我疑心这好色的摩尔人夺去了我在她心头的地位。这一种思想像毒药一样腐蚀我的肝肠，什么都不能使我心满意足，除非在他身上发泄这一口怨气，他夺去我的人，我也叫他有了妻子享受不成；即使不能做到这一点，我也要叫这摩尔人心里长起根深蒂固的嫉妒来，没有一种理智的药饵可以把它治疗。为了达到这一个目的，我已经利用这威尼斯的瘟生做我的鹰犬；要是他果然听我的唆使，我

Abuse him to the Moor in the rank garb
For I fear Cassio with my nightcap too,
Make the Moor thank me, love me, and reward me,
For making him **egregiously**① an ass,
And practicing upon his peace and quiet,
Even to madness. 'tis here, but yet confused:
Knavery's plain face is never seen till used.
Exit.

就可以抓住我们那位迈克尔·卡西奥的把柄，在这摩尔人面前诽谤他，因为我疑心卡西奥跟我的妻子也是有些暧昧的。这样我可以让这摩尔人感谢我，喜欢我，报答我，因为我叫他做了一头大大的驴子，用诡计捣乱他的平和安宁，使他因气愤而发疯。方针已经决定，前途未可预料；恶人的面目必须到时才揭晓。（下）

---

① egregious [i'gri:dʒiəs] *a.* 极坏的

Scene II. A street.

*Enter a Herald with a **proclamation**①; people following.*

Herald. It is Othello's pleasure, our noble and valiant general. That upon certain tidings now arrived, importing the mere **perdition**② of the Turkish fleet, every man put himself into triumph; some to dance, some to make bonfires, each man to what sport and **revels**③ his addiction leads him; for besides these beneficial news, it is the celebration of his **nuptial**④. So much was his pleasure should be proclaimed. All offices are open, and there is full liberty of **feasting**⑤ from this present hour of five, till the bell have told eleven. Heaven bless the isle of Cyprus, and our noble general Othello!

Exeunt.

第二场　街道

① proclamation [ˌprɔkləˈmeiʃən] *n.* 公告，布告

② perdition [pəˈdiʃən] *n.* 永灭；沉沦

③ revel [ˈrevəl] *v.* 狂欢；欢宴

④ nuptial [ˈnʌpʃəl] *n.* 婚礼

⑤ feast [fiːst] *v.* 参加宴会，受到款待

传令官持告示上；民众随后。

传令官　我们尊贵的英勇的元帅奥赛罗有令，根据最近接到的消息，土耳其舰队已经全军覆没，全体军民听到这一个捷音，理应同伸庆祝：跳舞的跳舞，燃放焰火的燃放焰火，每个人都可以随他自己的高兴尽情欢乐；因为除了这些可喜的消息以外，我们同时还要祝贺我们元帅的新婚。帅府中一切门禁完全撤除，从下午五时起，直到深夜十一时，无论何人，可以自由出入，饮酒宴乐。上天祝福塞浦路斯岛和我们尊贵的元帅奥赛罗！　（同下）

Scene III. A hall in the castle.

Enter Othello, Desdemona, Cassio and Attendants.

Othello. Good Michael, look you to the guard tonight.
   Let's teach ourselves that honorable stop,
   Not to outsport discretion.

Cassio. Iago hath direction what to do;
   But notwithstanding with my personal eye
   Will I look to 't.

Othello. Iago is most honest.
   Michael, good night. Tomorrow with your earliest,
   Let me have speech with you. Come, my dear love,
   The purchase made, the fruits are to **ensue**①;
   That profit's yet to come 'tween me and you.
   Good night.
   Exeunt Othello, Desdemona and Attendants.
   Enter Iago.

Cassio. Welcome Iago; we must to the watch.

Iago. Not this hour, lieutenant; 'tis not yet ten o' the clock. Our general cast us thus early for the love of his Desdemona; who let us not therefore blame. He hath not yet made wanton the night with her, and she is sport

第三场　城堡中的厅堂

奥赛罗、苔丝狄蒙娜、卡西奥及侍从等上。

奥赛罗　好迈克尔，今天请你留心警备；我们必须随时谨慎，免得因为纵乐无度而肇成意外。

卡西奥　我已经吩咐伊阿古怎样办了，我自己也要亲自督察照看。

奥赛罗　伊阿古是个忠实可靠的汉子。迈克尔，晚安；明天你一早就来见我。（向苔丝狄蒙娜）来，我的爱人，我们已经把彼此心身互相交换，愿今后开花结果，恩情美满。晚安！（奥赛罗、苔丝狄蒙娜及侍从等下）

伊阿古上。

卡西奥　欢迎，伊阿古；我们该守夜去了。

伊阿古　时候还早哪，副将；现在还不到十点钟。咱们主帅因为舍不得他的新夫人，所以这么早就打发我们出去；可是我们也怪不得他，他还没有跟她真个

① ensue [in'sju:] *v.* 依次跟着；随后而来

ACT II

for Jove.

Cassio. She's a most exquisite lady.

Iago. And I'll warrant her, full of game.

Cassio. Indeed she's a most fresh and delicate creature.

Iago. What an eye she has? Methinks it sounds a **parley**① to provocation.

Cassio. An inviting eye; and yet methinks right modest.

Iago. And when she speaks, is it not an **alarum**② to love?

Cassio. She is indeed perfection.

Iago. Well, happiness to their sheets. Come, lieutenant, I have a **stoup**③ of wine, and here without are a brace of Cyprus Gallants, that would fain have a measure to the health of black Othello.

Cassio. Not tonight, good Iago. I have very poor and unhappy brains for drinking. I could well wish courtesy would invent some other custom of entertainment.

Iago. Oh, they are our friends! But one cup; I'll drink for you.

Cassio. I have drunk but one cup tonight, and that was craftily qualified too, and behold what innovation it makes here. I am unfortunate in the **infirmity**④, and dare not task my weakness with any more.

Iago. What man? 'tis a night of revels, the gallants desire it.

Cassio. Where are they?

Iago. Here at the door; I pray you, call them in.

Cassio. I'll do 't, but it dislikes me.

Exit.

Iago. If I can fasten but one cup upon him,
With that which he hath drunk tonight already,
He'll be as full of quarrel and offence
As my young Mistress' dog. Now my sick fool Roderigo,
Whom love hath turn'd almost the wrong side out,
To Desdemona hath tonight **caroused**⑤,
Potations⑥ pottle-deep; and he's to watch.

① parley ['pɑ:li] *n.* 会谈
② alarum [ə'lɛərəm] *n.* [英国古语、诗歌用语] 武装动员令
③ stoup [stu:p] *n.* 一大杯的量
④ infirmity [in'fə:məti] *n.* 弱点
⑤ carouse [kə'rauz] *v.* 痛饮
⑥ potation [pəu'teiʃən] *n.* 一饮，一饮的量

销魂，而她这个人，任是天神见了她也要动心的。

卡西奥 她是一位人间无比的佳人。

伊阿古 我可以担保她也是一个非常风流的人儿。

卡西奥 她的确是一个娇艳可爱的女郎。

伊阿古 她的眼睛多么迷人！简直在向人挑战。

卡西奥 一双动人的眼睛；可是却有一种端庄贞静的神气。

伊阿古 她说话的时候，不就是爱情的警报吗？

卡西奥 她真是十全十美。

伊阿古 好，愿他们被窝里快乐！来，副将，我还有一瓶酒；外面有两个塞浦路斯的绅士，要想为黑将军祝饮一杯。

卡西奥 今夜可不能奉陪了，好伊阿古。我一喝了酒，头脑就会糊涂起来。我希望有人能够发明喝酒以外的欢庆方式。

伊阿古 啊，他们都是我们的朋友；喝一杯吧，我也可以代你喝。

卡西奥 我今晚只喝了一杯，就是那一杯也被我偷偷地冲了些水，可是我的头已经有点儿昏啦。我知道自己的弱点，实在不敢再多喝了。

伊阿古 哎哟，朋友！这是一个狂欢的良夜，不要让那些绅士们扫兴吧。

卡西奥 他们在什么地方？

伊阿古 就在这儿门外；请你去叫他们进来吧。

卡西奥 我去就去，可是我心里是不愿意的。（下）

伊阿古 他今晚已经喝过了一些酒，我只要再灌他一杯下去，他就会像小狗一样到处招惹是非。我们那位为情憔悴的傻瓜罗德利哥今晚为了苔丝狄蒙娜也喝了几大杯的酒，我已经派他守夜了。还有三个心性高傲，重视荣誉的塞浦路斯少年，都是这座尚武

ACT II

Three lads of Cyprus, noble swelling spirits,
That hold their honors in a wary distance,
The very elements of this warlike isle,
Have I tonight fluster'd with flowing cups,
And they watch too.
Now 'mongst this flock of drunkards,
Am I to put our Cassio in some action
That may offend the isle. But here they come.
If consequence do but approve my dream,
My boat sails freely, both with wind and stream.
Enter Cassio; with him Montano and Gentlemen.
Servants following with wine.

Cassio. 'Fore God, they have given me a rouse already.

Mont. Good faith, a little one; not past a pint, as I am a soldier.

Iago. Some wine, ho!
[*Sings.*] And let me the **canakin**① **clink**②, clink;
And let me the canakin clink.
A soldier's a man;
Oh, man's life's but a **span**③;
Why then let a soldier drink.
Some wine, boys!

Cassio. 'Fore God, an excellent song.

Iago. I learned it in England, where indeed they are most potent in potting. Your Dane, your German, and your swag-bellied Hollander Drink, ho! — are nothing to your English.

Cassio. Is your Englishman so expert in his drinking?

Iago. Why, he drinks you with facility your Dane dead drunk. He sweats not to overthrow your **Almain**④; he gives your Hollander a vomit **ere**⑤ the next pottle can be filled.

Cassio. To the health of our general!

的岛上的优秀人物,我也把他们灌得酩酊大醉;他们今晚也是要守夜的。在这一群醉汉中间,我要叫我们这位卡西奥干出一些可以激起这岛上公愤的事来。可是他们来了。

　　　　卡西奥率蒙塔诺及绅士等重上;众仆持酒后随。

卡西奥　上帝可以作证,他们已经灌了我一满杯啦。

蒙塔诺　真的,只是小小的一杯,顶多也不过一品脱的分量;我是一个军人,从来不会说谎的。

伊阿古　喂,酒来!(唱)

　　　　一瓶一瓶复一瓶,
　　　　饮酒击瓶叮当鸣。
　　　　我为军人岂无情,
　　　　人命倏忽如烟云,
　　　　聊持杯酒遣浮生。

　　　　孩子们,酒来!

卡西奥　好一支歌儿!

伊阿古　这一支歌是我在英格兰学来的。英格兰人的酒量才厉害呢;什么丹麦人,德国人,大肚子的荷兰人——酒来!——比起英格兰人来都不算什么。

卡西奥　你那英格兰人果然这样善于喝酒吗?

伊阿古　嘿,他会不动声色地把丹麦人灌得烂醉如泥,面不流汗地把德国人灌得不省人事,还没有倒满下一杯,那荷兰人已经呕吐狼藉了。

卡西奥　祝我们的主帅健康!

① canakin ['kænəkin] *n.* 小罐;小杯
② clink [kliŋk] *v.* 叮当作响
③ span [spæn] *n.* 一段时间;短暂的时间

④ Almain ['ælmein] *n., a.* [废语] 日耳曼(的)
⑤ ere [εə] *prep.* [古语、诗歌用语] 在……之前;在……以前

Mont. I am for it, lieutenant, and I'll do you justice.

Iago. O sweet England!

[*Sings.*] King Stephen was and-a worthy peer,

His **breeches**① cost him but a crown;

He held them sixpence all too dear,

With that he call'd the tailor lown.

He was a **wight**② of high renown,

And thou art but of low degree.

'Tis pride that pulls the country down;

Then take thine **auld**③ cloak about thee.

Some wine, hoa!

Cassio. Why, this is a more exquisite song than the other.

Iago. Will you hear't again?

Cassio. No, for I hold him to be unworthy of his place that does those things. Well: God's above all, and there be souls must be saved, and there be souls must not be saved.

Iago. It's true, good lieutenant.

Cassio. For mine own part—no offense to the General, nor any man of quality—I hope to be saved.

Iago. And so do I too, lieutenant.

Cassio. Ay, but, by your leave, not before me. The lieutenant is to be saved before the ancient. Let's have no more of this; let's to our affairs. God forgive us our sins! Gentlemen, let's look to our business. Do not think, gentlemen, I am drunk: this is my ancient, this is my right hand, and this is my left. I am not drunk now; I can stand well enough, and I speak well enough.

All. Excellent well.

Cassio. Why, very well then; you must not think then that I am drunk.

Exit.

Mont. To the platform, masters; come, let's set the watch.

① breeches ['britʃiz; 'briːtʃiz] n. 马裤

② wight [wait] n. [古语] 人

③ auld [ɔːld] a. [苏格兰方言] 旧的

蒙塔诺　赞成，副将，您喝我也喝。

伊阿古　可爱的英格兰！

　　　　斯蒂芬皇帝是英主，
　　　　做条裤子用五先令；
　　　　他嫌多花了六便士，
　　　　因此他破口骂裁缝。
　　　　他为人是大名鼎鼎，
　　　　你不过是无名小卒；
　　　　虚荣把国家社稷倾，
　　　　我劝你还穿旧衣服。

　　喂，酒来！

卡西奥　呃，这支歌比方才唱的那一支更好听。

伊阿古　你要再听一遍吗？

卡西奥　不，因为我认为他这样地位的人做出这种事情来是有失体统的。好，上帝在我们头上，有的灵魂必须得救，有的灵魂就不能得救。

伊阿古　对了，副将。

卡西奥　讲到我自己——我并没有冒犯我们主帅或是无论哪一位大人物的意思——我是希望能够得救的。

伊阿古　我也这样希望，副将。

卡西奥　嗯，可是，对不起，你不能比我先得救；副将得救了，然后才是旗官得救。咱们别提这种话啦，还是去干我们的事吧。上帝赦免我们的罪恶！各位先生，我们不要忘记了我们的事情。不要以为我是醉了，各位先生。这是我的旗官；这是我的右手，这是我的左手。我现在并没有醉；我站得很稳，我说话也很清楚。

众人　非常清楚。

卡西奥　那么很好；你们可不要以为我醉了。（下）

蒙塔诺　各位朋友，来，我们到露台上守望去。

Iago. You see this fellow that is gone before;
He is a soldier, fit to stand by Caesar,
And give direction. And do but see his vice;
'Tis to his virtue a just **equinox**①,
The one as long as the other. 'tis pity of him.
I fear the trust Othello puts him in,
On some odd time of his infirmity
Will shake this Island.

Mont. But is he often thus?

Iago. 'Tis evermore the prologue to his sleep.
He'll watch the **horologe**② a double set,
If drink rock not his cradle.

Mont. It were well
The general were put in mind of it.
Perhaps he sees it not, or his good nature
Prizes the virtue that appears in Cassio,
And looks not on his evils: is not this true?
Enter Roderigo.

Iago. [*Aside to him.*] How now, Roderigo?
I pray you, after the lieutenant; go.
Exit Roderigo.

Mont. And 'tis great pity that the noble Moor
Should hazard such a place as his own second
With one of an ingraft infirmity.
It were an honest action to say
So to the Moor.

Iago. Not I, for this fair island.
I do love Cassio well, and would do much.
To cure him of this evil. But hark, What noise?
[*Within.*] Help, help.

第二幕

① equinox ['i:kwinɔks] *n.* 昼夜平分时

伊阿古　你们看刚才出去的这一个人；讲到指挥三军的才能，他可以和恺撒争一日之雄；可是你们瞧他这一种酗酒的样子，它正好和他的长处互相抵消。我真为他可惜！我怕奥赛罗对他如此信任，也许有一天会被他误了大事，使全岛大受震动的。

② horologe ['hɔrələdʒ] *n.* 计时器

蒙塔诺　可是他常常是这样的吗？

伊阿古　他喝醉了酒总要睡觉；要是没有酒替他催眠，他可以一昼夜打起精神不睡。

蒙塔诺　这种情形应该向元帅提起；也许他没有觉察，也许他秉性仁恕，因为看重卡西奥的才能而忽略了他的短处。这句话对不对？

　　　　　罗德利哥上。

伊阿古　（向罗德利哥旁白）怎么，罗德利哥！你快追上那副将后面去吧；去。（罗德利哥下）

蒙塔诺　这高贵的摩尔人竟会让一个染上这种恶癖的人做他的辅佐，真是一件令人抱憾的事。谁能够老实对他这样说，才是一个正直的汉子。

伊阿古　即使把这一座大好的岛送给我，我也不愿意说；我很爱卡西奥，要是有办法，我愿意尽力帮助他除去这一种恶癖。可是听！什么声音？（内呼声："救命！救命！"）

ACT II

Enter Cassio, pursuing Roderigo.

Cassio. 'Zounds, you rogue! You rascal!

Mont. What's the matter, lieutenant?

Cassio. A knave teach me my duty? But I'll beat the knave into a twiggen bottle.

Rod. Beat me?

Cassio. Dost thou prate, Rogue?

Strikes Roderigo.

Mont. [*Staying him.*] Nay, good lieutenant; I pray you, sir, hold your hand.

Cassio. Let me go, sir, or I'll knock you o'er the **mazzard**①.

Mont. Come, come, you're drunk.

Cassio. Drunk?

They fight.

Iago. [*Aside to Roderigo.*] Away I say; go out and cry a **mutiny**②.

Exit Roderigo.

Nay, good lieutenant. God's will, gentlemen!

Help, hoa! Lieutenant! Sir Montan! Sir!

Help masters. Here's a goodly watch indeed.

A bell rings.

Who's that that rings the bell. Diablo, hoa!

The town will rise. God's will, lieutenant, hold!

You will be shamed forever.

Enter Othello and Attendants.

Othello. What is the matter here?

Mont. 'Zounds, I bleed still; I am hurt to the death.

Othello. Hold for your lives.

Iago. Hold hoa! Lieutenant — sir — Montano — gentlemen —

Have you forgot all place of sense and duty?

Hold! The general speaks to you: hold for shame!

Othello. Why, how now hoa? From whence ariseth this?

①　mazzard ['mæzəd] *n.* [古语] 头，头颅；脸

②　mutiny ['mju:tini] *n.* 叛变；暴动

　　　　　　　　　卡西奥驱罗德利哥重上。

卡西奥　混蛋！狗贼！

蒙塔诺　什么事，副将？

卡西奥　一个混蛋竟敢教训起我来！我要把这混蛋打进一只瓶子里去。

罗德利哥　打我！

卡西奥　你还要利嘴吗，狗贼？（打罗德利哥）

蒙塔诺　（拉卡西奥）不，副将，请您住手。

卡西奥　放开我，先生，否则我要一拳打到你的头上来了。

蒙塔诺　得啦得啦，你醉了。

卡西奥　醉了！（与蒙塔诺斗）

伊阿古　（向罗德利哥旁白）快走！到外边去高声嚷叫，说是出了乱子啦。（罗德利哥下）不，副将！天啊，各位先生！喂，来人！副将！蒙塔诺！帮帮忙，各位朋友！这算是守的什么夜呀！（钟鸣）谁在那儿打钟？该死！全市的人都要起来了。天啊！副将，住手！你的脸要从此丢尽啦。

　　　　　　　　　奥赛罗及侍从等重上。

奥赛罗　这儿出了什么事情？

蒙塔诺　他妈的！我的血流个不停；我受了重伤啦。

奥赛罗　要活命的快住手！

伊阿古　喂，住手，副将！蒙塔诺！各位先生！你们忘记你们的地位和责任了吗？住手！主帅在对你们说话；还不住手！

奥赛罗　怎么，怎么！为什么闹起来的？难道我们都

ACT II

>Are we turn'd Turks, and to ourselves do that
>Which heaven hath forbid the Ottomites?
>For Christian shame, put by this barbarous brawl.
>He that stirs next to carve for his own rage,
>Holds his soul light; he dies upon his motion.
>Silence that dreadful bell; it frights the Isle
>From her propriety. What is the matter, Masters?
>Honest Iago, that look'st dead with grieving,
>Speak: who began this? On thy love, I charge thee.

Iago. I do not know. Friends all but now, even now,
In quarter, and in terms like bride and groom
Devesting① them for bed; and then, but now
As if some planet had unwitted men,
Swords out, and tilting one at other's breast,
In opposition bloody. I cannot speak
Any beginning to this **peevish**② odds.
And would in action glorious, I had lost
Those legs that brought me to a part of it.

Othello. How comes it, Michael, you are thus forgot?

Cassio. I pray you, pardon me; I cannot speak.

Othello. Worthy Montano, you were wont be civil;
The gravity and stillness of your youth
The world hath noted, and your name is great
In mouths of wisest censure. What's the matter,
That you **unlace**③ your reputation thus,
And spend your rich opinion, for the name
Of a night-brawler? Give me answer to it.

Mont. Worthy Othello, I am hurt to danger.
Your officer, Iago, can inform you,
While I spare speech which something now offends me,

变成野蛮人了吗？上天不许异教徒攻打我们，我们倒自相残杀起来了吗？为了基督徒的面子，停止这场粗暴的争吵；谁要是一味怄气，再敢动一动，他就是看轻他自己的灵魂，他一举手我就叫他死。叫他们不要打那可怕的钟；它会扰乱岛上的人心。各位，究竟是怎么一回事？正直的伊阿古，瞧你懊恼得脸色惨淡，告诉我，谁开始这场争闹的？凭着你的忠心，老实对我说。

伊阿古 我不知道，刚才还是好好的朋友，像正在宽衣解带的新夫妇一般相亲相爱，一下子就好像受到什么星光的刺激，迷失了他们的本性似的，大家拔出剑来，向彼此的胸前直刺过去，拼个你死我活了。我说不出这场任性的争吵是怎么开始的；只怪我这双腿不曾在光荣的战阵上失去，那么我也不会踏进这种是非中间了！

奥赛罗 迈克尔，你怎么会这样忘记你自己的身份？
卡西奥 请您原谅我；我没有话可说。
奥赛罗 尊贵的蒙塔诺，您一向是个温文知礼的人，您的少年端重为举世所钦佩，在贤人君子之间，您有很好的名声；为什么您会这样自贬身价，牺牲您的宝贵的名誉，让人家说您是个在深更半夜里酗酒闹事的家伙？给我一个回答。

蒙塔诺 尊贵的奥赛罗，我伤得很厉害，不能多说话；您的贵部下伊阿古可以告诉您我所知道的一切。其实我也不知道我在今夜说错了什么话或是做错了

① devest [di'vest] v. 脱掉……的衣服

② peevish ['pi:viʃ] a. 易怒的

③ unlace [ʌn'leis] v. 解开……的带子

ACT II

        Of all that I do know, nor know I aught
        By me that's said or done amiss this night,
        Unless self-charity be sometimes a vice,
        And to defend ourselves it be a sin,
        When violence assails us.

Othello. Now, by heaven,
        My blood begins my safer guides to rule,
        And passion having my best judgement collied,
        Assays to lead the way. If I once stir,
        Or do but lift this arm, the best of you
        Shall sink in my rebuke. Give me to know
        How this foul **rout**① began, who set it on,
        And he that is approved in this offense,
        Though he had twinn'd with me, both at a birth,
        Shall lose me. What in a town of war,
        Yet wild, the people's hearts brimful of fear,
        To manage private and domestic quarrel,
        In night, and on the court and guard of safety?
        'Tis monstrous. Iago, who began 't?

Mont. If partially **affined**②, or leagued in office,
        Thou dost deliver more or less than truth,
        Thou art no soldier.

Iago. Touch me not so near,
        I had rather have this tongue cut from my mouth,
        Than it should do offense to Michael Cassio.
        Yet, I persuade myself, to speak the truth,
        Shall nothing wrong him. Thus it is general.
        Montano and myself being in speech,
        There comes a fellow crying out for help,
        And Cassio following him with determined sword,

什么事,除非在暴力侵凌的时候,自卫是一桩罪恶。

奥赛罗　苍天在上,我现在可再也遏制不住我的怒气了。我只要动一动,或是举一举这一只胳臂,就可以叫你们中间最有本领的人在我的一怒之下丧失了生命。让我知道这一场可耻的骚乱①是怎么开始的,谁是最初肇起事端来的人;要是证实了哪一个人是启衅的罪魁,即使他是我的孪生兄弟,我也不能放过他。什么!一个新遭战乱的城市,秩序还没有恢复,人民的心里充满了恐惧,你们却在深更半夜,在全岛治安所系的所在为了私人间的细故争吵起来!岂有此理!伊阿古,谁是肇事的人?

蒙塔诺　你要是意存偏袒,或是同僚相护②,所说的话和事实不尽符合,你就不是个军人。

伊阿古　不要这样逼我;我宁愿割下自己的舌头,也不愿让它说迈克尔·卡西奥的坏话;可是事已如此,我想说老实话也不算对不起他。是这样的,主帅,蒙塔诺跟我正在谈话,忽然跑进一个人来高呼救命,后面跟着卡西奥,杀气腾腾地提着剑,好像一定要杀死他才甘心似的;那时候这位先生就挺身前去拦住卡西奥,请他息怒;我自己追赶那个叫喊的人,因为恐怕他在外边大惊小怪,扰

---

① rout [raut] *n.* 骚乱

② affined [əˈfaind] *a.* 有密切关系的

ACT II

To execute upon him. Sir, this gentleman,
Steps in to Cassio and **entreats**① his pause.
Myself the crying fellow did pursue,
Lest by his clamor, as it so fell out,
The town might fall in fright. He, swift of foot,
Outran my purpose; and I return'd the rather
For that I heard the clink and fall of swords,
And Cassio high in oath, which till tonight
I ne'er might say before. When I came back
For this was brief, I found them close together,
At blow and thrust, even as again they were
When you yourself did part them.
More of this matter cannot I report.
But men are men; the best sometimes forget.
Though Cassio did some little wrong to him,
As men in rage strike those that wish them best,
Yet surely Cassio, I believe, received
From him that fled some strange indignity,
Which patience could not pass.

Othello. I know Iago,
Thy honesty and love doth **mince**② this matter,
Making it light to Cassio: Cassio, I love thee,
But never more be officer of mine.
Enter Desdemona, attended.
Look, if my gentle love be not raised up:
I'll make thee an example.

Desde. What's the matter?

Othello. All's well, sweeting; come away to bed.
Sir, for your hurts, myself will be your surgeon.
Lead him off.

① entreat [in'tri:t] v. 请求

② mince [mins] v. 细分、切细

乱人心,可是他跑得快,我追不上,又听见背后刀剑碰撞和卡西奥高声咒骂的声音,所以就回来了;我从来没有听见他这样骂过人;我本来追得不远,一转身就看见他们在这儿你一刀我一剑地厮杀得难解难分,正像您到来喝开他们的时候一样。我所能报告的就是这几句话。人总是人,圣贤也有错误的时候;一个人在愤怒之中,就是好朋友也会翻脸不认。虽然卡西奥给了他一点小小的伤害,可是我相信卡西奥一定从那逃走的家伙手里受到什么奇耻大辱,所以才会动起那么大的火性来的。

奥赛罗 伊阿古,我知道你的忠实和义气,是你把这件事情轻描淡写,替卡西奥减轻他的罪名。卡西奥,你是我的好朋友,可是从此以后,你不是我的部属了。

    苔丝狄蒙娜率侍从重上。

奥赛罗 瞧!我的温柔的爱人也给你们吵醒了!(向卡西奥)我要拿你做一个榜样。

苔丝狄蒙娜 什么事?

奥赛罗 现在一切都没事了,爱人;去睡吧。先生,您受的伤我愿意亲自替您医治。把他扶出去。(侍从扶蒙塔诺下)伊阿古,你去巡视市街,安定安定受

ACT II

Exit Montano, attended.

Iago, look with care about the town,
And silence those whom this vile brawl distracted.
Come, Desdemona, 'tis the soldiers' life.
To have their **balmy**① **slumbers**② waked with **strife**③.

Exeunt all but Iago and Cassio.

Iago. What, are you hurt, Lieutenant?

Cassio. Ay, past all surgery.

Iago. Marry, heaven forbid!

Cassio. Reputation, reputation, reputation, Oh, I have lost my reputation, I have lost the immortal part of myself, and what remains is **bestial**④. My reputation, Iago, my reputation!

Iago. As I am an honest man, I thought you had received some bodily wound; there is more sense in that than in reputation. Reputation is an idle and most false **imposition**⑤; often got without merit and lost without deserving. You have lost no reputation at all, unless you repute yourself such a loser. What man, there are ways to recover the general again. You are but now cast in his mood, a punishment more in policy than in malice; even so as one would beat his offenseless dog to **affright**⑥ an imperious lion. Sue to him again, and he's yours.

Cassio. I will rather sue to be despised than to deceive so good a commander with so slight, so drunken, and so indiscreet an officer. Drunk? And speak parrot? And **squabble**⑦? Swagger? Swear? And discourse fustian with one's own shadow? Oh thou invisible spirit of wine, if thou hast no name to be known by, let us call thee devil.

Iago. What was he that you followed with your sword?
What had he done to you?

Cassio. I know not.

Iago. Is 't possible?

① balmy ['bɑ:mi] *a.* 宜人的
② slumber ['slʌmbə] *n.* 睡眠
③ strife [straif] *n.* 争吵，冲突
④ bestial ['bestjəl] *a.* 畜生般的
⑤ imposition [,impə'ziʃən] *n.* 欺骗，哄骗
⑥ affright [ə'frait] *v.* 吓唬
⑦ squabble ['skwɔbl] *v.*（为小事）争论，争吵

惊的人心。来，苔丝狄蒙娜。难圆的是军人的好梦，才合眼又被杀声惊动。（除伊阿古、卡西奥外均下）

伊阿古 什么！副将，你受伤了吗？

卡西奥 嗯，我的伤是无药可救的了。

伊阿古 哎哟，上天保佑没有这样的事！

卡西奥 名誉，名誉，名誉！啊，我的名誉已经一败涂地了！我已经失去我的生命中不死的一部分，留下来的也就跟畜生没有分别了。我的名誉，伊阿古，我的名誉。

伊阿古 我是个老实人，我还以为你受到了什么身体上的伤害，那是比名誉的损失痛苦得多的。名誉是一件无聊的骗人的东西；得到它的人未必有什么功德，失去它的人也未必有什么过失。你的名誉仍旧是好端端的，除非你自己以为它已经扫地了。嘿，朋友，你要恢复主帅对你的欢心，尽有办法呢。你现在不过一时遭逢他的恼怒，他给你的这一种处分，与其说是表示对你的不满，还不如说是遮掩世人耳目的政策，正像有人为吓退一头凶恶的狮子而故意鞭打他的驯良的狗一样。你只要向他恳求恳求，他一定会回心转意的。

卡西奥 我宁愿恳求他唾弃我，也不愿蒙蔽他的聪明，让这样一位贤能的主帅手下有这么一个酗酒放荡的不肖将校。纵饮无度！胡言乱道！吵架！吹牛！赌咒！跟自己的影子说些废话！啊，你空虚缥缈的旨酒的精灵，要是你还没有一个名字，让我们叫你作魔鬼吧！

伊阿古 你提着剑追逐不舍的那个人是谁？他怎么冒犯了你？

卡西奥 我不知道。

伊阿古 你怎么会不知道？

ACT II

Cassio. I remember a mass of things, but nothing distinctly; a quarrel, but nothing wherefore. Oh God, That men should put an enemy in their mouths, to steal away their brains! that we should with joy, pleasance, **revel**①, and applause transform ourselves into beasts!

Iago. Why? But you are now well enough. How came you thus recovered?

Cassio. It hath pleased the devil drunkenness, to give place to the devil **wrath**②: one unperfectness shows me another, to make me frankly despise myself.

Iago. Come, you are too severe a moraler. As the time, the place, and the condition of this country stands, I could heartily wish this had not befallen; but since it is as it is, mend it for your own good.

Cassio. I will ask him for my place again; he shall tell me I am a drunkard! Had I as many mouths as **Hydra**③, such an answer would stop them all. To be now a sensible man, by and by a fool, and presently a beast. Oh strange! Every **inordinate**④ cup is unblest, and the ingredient is a devil.

Iago. Come, come, good wine is a good familiar creature, if it be well used. Exclaim no more against it. And good lieutenant, I think you think I love you.

Cassio. I have well approved it, sir. I drunk!

Iago. You or any man living may be drunk at a time, man. I'll tell you what you shall do: Our general's wife is now the general. I may say so in this respect, for that he hath devoted and given up himself to the contemplation, mark and denotement of her parts and graces. Confess yourself freely to her; **importune**⑤ her help to put you in your place again. She is of so free, so kind, so apt, so blessed a disposition, she holds it a vice in her goodness, not to do more than she is requested. This broken joint between you and her husband, entreat her to **splinter**⑥. And my fortunes against any lay worth naming, this crack of your love shall

① revel ['revəl] v. 狂欢

② wrath [rɔθ] n. 愤怒

③ Hydra ['haidrə] n. 九头蛇

④ inordinate [i'nɔ:dinət] a. 无节制的

⑤ importune [im'pɔ:tju:n] v. 不断恳求

⑥ splinter ['splintə] n. 裂片

卡西奥 我记得一大堆的事情，可是全都是模模糊糊的；我记得跟人家吵起来，可是不知道为了什么。上帝啊！人们居然会把一个仇敌放进自己的嘴里，让它偷去他们的头脑，在欢天喜地之中，把我们自己变成了畜生！

伊阿古 可是你现在已经很清醒了；你怎么会明白过来的？

卡西奥 气鬼一上了身，酒鬼就自动退让；一件过失引起了第二件过失，简直使我自己也瞧不起自己了。

伊阿古 得啦，你也太认真了。照此地的环境说起来，我但愿没有这种事情发生；可是既然事已如此，以后留心改过就是了。

卡西奥 我要向他请求恢复我的原职；他会对我说我是一个酒棍！即使我有一百张嘴，这样一个答复也会把它们一起封住。现在还是一个清清楚楚的人，不一会儿就变成个傻子，然后立刻就变成一头畜生！啊，奇怪！每一杯过量的酒都是魔鬼酿成的毒水。

伊阿古 算了，算了，好酒只要不滥喝，也是一个很好的伙伴；你也不用咒骂它了。副将，我想你一定把我当作一个好朋友看待。

卡西奥 我很信任你的友谊。我醉了！

伊阿古 朋友，一个人有时候多喝了几杯，也是免不了的。让我告诉你一个办法。我们主帅的夫人现在是我们真正的主帅；我可以这样说，因为他心里只念着她的好处，眼睛里只看见她的可爱。你只要在她面前坦白忏悔，恳求恳求她，她一定会帮助你官复原职。她的性情是那么慷慨仁慈，那么体贴人心，人家请她出十分力，她要是没有出到十二分，就觉得好像对不起人似的。你请她替你弥缝弥缝你跟她的丈夫之间的这一道裂痕，我可以拿我的全部财产

grow stronger than it was before.

Cassio. You advise me well.

Iago. I protest, in the sincerity of love and honest kindness.

Cassio. I think it freely; and betimes in the morning, I will beseech the virtuous Desdemona to undertake for me. I am desperate of my fortunes if they check me.

Iago. You are in the right. Good night lieutenant, I must to the watch.

Cassio. Good night, honest Iago.

Exit.

Iago. And what's he then that says I play the villain?
When this advice is free I give and honest,
Probal to thinking, and indeed the course
To win the Moor again. For 'tis most easy
The inclining Desdemona to subdue
In any honest suit. She's framed as fruitful
As the free elements. And then for her
To win the Moor, were 't to **renounce**① his **baptism**②,
All seals and symbols of redeemed sin:
His soul is so **enfetter'd**③ to her love,
That she may make, unmake, do what she list,
Even as her appetite shall play the god,
With his weak function. How am I then a villain,
To counsel Cassio to this parallel course,
Directly to his good? Divinity of hell,
When devils will the blackest sins put on,
They do suggest at first with heavenly shows,
As I do now. For whiles this honest fool
Plies Desdemona to repair his fortune,
And she for him, pleads strongly to the Moor,
I'll pour this **pestilence**④ into his ear,

打赌，你们的交情一定反而会因此格外加强的。

卡西奥　你的主意出得很好。

伊阿古　我发誓这一种意思完全出于一片诚心。

卡西奥　我充分信任你的善意；明天一早我就请求贤德的苔丝狄蒙娜替我尽力说情。要是我在这儿给他们革退了，我的前途也就从此毁了。

伊阿古　你说得对。晚安，副将；我还要守夜去呢。

卡西奥　晚安，正直的伊阿古！（下）

伊阿古　谁说我做事奸恶？我贡献给他的这番意见，不是光明正大，很合理，而且的确是挽回这摩尔人的心意的最好办法吗？只要是正当的请求，苔丝狄蒙娜总是有求必应的；她的为人是再慷慨再热心不过的了。至于叫她去说动这摩尔人，更是不费吹灰之力；他的灵魂已经完全成为她的爱情的俘虏，无论她要做什么事，或是把已经做成的事重新推翻，即使叫他抛弃他的信仰和一切得救的希望，他也会唯命是从，让她的喜恶主宰他的无力反抗的身心。我既然向卡西奥指示了这一条对他有利的方策，谁还能说我是个恶人呢？佛面蛇心的鬼魅！恶魔往往用神圣的外表，引诱世人干最恶的罪行，正像我现在所用的手段一样；因为当这个老实的呆子恳求苔丝狄蒙娜为他转圜，当她竭力在那摩尔人面前替他说情的时候，我就要用毒药灌进那摩尔人的耳中，说是她所以要运动卡西

---

① renounce [ri'nauns] *v.* 宣布放弃（要求、权力、信仰等）

② baptism ['bæptizəm] *n.*【基督教】洗礼

③ enfetter [in'fetə] *v.* 给……上脚镣

④ pestilence ['pestiləns] *n.* 疫，有毒害的事物

ACT II

        That she repeals him for her body's lust;
        And by how much she strives to do him good,
        She shall undo her credit with the Moor.
        So will I turn her virtue into pitch,
        And out of her own goodness make the net,
        That shall **enmesh**① them all.
        Enter Roderigo.
        How now, Roderigo?

Rod. I do follow here in the chase, not like a hound that hunts, but one that **fills up**② the cry. My money is almost spent; I have been tonight exceedingly well **cudgeled**③; and I think the issue will be, I shall have so much experience for my pains; and so, with no money at all and a little more wit, return again to Venice.

Iago. How poor are they that have not patience?
        What wound did ever heal but by degrees?
        Thou know'st we work by wit and not by witchcraft,
        And wit depends on **dilatory**④ time.
        Does 't not go well? Cassio hath beaten thee,
        And thou by that small hurt hast cashier'd Cassio.
        Though other things grow fair against the sun,
        Yet fruits that blossom first, will first be ripe.
        Content thyself awhile. By the mass, 'tis morning;
        Pleasure and action make the hours seem short.
        Retire thee; go where thou art **billeted**⑤.
        Away, I say, thou shalt know more hereafter.
        Nay, get thee gone.
        Exit Roderigo.
        Two things are to be done:
        My wife must move for Cassio to her mistress: I'll set her on;
        Myself a while to draw the Moor apart,

奥复职，只是为了恋奸情热的缘故。这样她越是忠于所托，越是会加强那摩尔人的猜疑；我就利用她的善良的心肠污毁她的名誉，让他们一个个都落进了我的罗网之中。

罗德利哥重上。

① enmesh [in'meʃ] v. 使陷入网中，缠住

伊阿古　啊，罗德利哥！

罗德利哥　我在这儿给你们驱来赶去，不像一头追寻狐兔的猎狗，倒像是替你们凑凑热闹的。我的钱也差不多花光了，今夜我还挨了一顿痛打；我想这番教训，大概就是我费去不少辛苦换来的代价了。现在我的钱囊已经空空如也，我的头脑里总算增加了一点智慧，我要回威尼斯去了。

② fill up（使）装满
③ cudgel ['kʌdʒəl] v. 棒打

伊阿古　没有耐性的人是多么可怜！什么伤口不是慢慢地平复起来的？你知道我们干事情全赖计谋，并不是用的魔法；用计谋就必须等待时机成熟。一切不是进行得很顺利吗？卡西奥固然把你打了一顿，可是你受了一点小小的痛苦，已经使卡西奥把官职都丢了。虽然在太阳光底下，各种草木都欣欣向荣，可是最先开花的果子总是最先成熟。你安心点儿吧。哎哟，天已经亮啦；又是喝酒，又是打架，闹哄哄的就让时间飞过去了。你去吧，回到你的宿舍里去，去吧，有什么消息我再来告诉你；去吧。（罗德利哥下）我还要做两件事情：第一是叫我的妻子在她的女主人面前替卡西奥说两句好话；同时我就去设法把那摩尔人骗开，等到

④ dilatory ['dilətəri] a. 迟误的，拖拉的

⑤ billet ['bilit] v. 为……提供宿舍

And bring him jump when he may Cassio find
Soliciting① his wife. Ay, that's the way;
Dull not device by coldness and delay.
Exit.

卡西奥去向他的妻子请求的时候，再让他亲眼看见这幕把戏。好，言之有理；不要迁延不决，耽误了锦囊妙计。（下）

① solicit [sə'lisit] v. 请求

ACT III

第三幕

Scene I. Before the castle.

Enter Cassio and some Musicians.

Cassio. Masters, play here, I will content your pains; something that's brief; and bid good morrow, general.

Enter Clown.

Clown. Why, Masters, have your instruments been in Naples, that they speak i' the nose thus?

Musician. How, sir, how?

Clown. Are these, I pray you, **wind instruments**①?

Musician. Ay, marry are they, sir.

Clown. Oh, **thereby**② hangs a tale.

Musician. Whereby hangs a tale, sir?

Clown. Marry sir, by many a wind instrument that I know. But masters, here's money for you; and the general so likes your music, that he desires you for love's sake, to make no more noise with it.

Musician. Well, sir, we will not.

Clown. If you have any music that may not be heard, to 't again; but as they say, to hear music the general does not greatly care.

Musician. We have none such, sir.

第一场　城堡前

　　　　　　卡西奥及若干乐工上。

卡西奥　列位朋友，就在这儿奏起来吧；我会酬劳你们的。奏一支简短一些的乐曲，敬祝我们的主帅晨安。（音乐）

　　　　　　小丑上。

小丑　怎么，列位朋友，你们的乐器都曾到过那不勒斯，所以这样嗡咙嗡咙地用鼻音说话吗？

乐工甲　怎么，大哥，怎么？

小丑　请问这些都是管乐器吗？

乐工甲　正是，大哥。

小丑　啊，怪不得下面有个那玩意儿。

乐工甲　怪不得有个什么玩意儿，大哥？

小丑　我说，有好多管乐器就都是这么回事。可是，列位朋友，这儿是赏给你们的钱；将军非常喜欢你们的音乐，他请求你们千万不要再奏下去了。

乐工甲　好，大哥，那么我们不奏了。

小丑　要是你们会奏听不见的音乐，请奏起来吧；可是正像人家说的，将军对于听音乐这件事不大感兴趣。

乐工甲　我们不会奏那样的音乐。

---

① wind instrument【音乐】管乐器

② thereby [,ðɛəˈbai; ˈðɛəbai] *ad.* 因此

ACT III

Clown. Then put up your pipes in your bag, for I'll away.
　　Go, vanish into air, away!
　　Exeunt Musicians.
Cassio. Dost thou hear, my honest friend?
Clown. No, I hear not your honest friend; I hear you.
Cassio. Prithee, keep up thy **quillets**①. There's a poor piece of gold for thee.
　　If the gentlewoman that attends the general's wife be stirring, tell her
　　there's one Cassio entreats her a little favor of speech. Wilt thou do this?
Clown. She is stirring, sir. If she will stir hither, I shall seem to **notify**② unto her.
Cassio. Do, good my friend.
　　Exit Clown.
　　Enter Iago.
　　In happy time, Iago.
Iago. You have not been a-bed, then?
Cassio. Why, no; the day had broke
　　Before we parted. I have made bold, Iago,
　　To send in to your wife. My suit to her is,
　　That she will to virtuous Desdemona
　　Procure me some access.
Iago. I'll send her to you presently;
　　And I'll devise a mean to draw the Moor
　　Out of the way, that your **converse**③ and business
　　May be more free.
Cassio. I humbly thank you for 't.
　　Exit Iago.
　　I never knew
　　A Florentine more kind and honest.
　　Enter Emilia.
Emilia. Good morrow, good lieutenant. I am sorry
　　For your displeasure, but all will sure be well.

第三幕

小丑 那么把你们的笛子藏起来,因为我要去了。去,消灭在空气里吧;去!(乐工等下)

卡西奥 你听没听见,我的好朋友?

小丑 不,我没有听见您的好朋友;我只听见您。

卡西奥 少说笑话。这一块小小的金币你拿了去;要是侍候将军夫人的那位奶奶已经起身,你就告诉她有一个卡西奥请她出来说话。你肯不肯?

小丑 她已经起身了,先生;要是她愿意出来,我就告诉她。

卡西奥 谢谢你,我的好朋友。(小丑下)
　　伊阿古上。

卡西奥 来得正好,伊阿古。

伊阿古 你还没有上过床吗?

卡西奥 没有;我们分手的时候,天早就亮了。伊阿古,我已经大胆叫人去请你的妻子出来;我想请她替我设法见一见贤德的苔丝狄蒙娜。

伊阿古 我去叫她立刻出来见你。我还要想一个法子把那摩尔人调开,好让你们谈话方便一些。

卡西奥 多谢你的好意。(伊阿古下)我从来没有认识过一个比他更善良正直的佛罗伦萨人。
　　埃米莉亚上。

埃米莉亚 早安,副将!听说您误触主帅之怒,真是一件令人懊恼的事;可是一切就会转祸为福的。将军

① quillet ['kwilit] *n.* 遁词,托词

② notify ['nəutifai] *v.* 通知,通告;报告

③ converse [kən'və:s] *n.* (非正式)谈话

· 121 ·

ACT III

        The general and his wife are talking of it,
        And she speaks for you stoutly. The Moor replies
        That he you hurt is of great fame in Cyprus
        And great **affinity**① and that in wholesome wisdom
        He might not but refuse you; but he protests he loves you
        And needs no other suitor but his likings
        To take the safest occasion by the front
        To bring you in again.

Cassio.   Yet, I beseech you,
        If you think fit, or that it may be done,
        Give me advantage of some brief discourse
        With Desdemona alone.

Emilia.   Pray you, come in.
        I will bestow you where you shall have time
        To speak your **bosom**② freely.

Cassio.   I am much bound to you.
        Exeunt.

① affinity [ə'finəti] *n.* 密切关系

② bosom ['buzəm] *n.* 胸怀、内心

和他的夫人正在谈起此事，夫人竭力替您辩白。将军说，被您伤害的那个人，在塞浦路斯是很有名誉很有势力的，为了避免受人非难起见，他不得不把您斥革；可是他说他很喜欢您，即使没有别人替您说情，他也会留心着一有适当的机会，就让您恢复原职的。

卡西奥　可是我还要请求您一件事；要是您认为没有妨碍，或是可以办得到的话，请您设法让我独自见一见苔丝狄蒙娜，跟她作一次简短的谈话。

埃米莉亚　请您进来吧；我可以带您到一处可以让您从容吐露您的心曲的所在。

卡西奥　那真使我感激万分了。（同下）

Scene II. A room in the castle.

Enter Othello, Iago and Gentlemen.

Othello. These letters give, Iago, to the pilot,
And by him do my duties to the Senate.
That done, I will be walking on the works;
Repair there to me.

Iago. Well, my good lord, I'll do 't.

Othello. This **fortification**①, gentlemen, shall we see 't?

Gentlemen. We'll wait upon your lordship.

Exeunt.

第二场　城堡中的一室

奥赛罗、伊阿古及绅士等上。

奥赛罗　伊阿古,这几封信你拿去交给舵师,叫他回去替我呈上元老院。我就在堡垒上走走;你把事情办好以后,就到那边来见我。

伊阿古　是,主帅,我就去。

奥赛罗　各位,我们要不要去看看这儿的防务①?

众人　我们愿意奉陪。(同下)

---

① fortification [ˌfɔːtɪfɪˈkeɪʃ(ə)n] *n.* 防务

Scene III. The garden of the castle.

Enter Desdemona, Cassio and Emilia.

Desde.   Be thou assured, good Cassio, I will do
    All my abilities in thy behalf.
Emilia.   Good madam do:
    I warrant it grieves my husband,
    As if the cause were his.
Desde.   O, that's an honest fellow. Do not doubt, Cassio,
    But I will have my lord and you again
    As friendly as you were.
Cassio.   Bounteous madam,
    Whatever shall become of Michael Cassio,
    He's never anything but your true servant.
Desde.   I know 't: I thank you. You do love my lord:
    You have known him long; and be you well assured
    He shall in strangeness stand no farther off,
    Than in a politic distance.
Cassio.   Ay, but, lady,
    That policy may either last so long,
    Or feed upon such nice and waterish diet,

第三场　城堡中的花园

　　　　　　苔丝狄蒙娜、卡西奥及埃米莉亚上。

苔丝狄蒙娜　好卡西奥,你放心吧,我一定尽力替你说情就是了。

埃米莉亚　好夫人,请您千万出力。不瞒您说,我的丈夫为了这件事情,也懊恼得不得了,就像是他自己身上的事情一般。

苔丝狄蒙娜　啊!你的丈夫是一个好人。放心吧,卡西奥,我一定会设法使我的丈夫对你恢复原来的友谊。

卡西奥　大恩大德的夫人,无论迈克尔·卡西奥将来会有什么成就,他永远是您的忠实的仆人。

苔丝狄蒙娜　我知道;我感谢你的好意。你爱我的丈夫,你又是他的多年的知交;放心吧,他除了表面上因为避免嫌疑而对你略示疏远以外,绝不会真把你见外的。

卡西奥　您说得很对,夫人;可是避嫌这一个权宜之计可能因为什么细故或偶然事件而拖很长时间。我现在又失去了在帐下供奔走的机会,日久之后,有人

ACT III

        Or breed itself so out of circumstances,

        That I being absent and my place supplied,

        My General will forget my love and service.

Desde. Do not doubt that. Before Emilia here,

        I give thee warrant of thy place. Assure thee,

        If I do vow a friendship, I'll perform it

        To the last article. My lord shall never rest;

        I'll watch him tame and talk him out of patience;

        His bed shall seem a school, his board a shrift;

        I'll **intermingle**① everything he does

        With Cassio's suit: therefore be merry, Cassio,

        For thy solicitor shall rather die,

        Than give thy cause away.

        Enter Othello and Iago, at a distance.

Emilia. Madam, here comes my lord.

Cassio. Madam, I'll take my leave.

Desde. Nay, stay and hear me speak.

Cassio. Madam, not now. I am very **ill at ease**②,

        Unfit for mine own purposes.

Desde. Well, do your **discretion**③.

        Exit Cassio.

Iago. Ha! I like not that.

Othello. What dost thou say?

Iago. Nothing, my lord; or if I know not what.

Othello. Was not that Cassio parted from my wife?

Iago. Cassio, my lord? No sure, I cannot think it,

        That he would steal away so guilty-like,

        Seeing you coming.

Othello. I do believe 'twas he.

Desde. How now my lord?

代替了我的地位，恐怕主帅就要把我的忠诚和微劳一起忘记了。

苔丝狄蒙娜 那你不用担心；当着埃米莉亚的面，我保证你一定可以恢复原职。请你相信我，要是我发誓帮助一个朋友，我一定会帮助他到底。我的丈夫将要不得安息，无论睡觉吃饭的时候，我都要在他耳旁聒噪；无论他干什么事，我都要插进嘴去替卡西奥说情。所以高兴起来吧，卡西奥，因为你的辩护人是宁死不愿放弃你的权益的。

奥赛罗及伊阿古自远处上。

埃米莉亚 夫人，将军来了。
卡西奥 夫人，我告辞了。
苔丝狄蒙娜 啊，等一等，听我说。
卡西奥 夫人，改日再谈吧；我现在心里很不自在，见了主帅恐怕反多不便。
苔丝狄蒙娜 好，随您的便。（卡西奥下）
伊阿古 吓！我不喜欢那种样子。
奥赛罗 你说什么？
伊阿古 没有什么，主帅；要是——我不知道。
奥赛罗 那从我妻子身边走开去的，不是卡西奥吗？
伊阿古 卡西奥，主帅？不，我想他一定不会看见您来了，就好像做了什么亏心事似的偷偷地溜走的。
奥赛罗 我相信是他。
苔丝狄蒙娜 啊，我的主！刚才有人在这儿向我请托，他因为失去了您的欢心，非常抑郁不快呢。

① intermingle [ˌɪntəˈmɪŋgl] v. 使掺和

② ill at ease 局促不安，不自在，不舒服

③ discretion [dɪsˈkreʃən] n. 斟酌处理（或决定、选择）的自由（或权限）

ACT III

> I have been talking with a suitor here,
> A man that **languishes**① in your displeasure.

Othello. Who is 't you mean?

Desde. Why your lieutenant, Cassio. Good my lord,
> If I have any grace or power to move you,
> His present reconciliation take.
> For if he be not one that truly loves you,
> That errs in ignorance and not in cunning,
> I have no judgement in an honest face.
> I prithee call him back.

Othello. Went he hence now?

Desde. Ay, sooth; so humbled,
> That he hath left part of his grief with me
> To suffer with him. Good love, call him back.

Othello. Not now, sweet Desdemona; some other time.

Desde. But shall 't be shortly?

Othello. The sooner, sweet, for you.

Desde. Shall 't be tonight at supper?

Othello. No, not tonight.

Desde. Tomorrow dinner then?

Othello. I shall not dine at home;
> I meet the Captains at the Citadel.

Desde. Why then tomorrow night, on Tuesday morn,
> On Tuesday noon, or night, on Wednesday morn.
> I prithee name the time, but let it not
> Exceed three days. **In faith**②, he's **penitent**③;
> And yet his **trespass**④, in our common reason
> Save that, they say the wars must make example,
> Out of their best, is not almost a fault
> To incur a private check. When shall he come?

① languish ['læŋwiʃ] v. 失去活力

奥赛罗 你说的是什么人？

苔丝狄蒙娜 就是您的副将卡西奥呀。我的好夫君，要是我还有几分面子，或是几分可以左右您的力量，请您立刻对他恢复原来的恩宠吧；因为他倘不是一个真心爱您的人，他的过失倘不是无心而是有意的，那么我就是看错了人啦。请您叫他回来吧。

奥赛罗 他刚才从这儿走开吗？

苔丝狄蒙娜 嗯，是的；他是那样满含着羞愧，使我也不禁对他感到同情的悲哀。爱人，叫他回来吧。

奥赛罗 现在不必，亲爱的苔丝狄蒙娜；慢慢再说吧。

苔丝狄蒙娜 可是那不会太久吗？

奥赛罗 亲爱的，为了你的缘故，我叫他早一点复职就是了。

苔丝狄蒙娜 能不能在今天晚餐的时候？

奥赛罗 不，今晚可不能。

苔丝狄蒙娜 那么明天午餐的时候？

奥赛罗 明天我不在家里午餐；我要跟将领们在营中会面。

苔丝狄蒙娜 那么明天晚上吧；或是星期二早上，星期二中午，晚上，星期三早上，随您指定一个时间，可是不要超过三天以上。他对于自己的行为失检，的确非常悔恨；固然在这种战争的时期，必须惩办典型，以儆效尤，可是照我们平常的眼光看来，他的过失实在是微乎其微，不必受什么处分。什么时候让他来？告诉我，奥赛罗。要是您有什么事情要求我，我想我决不会拒绝您。或是这样吞吞吐吐的。什么！迈克尔·卡西奥，您向我求婚的时候，是他

② in faith 的确，确实

③ penitent ['penitənt] a. 悔过的

④ trespass ['trespəs; -pæs] n. 冒犯，过失

ACT III

        Tell me, Othello. I wonder in my soul,
        What you would ask me, that I should deny,
        Or stand so **mammering**① on? What? Michael Cassio,
        That came awooing with you, and so many a time
        When I have spoke of you **dispraisingly**②
        Hath ta'en your part, to have so much to do
        To bring him in? Birlady, I could do much.

Othello.   Prithee no more. Let him come when he will;
        I will deny thee nothing.

Desde.   Why, this is not a **boon**③;
        'Tis as I should entreat you wear your gloves,
        Or feed on nourishing dishes, or keep you warm,
        Or sue to you to do a peculiar profit
        To your own person. Nay, when I have a suit
        Wherein I mean to touch your love indeed,
        It shall be full of poise and difficult weight,
        And fearful to be granted.

Othello.   I will deny thee nothing,
        Whereon, I do beseech thee, grant me this,
        To leave me but a little to myself.

Desde.   Shall I deny you? No: farewell, my lord.

Othello.   Farewell my Desdemona; I'll come to thee straight.

Desde.   Emilia, come. Be as your fancies teach you;
        Whate'er you be, I am obedient.
        Exeunt Desdemona and Emilia.

Othello.   Excellent wretch: Perdition catch my soul,
        But I do love thee: and when I love thee not,
        Chaos is come again.

Iago.   My noble lord.

Othello.   What dost thou say, Iago?

① mammer ['mæmə] v. 口吃，犹豫不决

② dispraise [dis'preiz] v. 贬低

③ boon [bu:n] n. 恩赐

陪着您来的；好多次我表示对您不满意的时候，他总是为您辩护，现在我请您把他重新叙用，却会这样为难！相信我，我可以——

奥赛罗　好了，不要说下去了。让他随便什么时候来吧；你要什么我总不愿拒绝的。

苔丝狄蒙娜　这并不是一个恩惠，就好像我请求您戴上您的手套，劝您吃些富于营养的菜肴，穿些温暖的衣服，或是叫您做一件对您自己有益的事情一样。不，要是我真的向您提出什么要求，来试探试探您的爱情，那一定要是一件非常棘手而难以应允的事。

奥赛罗　我什么都不愿拒绝你；可是现在你必须答应暂时离开我一会儿。

苔丝狄蒙娜　我会拒绝您的要求吗？不。再会，我的主。
奥赛罗　再会，我的苔丝狄蒙娜；我马上就来看你。
苔丝狄蒙娜　埃米莉亚，来吧。您爱怎么样就怎么样，我总是服从您的。（苔丝狄蒙娜、埃米莉亚同下）

奥赛罗　可爱的女人！要是我不爱你，我的灵魂永堕地狱！当我不爱你的时候，世界也要复归于混沌了。

伊阿古　尊贵的主帅——
奥赛罗　你说什么，伊阿古？

ACT III

Iago.   Did Michael Cassio, when you woo'd my lady,
    Know of your love?
Othello.   He did, from first to last. Why dost thou ask?
Iago.   But for a satisfaction of my thought;
    No further harm.
Othello.   Why of thy thought, Iago?
Iago.   I did not think he had been acquainted with her.
Othello.   O yes, and went between us very oft.
Iago.   Indeed?
Othello.   Indeed? Ay, indeed. **Discern'st**① thou aught in that?
    Is he not honest?
Iago.   Honest, my lord?
Othello.   Honest? Ay, honest.
Iago.   My lord, for aught I know.
Othello.   What dost thou think?
Iago.   Think, my lord?
Othello.   Think, my lord? By heaven, he echoes me,
    As if there were some monster in his thought
    Too hideous to be shown. Thou dost mean something.
    I heard thee say even now, thou like'st not that,
    When Cassio left my wife. What didst not like?
    And when I told thee, he was of my counsel,
    In my whole course of wooing, thou criedst, indeed?
    And didst contract and **purse**② thy brow together,
    As if thou then hadst shut up in thy brain
    Some horrible **conceit**③. If thou dost love me,
    Show me thy thought.
Iago.   My lord, you know I love you.
Othello.   I think thou dost;
    And for I know thou'rt full of love and honesty,

① discern [di'sə:n] v.（用视觉或其他感觉或智力）看出

② purse [pə:s] v. 使皱起，使缩拢

③ conceit [kən'si:t] n. 想法，意见，私见

伊阿古 当您向夫人求婚的时候，迈克尔·卡西奥也知道你们的恋爱吗？

奥赛罗 他从头到尾都知道。你为什么问起？

伊阿古 不过是为了解释我心头的一个疑惑，并没有其他用意。

奥赛罗 你有什么疑惑，伊阿古？

伊阿古 我以为他从来跟夫人是不相识的。

奥赛罗 啊，不，他常常在我们两人之间传递消息。

伊阿古 当真！

奥赛罗 当真！嗯，当真。你觉得有什么不对吗？他这人不老实吗？

伊阿古 老实，我的主帅？

奥赛罗 老实！嗯，老实。

伊阿古 主帅，照我所知道的——

奥赛罗 你有什么意见？

伊阿古 意见，我的主帅！

奥赛罗 意见，我的主帅！天啊，他在学我的舌，好像在他的思想之中，藏着什么丑恶得不可见人的怪物似的。你的话里含着意思。刚才卡西奥离开我的妻子的时候，我听见你说，你不喜欢那种样子，你不喜欢什么样子呢？当我告诉你在我求婚的全部过程中，他都参与我们的秘密的时候，你又喊着说，"当真！"蹙紧了你的眉头，好像在把一个可怕的思想关锁在你的脑筋里一样。要是你爱我，把你所想到的事告诉我吧。

伊阿古 主帅，您知道我是爱您的。

奥赛罗 我相信你的话；因为我知道你是一个忠诚正直的人，从来不让一句没有忖度过的话轻易出口，所

ACT III

>   And weigh'st thy words before thou givest them breath,
>   Therefore these stops of thine fright me the more;
>   For such things in a false disloyal knave
>   Are tricks of custom; but in a man that's just
>   They're close **dilations**①, working from the heart,
>   That passion cannot rule.

Iago. For Michael Cassio,
>   I dare be sworn, I think that he is honest.

Othello. I think so too.

Iago. Men should be what they seem;
>   Or those that be not, would they might seem none.

Othello. Certain, men should be what they seem.

Iago. Why then I think Cassio's an honest man.

Othello. Nay, yet there's more in this?
>   I prithee speak to me, as to thy thinkings,
>   As thou dost **ruminate**②, and give thy worst of thoughts
>   The worst of words.

Iago. Good my lord, pardon me;
>   Though I am bound to every act of duty,
>   I am not bound to that: all slaves are free:
>   Utter my thoughts? Why say, they are vile and false?
>   As where's that palace, whereinto foul things
>   Sometimes **intrude**③ not? Who has a breast so pure,
>   But some uncleanly apprehensions
>   Keep leets and law-days, and in session sit
>   With **meditations**④ lawful?

Othello. Thou dost conspire against thy friend, Iago,
>   If thou but think'st him wrong'd and makest his ear
>   A stranger to thy thoughts.

Iago. I do beseech you,

第三幕

以你这种吞吞吐吐的口气格外使我惊疑。在一个奸诈的小人，这些不过是一套玩惯了的戏法；可是在一个正人君子，那就是从心底里不知不觉自然流露出来的秘密的抗议。

① dilation [dai'leiʃən; di-] *n.* 膨胀

伊阿古 讲到迈克尔·卡西奥，我敢发誓我相信他是忠实的。

奥赛罗 我也这样想。

伊阿古 人们的内心应该跟他们的外表一致，有的人却不是这样；要是他们能够脱下了假面，那就好了！

奥赛罗 不错，人们的内心应该跟他们的外表一致。

伊阿古 所以我想卡西奥是个忠实的人。

奥赛罗 不，我看你还有一些别的意思。请你老老实实把你的思想告诉我，尽管用最坏的字眼，说出您所想到的最坏的事情。

② ruminate ['ru:mineit] *v.* 深思

伊阿古 我的好主帅，请原谅我；凡是我名分上应尽的责任，我当然不敢躲避，可是您不能勉强我做那一切奴隶们也没有那种义务的事。吐露我的思想？也许它们是邪恶而卑劣的；哪一座庄严的宫殿里，不会有时被下贱的东西闯入呢？哪一个人的心胸这样纯洁，没有一些污秽的念头和正大的思想分庭抗礼呢？

③ intrude [in'tru:d] *v.* 侵入

④ meditation [medi'teiʃən] *n.* 沉思

奥赛罗 伊阿古，要是你以为你的朋友受人欺侮了，可是却不让他知道你的思想，这不成合谋卖友了吗？

伊阿古 也许我是以小人之心度君子之腹，因为我是一

· 137 ·

ACT III

> Though I **perchance**① am vicious in my guess,
> As I confess it is my nature's plague
> To spy into abuses, and oft my jealousy
> Shapes faults that are not, that your wisdom
> From one that so imperfectly conceits,
> Would take no notice, nor build yourself a trouble
> Out of his **scattering**②, and unsure observance.
> It were not for your quiet, nor your good,
> Nor for my manhood, honesty, and wisdom,
> To let you know my thoughts.

Othello. What dost thou mean?

Iago. Good name in man and woman, dear my lord,
> Is the immediate jewel of their souls.
> Who steals my purse steals trash; 'tis something, nothing;
> 'Twas mine, 'tis his, and has been slave to thousands;
> But he that **filches**③ from me my good name,
> Robs me of that which not enriches him,
> And makes me poor indeed.

Othello. By heaven, I'll know thy thoughts.

Iago. You cannot, if my heart were in your hand;
> Nor shall not, whilst 'tis in my custody.

Othello. Ha?

Iago. Oh, beware, my lord, of jealousy!
> It is the green-eyed Monster, which doth mock
> The meat it feeds on. That cuckold lives in **bliss**④,
> Who, certain of his fate, loves not his wronger;
> But O, what damned minutes tells he o'er,
> Who dotes, yet doubts, Suspects, yet strongly loves?

Othello. O **misery**⑤!

Iago. Poor and content, is rich, and rich enough;

① perchance [pə'tʃɑːns] ad. 可能

② scattering ['skætəriŋ] a. 分散的

③ filch [filtʃ] v. 偷窃（不贵重小件物品），小偷小摸

④ bliss [blis] n. 极大的欢乐

⑤ misery ['mizəri] n. 痛苦

个秉性多疑的人，常常会无中生有，错怪了人家；所以请您还是不要把我的无稽的猜测放在心上，更不要因为我的胡乱的妄言而自寻烦恼。要是我让您知道了我的思想，一则将会破坏您的安静，对您没有什么好处；二则那会影响我的人格，对我也是一件不智之举。

奥赛罗 你的话是什么意思？

伊阿古 我的好主帅，无论男人女人，名誉是他们灵魂里面最切身的珍宝。谁偷窃我的钱囊，不过偷窃到一些废物，一些虚无的东西，它只是从我的手里转到他的手里，它也曾做过千万人的奴隶；可是谁偷去了我的名誉，那么他虽然并不因此而富足，我却因为失去它而成为赤贫了。

奥赛罗 凭着上天起誓，我一定要知道你的思想。

伊阿古 即使我的心在您的手里，您也不能知道我的思想；当它还在我的保管之下，我更不能让您知道。

奥赛罗 吓！

伊阿古 啊，主帅，您要留心嫉妒啊；那是一个绿眼的妖魔，谁做了它的牺牲，就要受它的玩弄。本来并不爱他的妻子的那种丈夫，虽然明知被他的妻子欺骗，算来还是幸福的；可是啊！一方面那样痴心疼爱，一方面又是那样满腹狐疑，这才是活活的受罪！

奥赛罗 啊，难堪的痛苦！

伊阿古 贫穷而知足，可以赛过富有；有钱的人要是时

　　　　　But riches fineless, is as poor as winter,
　　　　　To him that ever fears he shall be poor:
　　　　　Good God, the souls of all my tribe defend
　　　　　From jealousy.
Othello.　　Why? Why is this?
　　　　　Think'st thou, I'ld make a life of jealousy,
　　　　　To follow still the changes of the moon
　　　　　With fresh suspicions? No to be once in doubt,
　　　　　Is once to be resolved. Exchange me for a goat,
　　　　　When I shall turn the business of my soul
　　　　　To such exsufflicate and blown **surmises**①,
　　　　　Matching thy **inference**②. 'tis not to make me jealous
　　　　　To say my wife is fair, feeds well, loves company,
　　　　　Is free of speech, sings, plays and dances;
　　　　　Where virtue is, these are more virtuous.
　　　　　Nor from mine own weak merits, will I draw
　　　　　The smallest fear or doubt of her revolt;
　　　　　For she had eyes and chose me. No Iago,
　　　　　I'll see before I doubt; when I doubt, prove;
　　　　　And on the proof, there is no more but this,
　　　　　Away at once with love or jealousy!
Iago.　　I am glad of it, for now I shall have reason
　　　　　To show the love and duty that I bear you
　　　　　With franker spirit. Therefore, as I am bound,
　　　　　Receive it from me. I speak not yet of proof.
　　　　　Look to your wife; observe her well with Cassio;
　　　　　Wear your eye thus, not jealous nor secure.
　　　　　I would not have your free and noble nature,
　　　　　Out of self-bounty be abused: look to 't.
　　　　　I know our country **disposition**③ well;

时刻刻都在担心他会有一天变成穷人，那么即使他有无限的资财，实际上也像冬天一样贫困。天啊，保佑我们不要嫉妒吧！

奥赛罗　咦，这是什么意思？你以为我会在嫉妒里消磨我的一生，随着每一次月亮的变化，发生一次新的猜疑吗？不，我有一天感到怀疑，就要把它立刻解决。要是我会让这种捕风捉影的猜测支配我的心灵，像你所暗示的那样，我就是一头愚蠢的山羊。谁说我的妻子貌美多姿，爱好交际，口才敏慧，能歌善舞，又能弹一手好琴，绝不会使我嫉妒；对于一个贤淑的女子，这些是锦上添花的美妙的外饰。我也绝不因为我自己的缺点而担心她会背叛我；她倘不是独具慧眼，绝不会选中我的。不，伊阿古，我在没有亲眼看到以前，绝不妄起猜疑；当我感到怀疑的时候，我就要把它证实；果然有了确实的证据，我就一了百了，让爱情和嫉妒同时毁灭。

伊阿古　您这番话使我听了很是高兴，因为我现在可以用更坦白的精神，向您披露我的忠爱之忱了。我还不能给您确实的证据。注意尊夫人的行动；留心观察她对卡西奥的态度；用冷静的眼光看着他们，不要一味多心，也不要过于大意；我不愿您的慷慨豪迈的天性被人欺罔；留心着吧。我知道我们国家娘儿们的脾气；在威尼斯她们背着丈夫干的风流韵事，是不瞒天地的；她们可以不顾羞耻，干她们所要干的事，只要不让丈夫知道，

① surmise ['sə:maiz] n. 猜测，推测
② inference ['infərəns] n. 推断
③ disposition [dispə'ziʃən] n. 性格

ACT III

        In Venice, they do let heaven see the **pranks**①

        They dare not show their husbands; their best conscience,

        Is not to leave 't undone, but keep 't unknown.

Othello. Dost thou say so?

Iago. She did deceive her father, marrying you;

        And when she seem'd to shake and fear your looks,

        She loved them most.

Othello. And so she did.

Iago. Why, go to then.

        She that so young could give out such a seeming,

        To seel her father's eyes up close as oak,

        He thought 'twas witchcraft, but I am much to blame;

        I humbly do beseech you of your pardon

        For too much loving you.

Othello. I am bound to thee forever.

Iago. I see this hath a little dash'd your spirits.

Othello. Not a **jot**②, not a jot.

Iago. I'faith, I fear it has:

        I hope you will consider what is spoke

        Comes from my love. But I do see you're moved;

        I am to pray you not to strain my speech,

        To grosser issues nor to larger reach

        Than to suspicion.

Othello. I will not.

Iago. Should you do so, my lord,

        My speech should fall into such vile success

        Which my thoughts aim not at. Cassio's my worthy friend:

        My lord, I see you're moved.

Othello. No, not much moved.

        I do not think but Desdemona's honest.

① prank[præŋk] *n.* 胡闹

就可以问心无愧。

奥赛罗 你真的这样说吗？

伊阿古 她当初跟您结婚，曾经骗过她的父亲；当她好像对您的容貌战栗畏惧的时候，她的心里却在热烈地爱着它。

奥赛罗 她正是这样。

伊阿古 好，她这样小小的年纪就有这般能耐，做得不露一丝破绽，把她父亲的眼睛完全遮掩过去，使他疑心您用妖术把她骗走。——可是我不该说这种话；请您原谅我对您的过分的忠心吧。

奥赛罗 我永远感激你的好意。

伊阿古 我看这件事情有点儿令您扫兴。

② jot [dʒɔt] *n.* 最少量，一点儿

奥赛罗 一点不，一点不。

伊阿古 真的，我怕您在发恼啦。我希望您把我这番话当作善意的警戒。可是我看您真的在动怒啦。我必须请求您不要因为我这么说了，就武断地下了结论；不过是一点嫌疑，还不能就认为是事实哩。

奥赛罗 我不会的。

伊阿古 您要是这样，主帅，那么我的话就要引起不幸的后果，完全违反我的本意了。卡西奥是我的好朋友——主帅，我看您在动怒啦。

奥赛罗 不，并不怎么动怒。我想苔丝狄蒙娜是贞洁的。

Iago. Long live she so; and long live you to think so!

Othello. And yet, how nature erring from itself.

Iago. Ay, there's the point, as to be bold with you,
Not to affect many proposed matches
Of her own **clime**①, complexion and degree,
Whereto we see in all things nature tends:
Foh, one may smell in such a will most rank,
Foul disproportion, thoughts unnatural.
But pardon me, I do not in position
Distinctly speak of her; though I may fear,
Her will, **recoiling**② to her better judgement,
May fall to match you with her country forms,
And happily **repent**③.

Othello. Farewell, farewell:
If more thou dost perceive, let me know more;
Set on thy wife to observe. Leave me, Iago.

Iago. [*Going.*] My lord, I take my leave.

Othello. Why did I marry? This honest creature doubtless,
Sees and knows more, much more than he **unfolds**④.

Iago. [*Returning.*] My lord, I would I might entreat your honor
To scan this thing no further; leave it to time.
Although it be fit that Cassio have his place,
For sure he fills it up with great ability,
Yet if you please, to hold him off awhile,
You shall by that perceive him and his means.
Note if your lady strain his entertainment
With any strong or **vehement**⑤ **importunity**⑥;
Much will be seen in that. In the meantime,
Let me be thought too busy in my fears,
As worthy cause I have to fear I am,

① clime [klaim] n. [诗歌用语]（尤指气候宜人的）地带，地区

② recoil [ri'kɔil] v. 后退，退回

③ repent [ri'pent] v. 悔悟

④ unfold [ʌn'fəuld] v. 表明，吐露

⑤ vehement ['vi:imənt] a. 热烈的

⑥ importunity [impɔ:'tju:nəti] n. 纠缠，强求

伊阿古　但愿她永远如此！但愿您永远这样想！

奥赛罗　可是一个人往往容易迷失本性——

伊阿古　嗯，问题就在这儿，说句大胆的话，当初多少跟她同国族同肤色同阶级的人向她求婚，她都置之不理，这明明是违反常情的举动；嘿！从这儿就可以看到一个荒唐的意志，乖僻的习性和不近人情的思想。可是原谅我，我不一定指着她说；虽然我恐怕她因为一时的孟浪跟随了您，也许后来会觉得您在各方面不能符合她自己国中的标准而懊悔她的选择的错误。

奥赛罗　再会，再会。要是你还观察到什么，请让我知道；叫你的妻子留心察看。离开我，伊阿古。

伊阿古　主帅，我告辞了。（欲去）

奥赛罗　我为什么要结婚呢？这个诚实的汉子所看到所知道的事情，一定比他向我宣布出来的多得多。

伊阿古　（回转）主帅，我想请您最好把这件事情搁一搁，慢慢地再看吧。卡西奥虽然应该让他复职，因为他对于这一个职位是非常胜任的；可是您要是愿意对他暂时延宕一下，就可以借此窥探他的真相，看他钻的是哪一条门路。您只要注意尊夫人在您面前是不是着力替他说情，从那上头就可以看出不少情事。现在请您只把我的意见认作无谓的过虑——我相信我的确太多疑了——仍旧把尊夫人看成一

ACT III

        And hold her free, I do beseech your honor.

Othello.   Fear not my government.

Iago.   I once more take my leave.

        Exit.

Othello.   This fellow's of exceeding honesty,
        And knows all qualities with a learned spirit,
        Of human dealings. If I do prove her **haggard**①,
        Though that her jesses were my dear heartstrings,
        I'ld whistle her off, and let her down the wind
        To prey at Fortune. Haply, for I am black
        And have not those soft parts of conversation
        That **chamberers**② have, or for I am declined
        Into **the vale of year**③ yet that's not much,
        She's gone. I am abused, and my relief
        Must be to loathe her. Oh curse of marriage,
        That we can call these delicate creatures ours,
        And not their appetites! I had rather be a toad,
        And live upon the vapor of a **dungeon**④,
        Than keep a corner in the thing I love
        For others' uses. Yet, 'tis the plague to Great ones:
        Prerogatived⑤ are they less than the base;
        'Tis destiny unshunnable, like death.
        Even then this forked plague is fated to us,
        When we do quicken. Look where she comes:
        Enter Desdemona and Emilia.
        If she be false, then heaven mocks itself:
        I'll not believe 't.

Desde.   How now, my dear Othello?
        Your dinner, and the generous Islanders
        By you invited, do attend your presence.

个清白无罪的人。

奥赛罗 你放心吧，我不会失去自制的。

伊阿古 那么我告辞了。（下）

奥赛罗 这是一个非常诚实的家伙，对于人情世故是再熟悉不过的了。要是我能够证明她是一头没有驯服的野鹰，虽然我用自己的心弦把她系住，我也要放她随风远去，追寻她自己的命运。也许因为我生得黑丑，缺少绅士们温柔风雅的谈吐，也许因为我年纪老了点儿——虽然还不算顶老——所以她才会背叛我；我已经自取其辱，只好割断对她这一段痴情。啊，结婚的烦恼！我们可以在名义上把这些可爱的人儿称为我们所有，却不能支配她们的爱憎喜恶！我宁愿做一只蛤蟆，呼吸牢室中的浊气，也不愿占住了自己心爱之物的一角，让别人把它享用。可是那是富贵者也不能幸免的灾祸，他们并不比贫贱者享有更多的特权；那是像死一样不可逃避的命运，我们一生下来就已经在冥冥中注定了的。瞧！她来了。倘然她是不贞的，啊！那么上天在开自己的玩笑了。我不信。

苔丝狄蒙娜及埃米莉亚重上。

苔丝狄蒙娜 啊，我的亲爱的奥赛罗！您所宴请的那些岛上的贵人们都在等着您去就席哩。

---

① haggard ['hæɡəd] n. 野性未驯的鹰，悍鹰

② chamberer ['tʃeimbərə] n. 爱跟女人厮混的男人

③ the vale of years 老年

④ dungeon ['dʌndʒən] n. 地牢

⑤ prerogative [pri'rɔɡətiv] a. 有特权的

Othello. I am to blame.

Desde. Why do you speak so faintly?

Are you not well?

Othello. I have a pain upon my **forehead**① here.

Desde. Faith that's with watching; 'twill away again.

Let me but bind it hard, within this hour

It will be well.

Othello. Your napkin is too little;

He puts the handkerchief from him, and she drops it.

Let it alone. Come, I'll go in with you.

Desde. I am very sorry that you are not well.

Exeunt Othello and Desdemona.

Emilia. I am glad I have found this napkin;

This was her first remembrance from the Moor.

My **wayward**② husband hath a hundred times

Woo'd me to steal it. But she so loves the **token**③,

For he conjured her, she should ever keep it,

That she reserves it evermore about her,

To kiss and talk to. I'll have the work ta'en out,

And give 't Iago: what he will do with it

Heaven knows, not I;

I nothing, but to please his fantasy.

Enter Iago.

Iago. How now? What do you here alone?

Emilia. Do not you **chide**④; I have a thing for you.

Iago. A thing for me? It is a **common**⑤ thing —

Emilia. Hah?

Iago. To have a foolish wife.

Emilia. Oh, is that all? What will you give me now

For that same handkerchief?

① forehead ['fɔrhed] *n.* 前额，额

② wayward ['weiwəd] *a.* 任性的，古怪的

③ token ['təukən] *n.* 纪念品

④ chide [tʃaid] *v.* 责骂

⑤ common ['kɔmən] *a.* 劣等的，低级的

奥赛罗　是我失礼了。

苔丝狄蒙娜　您怎么说话这样没有劲？您不大舒服吗？

奥赛罗　我有点儿头痛。

苔丝狄蒙娜　那一定是因为睡少的缘故，不要紧的；让我替您绑紧了，一小时内就可以痊愈。

奥赛罗　你的手帕太小了。（苔丝狄蒙娜的手帕坠地）随它去；来，我跟你一块儿进去。

苔丝狄蒙娜　您身子不舒服，我很懊恼。（奥赛罗、苔丝狄蒙娜下）

埃米莉亚　我很高兴我拾到了这方手帕；这是她从那摩尔人手里第一次得到的礼物。我那古怪的丈夫向我说过了不知多少好话，要我把它偷了来；可是她非常喜欢这玩意儿，因为他叫她永远保存，不许遗失，所以她随时带在身边，一个人的时候就拿出来把它亲吻，对它说话。我要去把那花样描下来，再把它送给伊阿古；究竟他拿去有什么用，天才知道，我可不知道。我只不过为了讨他的喜欢。

　　　　伊阿古重上。

伊阿古　啊！你一个人在这儿干什么？

埃米莉亚　不要骂；我有一件好东西给你。

伊阿古　一件好东西给我？一件不值钱的东西——

埃米莉亚　吓！

伊阿古　娶了一个愚蠢的老婆。

埃米莉亚　啊！当真？要是我现在把那方手帕给了你，你给我什么东西？

ACT III

Iago. What handkerchief?

Emilia. What handkerchief?
     Why, that the Moor first gave to Desdemona,
     That which so often you did bid me steal.

Iago. Hast stol'n it from her?

Emilia. No faith; she let it drop by negligence,
     And to the advantage, I being here took 't up.
     Look, here it is.

Iago. A good **wench**①; give it me.

Emilia. What will you do with 't, that you have been so earnest
     To have me filch it?

Iago. Why, what is that to you?

Emilia. If 't be not for some purpose of import,
     Give 't me again. Poor lady, she'll run mad
     When she shall lack it.

Iago. Be not acknown on 't; I have use for it.
     Go, leave me.
     Exit Emilia.
     I will in Cassio's lodging lose this napkin,
     And let him find it. Trifles light as air
     Are to the jealous, confirmations strong,
     As proofs of holy writ; this may do something.
     The Moor already changes with my poison:
     Dangerous conceits are in their natures poisons,
     Which at the first are scarce found to distaste,
     But with a little act upon the blood,
     Burn like the mines of **sulphur**②. I did say so.
     Look, where he comes!
     Enter Othello.
     Not **poppy**③, nor **mandragora**④,

伊阿古 什么手帕？

埃米莉亚 什么手帕？就是那摩尔人第一次送给苔丝狄蒙娜，你老是叫我偷了来的那方手帕呀。

伊阿古 已经偷来了吗？

埃米莉亚 不，不瞒你说，她自己不小心掉了下来，我正在旁边，乘此机会就把它拾起来了。瞧，这不是吗？

伊阿古 好妻子，给我。

埃米莉亚 你一定要我偷了它来，究竟有什么用？

伊阿古 哼，那干你什么事？（夺帕）

埃米莉亚 要是没有重要的用途，还是把它还了我吧。可怜的夫人！她失去这方手帕，准要发疯了。

伊阿古 不要说出来；我自有用处。去，离开我。（埃米莉亚下）我要把这手帕丢在卡西奥的寓所里，让他找到它。像空气一样轻的小事，对于一个嫉妒的人，也会变成天书一样坚强的确证；也许这就可以引起一场是非。这摩尔人已经中了我的毒药的毒，他的心理上已经发生变化了；危险的思想本来就是一种毒药，虽然在开始的时候尝不到什么苦涩的味道，可是渐渐地在血液里活动起来，就会像硫矿一样轰然爆发。我已经说过了；瞧，他又来了！

　　奥赛罗重上。

① wench [wentʃ] *n.* 女孩，少妇

② sulphur ['sʌlfə] *n.* 硫

③ poppy ['pɔpi] *n.* 罂粟

④ mandragora [mæn'drægərə] *n.* 曼陀罗草

ACT III

  Nor all the drowsy **syrups**① of the world,
  Shall ever medicine thee to that sweet sleep
  Which thou owedst yesterday.
Othello. Ha, ha, false to me?
Iago. Why how now general? No more of that.
Othello. **Avaunt**② be gone! Thou hast set me on the rack.
  I swear 'tis better to be much abused,
  Than but to know 't a little.
Iago. How now, my lord?
Othello. What sense had I, in her stol'n hours of lust?
  I saw 't not, thought it not, it harm'd not me;
  I slept the next night well, was free and merry;
  I found not Cassio's kisses on her lips.
  He that is robb'd, not wanting what is stol'n,
  Let him not know 't and he's not robb'd at all.
Iago. I am sorry to hear this.
Othello. I had been happy if the general camp,
  Pioners and all, had tasted her sweet body,
  So I had nothing known. Oh now for ever
  Farewell the tranquil mind! Farewell content!
  Farewell the plumed troop and the big wars
  That make ambition virtue! Oh farewell,
  Farewell the **neighing**③ **steed**④ and the **shrill**⑤ trump,
  The spirit-stirring drum, the ear-piercing **fife**⑥,
  The royal banner, and all quality,
  Pride, pomp, and circumstance of glorious war!
  And O you mortal engines, whose rude throats
  The immortal Jove's dread clamors, counterfeit,
  Farewell! Othello's occupation's gone!
Iago. Is 't possible, my lord?

第三幕

① syrup ['sirəp] *n.* 糖浆

② avaunt [ə'vɔ:nt] *int.* [古语] 滚！

伊阿古　罂粟，曼陀罗，或是世上一切使人昏迷的药草，都不能使你得到昨天晚上你还安然享受的酣眠。

奥赛罗　吓！吓！对我不贞？

伊阿古　啊，怎么，主帅！别老想着那件事啦。

奥赛罗　去！滚开！你害得我好苦。与其知道得不明不白，还是糊里糊涂受人家欺弄的好。

伊阿古　怎么，主帅！

奥赛罗　她瞒着我跟人家私通，我不是一无知觉的吗？我没有看见，没有想到，它对我漠不相干；到了晚上，我还是睡得好好的，逍遥自得，无忧无虑，在她的嘴唇上找不到卡西奥吻过的痕迹。被盗的人要是不知道偷儿盗去了他什么东西，他就等于没有被盗一样。

伊阿古　我很抱歉听见您说这样的话。

奥赛罗　要是全营的将士，从最低微的工兵起，都曾领略过她的肉体美趣，只要我一无所知，我还是快乐的。啊！从今以后，永别了，宁静的心绪！永别了，平和的幸福！永别了，威武的大军、激发壮志的战争！啊，永别了！永别了，长嘶的骏马、锐利的号角、惊魂的鼙鼓、刺耳的横笛、庄严的大旗和一切战阵上的威仪！还有你，杀人的巨炮啊，你的残暴的喉管里模仿着天神乔武的怒吼，永别了！奥赛罗的事业已经完毕。

③ neigh [nei] *v.* （马）嘶

④ steed [sti:d] *n.* [诗歌用语、古语] 骏马

⑤ shrill [ʃril] *a.* 发出尖厉声响的

⑥ fife [faif] *n.* 短笛

伊阿古　难道以至于此吗，主帅？

· 153 ·

ACT III

Othello. Villain, be sure thou prove my love a whore;
    Be sure of it. Give me the **ocular**① proof;
    Or, by the worth of man's eternal soul,
    Thou hadst been better have been born a dog
    Than answer my waked wrath.

Iago. Is 't come to this?

Othello. Make me to see 't; or at the least so prove it,
    That the **probation**② bear no hinge nor loop,
    To hang a doubt on; or woe upon thy life.

Iago. My noble lord —

Othello. If thou dost slander her and torture me,
    Never pray more; abandon all **remorse**③;
    On horror's head; horrors accumulate;
    Do deeds to make heaven weep, all Earth amazed;
    For nothing canst thou to damnation add,
    Greater than that.

Iago. O grace! O heaven forgive me!
    Are you a man? Have you a soul or sense?
    God be wi' you; take mine office. Oh wretched fool,
    That livest to make thine honesty a vice!
    O monstrous world! **Take note**④, take note, O world,
    To be direct and honest, is not safe.
    I thank you for this profit, and from hence
    I'll love no friend, **sith**⑤ love breeds such offense.

Othello. Nay stay; thou shouldst be honest.

Iago. I should be wise; for honesty's a fool,
    And loses that it works for.

Othello. By the world,
    I think my wife be honest, and think she is not;
    I think that thou art just, and think thou art not.

① ocular ['ɔkjulə] a. 目击的

② probation [prəu'beiʃən] n. [废语] 证据

③ remorse [ri'mɔːs] n. 同情，怜悯

④ take note（对……）留意；注意

⑤ sith [siθ] conj. 既然

奥赛罗 恶人，你必须证明我的爱人是一个淫妇，您必须给我目击的证据；否则凭着人类永生的灵魂起誓，我的激起了的怒火将要喷射在你的身上，使你悔恨自己当初不曾投胎做一条狗！

伊阿古 竟会到了这样的地步吗？

奥赛罗 让我亲眼看见这种事实，或者至少给我无可置疑的切实的证据，否则我要活活要你的命！

伊阿古 尊贵的主帅——

奥赛罗 你要是故意捏造谣言，毁坏她的名誉，使我受到难堪的痛苦，那么你再不要祈祷吧；放弃一切恻隐之心，让各种残酷的罪恶丛集于你的残酷的一身，尽管做一些使上天悲泣，使人世惊愕的暴行吧，因为你现在已经罪大恶极，没有什么可以使你在地狱里沉沦得更深的了。

伊阿古 天啊！您是一个汉子吗？您有灵魂吗？您有知觉吗？上帝和您同在！我也不要做这劳什子的旗官了。啊，倒霉的傻瓜！你以为自己是个老实人，人家却把你的老实当作了罪恶！啊，丑恶的世界！注意，注意，世人啊！说老实话，做老实人，是一件危险的事哩。谢谢您给我这一个有益的教训；既然善意反而遭人嗔怪，从此以后，我再也不对什么朋友掬献我的真情了。

奥赛罗 不，且慢；你应该做一个老实的人。

伊阿古 我应该做一个聪明人；因为老实人就是傻瓜，虽然一片好心，结果还是不能取信于人。

奥赛罗 我想我的妻子是贞洁的，可是又疑心她不大贞洁；我想你是诚实的，可是又疑心你不大诚实。我

ACT III

        I'll have some proof. My name that was as flesh
        As Dian's visage, is now **begrimed**① and black
        As mine own face. If there be **cords**② or knives,
        Poison or fire, or suffocating streams,
        I'll not endure it. Would I were satisfied.

Iago.   I see you are **eaten up with**③ passion;
        I do repent me that I put it to you.
        You would be satisfied?

Othello.   Would? Nay, I will.

Iago.   And may: but how? How satisfied, my lord?
        Would you the supervisor grossly gape on?
        Behold her topp'd?

Othello.   Death and damnation. Oh!

Iago.   It were a tedious difficulty, I think,
        To bring them to that prospect. Damn them then,
        If ever mortal eyes do see them bolster
        More than their own. What then? How then?
        What shall I say? Where's satisfaction?
        It is impossible you should see this,
        Were they as prime as goats, as hot as monkeys,
        As salt as wolves in pride, and fools as gross
        As ignorance made drunk. But yet, I say,
        If **imputation**④ and strong circumstances,
        Which lead directly to the door of Truth,
        Will give you satisfaction, you may have 't.

Othello.   Give me a living reason she's disloyal.

Iago.   I do not like the office.
        But sith I am enter'd in this cause so far,
        Prick'd to 't by foolish honesty and love,
        I will go on. I lay with Cassio lately,

① begrime [bi'graimd] *a.* 污秽的

② cord [kɔːd] *n.* 绳子

③ eat up with 使纠缠于；使沉迷于

一定要得到一些证据。她的名誉本来是像黛安娜的容颜一样皎洁的，现在已经染上污垢，像我自己的脸一样黝黑了。要是这儿有绳子，刀子，毒药，火焰，或是使人窒息的河水，我一定不能忍受下去。但愿我能够扫空这一块疑团！

伊阿古 主帅，我看您完全被感情所支配了。我很后悔不该惹起您的疑心。那么您愿意知道究竟吗？

奥赛罗 愿意！嘿。我一定要知道。

伊阿古 那倒是可以的；可是怎样去知道它呢，主帅？你还是眼睁睁地当场看她被人奸污吗？

奥赛罗 啊！该死该死！

伊阿古 叫他们当场出丑，我想很不容易；他们干这种事，总是要避人眼目的。那么怎么样呢？我应该怎么说呢？怎样才可以拿到真凭实据？即使他们像山羊一样风骚，猴子一样好色，豺狼一样贪淫，即使他们是糊涂透顶的傻瓜，您也看不到他们这一幕把戏。可是我说，有了确凿的线索，就可以探出事实的真相；要是这一类间接的旁证可以替您解除疑惑，那倒是不难得到的。

奥赛罗 给我一个充分的理由，证明她已经失节。

伊阿古 我不喜欢这件差使；可是既然愚蠢的忠心已经把我拉进了这一桩纠纷里去，我也不能再守沉默了。最近我曾经和卡西奥同过榻；我因为牙痛不能

④ imputation [impjuː'teiʃən] *n.* 罪名

ACT III

        And being troubled with a raging tooth,
        I could not sleep.
        There are a kind of men, so loose of soul,
        That in their sleeps will mutter their affairs;
        One of this kind is Cassio.
        In sleep I heard him say, sweet Desdemona,
        Let us be wary, let us hide our loves;
        And then sir, would he **gripe**① and **wring**② my hand,
        Cry, "Oh sweet creature!" then kiss me hard,
        As if he pluck'd up kisses by the roots,
        That grew upon my lips; then laid his leg
        Over my thigh, and sigh'd and kiss'd; and then
        Cried, "Cursed fate that gave thee to the Moor!"

Othello. O, monstrous! monstrous!

Iago. Nay, this was but his dream.

Othello. But this denoted a **foregone**③ conclusion.
        'tis a shrewd doubt, though it be but a dream.

Iago. And this may help to thicken other proofs
        That do demonstrate thinly.

Othello. I'll tear her all to pieces.

Iago. Nay, but be wise; yet we see nothing done;
        She may be honest yet. Tell me but this;
        Have you not sometimes seen a handkerchief
        Spotted with strawberries in your wife's hand?

Othello. I gave her such a one; 'twas my first gift.

Iago. I know not that; but such a handkerchief,
        I am sure it was your wife's, did I today
        See Cassio wipe his beard with.

Othello. If it be that —

Iago. If it be that, or any that was hers,

入睡；世上有一种人，他们的灵魂是不能保守秘密的，往往会在睡梦之中吐露他们的私事，卡西奥也就是这一种人；我听见他在梦寐中说："亲爱的苔丝狄蒙娜，我们需要小心，不要让别人窥破了我们的爱情！"于是，主帅，他就紧紧地捏住我的手，嘴里喊："啊，可爱的人儿！"然后狠狠地吻着我，好像那些吻是长在我的嘴唇上，他恨不得把它们连根拔起一样；然后他又把他的脚搁在我的大腿上，叹一口气，亲一个吻，喊一声"该死的命运，把你给了那摩尔人！"

① gripe [graip] v. [古语] 握住，握紧
② wring [riŋ] v. 拧
③ foregone ['fɔːgɔn] a. 先前的

奥赛罗 啊，可恶！可恶！

伊阿古 不，这不过是他的梦。

奥赛罗 虽然只是一个梦，事情一定是做出来了。

伊阿古 这确实非常可疑；这也许可以进一步证实其他的疑窦。

奥赛罗 我要把她碎尸万段。

伊阿古 不，您不能太鲁莽了；我们还没有看见实际的行动；也许她还是贞洁的。告诉我这一点：您有没有看见过在尊夫人的手里有一方绣着草莓花样的手帕？

奥赛罗 我给过她这样一方手帕；那是我第一次送给她的礼物。

伊阿古 那我不知道；可是今天我看见卡西奥用这样一方手帕抹他的胡子，我相信它一定就是尊夫人的。

奥赛罗 假如就是那一方手帕——

伊阿古 假如就是那一方手帕，或者是其他她所用过的

It speaks against her with the other proofs.

Othello. O that the slave had forty thousand lives:
One is too poor, too weak for my revenge.
Now do I see 'tis true. Look here, Iago,
All my fond love thus do I blow to heaven.
'Tis gone.
Arise black **vengeance**①, from thy hollow hell,
Yield up, o love, thy crown and hearted throne
To tyrannous hate. Swell bosom with thy fraught,
For 'tis of **aspics'**② tongues.

Iago. Yet be content.

Othello. Oh blood, blood, blood!

Iago. Patience I say; your mind perhaps may change.

Othello. Never, Iago. Like to the **Pontic Sea**③,
Whose icy current and compulsive course,
Ne'er feels retiring ebb, but keeps due on
To the Propontic and the **Hellespont**④,
Even so my bloody thoughts, with violent pace,
Shall ne'er look back, ne'er ebb to humble love,
Till that a capable and wide revenge
Swallow them up. [*Kneels.*] Now, by **yond**⑤ marble heaven,
In the due reverence of a sacred vow,
I here engage my words.

Iago. Do not rise yet. [*Kneels.*]
Witness, you ever-burning lights above,
You elements that clip us round about,
Witness that here Iago doth give up
The execution of his wit, hands, heart,
To wrong'd Othello's service. Let him command,
And to obey shall be in me remorse,

① vengeance ['vendʒəns] *n.* 复仇

② aspic ['æspik] *n.* 毒舌

③ Pontic Sea 黑海

④ Hellespont ['helispɔnt] *n.* 赫勒斯庞特（达达尼尔海峡的古希腊名）

⑤ yond [jɔnd] *ad.* 在彼处

手帕，那么又是一个对她不利的证据了。

奥赛罗　啊，我但愿那家伙有四万条生命！单单让他死一次是发泄不了我的愤怒的。现在我明白这件事情全然是真的了。瞧，伊阿古，我把我的全部痴情向天空中吹散；它已经随风消失了。黑暗的复仇，从你的幽窟之中升起来吧！爱情啊，把你的王冠和你的心灵深处的宝座让给残暴的憎恨吧！涨起来吧，我的胸膛，因为你已经满载着毒蛇的螫舌！

伊阿古　请不要发恼。

奥赛罗　啊，血！血！血！

伊阿古　忍耐点儿吧；也许您的意见会改变过来的。

奥赛罗　决不，伊阿古。正像黑海的寒涛滚滚奔流，奔进马尔拉海，直冲达达尼尔海峡，永远不会后退一样，我的风驰电掣的流血的思想，在复仇的目的没充分达到以前，也决不会踟蹰回顾，化为绕指的柔情。（跪）苍天在上，我倘不能报复这奇耻大辱，誓不偷生人世。

伊阿古　且慢起来。（跪）亘古炳耀的日月星辰，环抱宇宙的风云雨雾，请你们为我作证：从现在起，伊阿古愿意尽心竭力，为被欺的奥赛罗效劳；无论他叫我做什么残酷的工作，我一切唯命是从。

What bloody business ever.

Othello.　I greet thy love,

　　Not with vain thanks, but with acceptance bounteous,

　　And will upon the instant put thee to 't.

　　Within these three days let me hear thee say,

　　That Cassio's not alive.

Iago.　My friend is dead, 'tis done at your request;

　　But let her live.

Othello.　Damn her **lewd**① **minx**②: O, damn her!

　　Come go with me apart; I will withdraw,

　　To furnish me with some swift means of death

　　For the fair devil. Now art thou my lieutenant.

Iago.　I am your own forever.

　　Exeunt.

奥赛罗 我不用空口的感谢接受你的好意,为了表示我的诚心的嘉纳,我要请你立刻履行你的诺言:在这三天以内,让我听见你说卡西奥已经不在人世。

伊阿古 我的朋友的死已经决定了,因为这是您的意旨;可是放她活命吧。

奥赛罗 该死的淫妇!啊,咒死她!来,跟我去;我要为这美貌的魔鬼想出一个干脆的死法。现在你是我的副将了。

伊阿古 我永远是您的忠仆。(同下)

① lewd [lju:d] *a.* 淫荡的
② minx [miŋks] *n.* 轻浮的姑娘

Scene IV. Before the castle.

Enter Desdemona, Emilia and Clown.

Desde. Do you know Sirrah, where lieutenant Cassio lies?

Clown. I dare not say he lies anywhere.

Desde. Why, man?

Clown. He's a soldier; and for one to say a soldier lies, is stabbing.

Desde. Go to! Where lodges he?

Clown. To tell you where he lodges, is to tell you where I lie.

Desde. Can anything be made of this?

Clown. I know not where he lodges, and for me to **devise**① a lodging, and say he lies here or he lies there, were to lie in mine own throat.

Desde. Can you inquire him out and be **edified**② by report?

Clown. I will **catechize**③ the world for him; that is, make questions and by them answer.

Desde. Seek him, bid him come hither. Tell him, I have moved my lord on his behalf and hope all will be well.

Clown. To do this, is within the compass of man's wit, and therefore I will

第四场　城堡前

　　　　　　　　苔丝狄蒙娜，埃米莉亚及小丑上。

苔丝狄蒙娜　喂，你知道卡西奥副将家在什么地方吗？

小丑　我不敢说他"假"在哪儿。

苔丝狄蒙娜　为什么？

小丑　他一个军人，说军人"假"，还不得挨他一刀。

苔丝狄蒙娜　行了！他住在哪儿？

小丑　我要告诉你他家哪儿，我就露出我"假"在哪儿了。

苔丝狄蒙娜　没头没脑的，什么意思？

小丑　我就不知道他住在哪儿。要是乱说一个地方，说他"假"在这儿，"假"在那儿，那就是存心说"假"话了。

苔丝狄蒙娜　你可以打听打听他在什么地方呀。

小丑　好，我就去到处向人家打听——那是说，去盘问人家，看他们怎么回答我。

苔丝狄蒙娜　找到了他，你就叫他到这儿来，对他说我已经替他在将军面前说过情了，大概可以得到圆满的结果。

小丑　干这件事是一个人的智力所能及的，所以我愿意

① devise [di'vaiz] *v.* 想出，发明

② edify ['edifai] *v.* 开导，启发
③ catechize ['kætikaiz] *v.* 盘问

ACT III

attempt the doing it.

Exit Clown.

Desde.   Where should I lose that handkerchief, Emilia?

Emilia.   I know not, madam.

Desde.   Believe me, I had rather have lost my purse

Full of **crusadoes**①. And but my noble Moor

Is true of mind and made of no such baseness,

As jealous creatures are, it were enough

To put him to ill thinking.

Emilia.   Is he not jealous?

Desde.   Who, he? I think the sun where he was born,

Drew all such humors from him.

Emilia.   Look, where he comes.

Desde.   I will not leave him now, till Cassio

Be call'd to him.

Enter Othello.

How is 't with you, my lord?

Othello.   Well my good lady. Oh hardness to **dissemble**②!

How do you, Desdemona?

Desde.   Well, my good lord.

Othello.   Give me your hand. This hand is **moist**③ my lady.

Desde.   It yet has felt no age nor known no sorrow.

Othello.   This argues fruitfulness and liberal heart;

Hot, hot and moist. This hand of yours requires

A sequester from liberty, fasting and prayer,

Much **castigation**④, exercise devout,

For here's a young and sweating devil here

That commonly rebels. 'tis a good hand,

A frank one.

Desde.   You may indeed say so;

① crusado [kru:'seidəu] n. 有十字架花样的银币

② dissemble [di'sembl] v. 掩饰

③ moist [mɔist] a. 潮湿的

④ castigation [kæsti'geiʃən] n. 惩责

去干它一下。（下）

苔丝狄蒙娜 我究竟在什么地方掉了那方手帕呢，埃米莉亚？

埃米莉亚 我不知道，夫人。

苔丝狄蒙娜 相信我，我宁愿失去我的一袋金币；倘然我的摩尔人不是这样一个光明磊落的汉子，倘然他也像那些多疑善妒的卑鄙男人一样，这是很可能引起他的疑心的。

埃米莉亚 他不会嫉妒吗？

苔丝狄蒙娜 谁！他？我想在他生长的地方，那灼热的阳光已经把这种气质完全从他身上吸去了。

埃米莉亚 瞧！他来了。

苔丝狄蒙娜 我在他没有跟卡西奥当面谈话以前，决不离开他一步。

　　　　　　奥赛罗上。

苔丝狄蒙娜 您好吗，我的主？

奥赛罗 好，我的好夫人。（旁白）啊，装假脸真不容易！——你好，苔丝狄蒙娜？

苔丝狄蒙娜 我好，我的好夫君。

奥赛罗 把你的手给我。这手很潮润呢，我的夫人。

苔丝狄蒙娜 它还没有感到老年的侵袭，也没有受过忧伤的损害。

奥赛罗 这一只手表明它的主人是多育子女而心肠慷慨的；这么热，这么潮。奉劝夫人努力克制邪心，常常斋戒祷告，反身自责，礼拜神明，因为这儿有一个年少风流的魔鬼，惯会在人们血液里捣乱。这是一只好手，一只很慷慨的手。

苔丝狄蒙娜 您真的可以这样说，因为就是这一只手把

ACT III

> For 'twas that hand that gave away my heart.

Othello. A liberal hand. The hearts of old gave hands;
> But our new heraldry is hands, not hearts.

Desde. I cannot speak of this. Come, now your promise.

Othello. What promise, Chuck?

Desde. I have sent to bid Cassio come speak with you.

Othello. I have a salt and sorry **rheum**① offends me;
> Lend me thy handkerchief.

Desde. Here my lord.

Othello. That which I gave you.

Desde. I have it not about me.

Othello. Not?

Desde. No findeed, my lord.

Othello. That's a fault. That handkerchief
> Did an Egyptian to my mother give;
> She was a **charmer**②, and could almost read
> The thoughts of people. She told her, while she kept it,
> 'Twould make her amiable and subdue my father
> Entirely to her love, but if she lost it
> Or made a gift of it, my father's eye
> Should hold her loathed and his spirits should hunt
> After new fancies. She dying gave it me,
> And bid me, when my fate would have me wive,
> To give it her. I did so, and take heed on 't;
> Make it a darling, like your precious eye;
> To lose 't or give 't away, were such perdition,
> As nothing else could match.

Desde. Is 't possible?

Othello. 'Tis true; there's magic in the web of it.
> A **sibyl**③ that had number'd in the world

我的心献给您的。

奥赛罗 一只慷慨的手。从前的姑娘把手给人，同时把心也一起给了他；现在时世变了，得到一位姑娘的手的，不一定能够得到她的心。

苔丝狄蒙娜 这种话我不会说。来，您答应我的事怎么样啦？

奥赛罗 我答应你什么，乖乖？

苔丝狄蒙娜 我已经叫人去请卡西奥来跟您谈谈了。

奥赛罗 我的眼睛有些胀痛，老是淌着眼泪，把你的手帕借给我一用。

苔丝狄蒙娜 这儿，我的主。

奥赛罗 我给你的那一方呢？

苔丝狄蒙娜 我没有带在身边。

奥赛罗 没有带？

苔丝狄蒙娜 真的没有带，我的主。

奥赛罗 那你可错了。那方手帕是一个埃及女人送给我的母亲的；她是一个能够洞察人心的女巫，她对我的母亲说，当她保存着这方手帕的时候，它可以使她得到我的父亲的欢心，享受专房的爱宠，可是她要是失去了它，或是把它送给旁人，我的父亲就要对她发生憎厌，他的心就要另觅新欢了。她在临死的时候把它传给我，叫我有了妻子以后，就把它交给新妇。我遵照她的吩咐给了你，所以你必须格外小心，珍惜它像珍惜你自己宝贵的眼睛一样；万一失去了，或是送给别人，那就难免遭到一场无比的灾祸。

苔丝狄蒙娜 真会有这种事吗？

奥赛罗 真的，这一方小小的手帕，却有神奇的魔力织在里面；它是一个二百岁的神巫在一阵心血来潮的

① rheum [ru:m] *n.* 鼻炎，感冒

② charmer ['tʃɑ:mə] *n.* 魔术师

③ sibyl ['sibil] *n.* 女巫

ACT III

        The sun to course, two hundred compasses,
        In her **prophetic**① fury sew'd the work;
        The worms were hallow'd that did breed the silk,
        And it was dyed in **mummy**②, which the skillful
        Conserved of maiden's hearts.

Desde. Indeed? Is 't true?

Othello. Most **veritable**③, therefore look to 't well.

Desde. Then would to God that I had never seen 't!

Othello. Ha? Wherefore?

Desde. Why do you speak so startingly and rash?

Othello. Is 't lost? Is 't gone? Speak, is it out o' the way?

Desde. Heaven bless us!

Othello. Say you?

Desde. It is not lost; but what an if it were?

Othello. How?

Desde. I say it is not lost.

Othello. Fetch 't, let me see it.

Desde. Why so I can, sir, but I will not now.
        This is a trick to put me from my suit.
        Pray you, let Cassio be received again.

Othello. Fetch me the handkerchief: my mind **misgives**④.

Desde. Come, come,
        You'll never meet a more sufficient man.

Othello. The handkerchief.

Desde. A man that all his time
        Hath founded his good fortunes on your love,
        Shared dangers with you.

Othello. The handkerchief.

Desde. **In sooth**⑤, you are to blame.

① prophetic [prəʊ'fetɪk] a. 预言的

② mummy ['mʌmi] n. 褐色颜料

③ veritable ['verɪtəbl] a. 真正的

时候缝就的；它那一缕缕的丝线，也不是世间的凡蚕所吐；织成以后，它曾经在用处女的心炼成的丹液里浸过。

苔丝狄蒙娜 当真！这是真的吗？

奥赛罗 绝对的真实；所以留心藏好它吧。

苔丝狄蒙娜 上帝啊，但愿我从来没有见过它！

奥赛罗 吓！为什么？

苔丝狄蒙娜 您为什么说得这样暴躁？

奥赛罗 它已经失去了吗？不见了吗？说，它是不是已经丢了？

苔丝狄蒙娜 上天祝福我们！

奥赛罗 你说。

苔丝狄蒙娜 它没有失去；可是要是失去了，那可怎么样呢？

奥赛罗 怎么！

苔丝狄蒙娜 我说它没有失去。

奥赛罗 去把它拿来给我看。

苔丝狄蒙娜 我可以把它拿来，可是现在我不高兴。这是一个诡计，要想把我的要求赖了过去，请您把卡西奥重新录用了吧。

④ misgive [mɪs'gɪv] v. 产生疑虑

奥赛罗 给我把那手帕拿来。我疑心起来了。

苔丝狄蒙娜 得啦，得啦，您再也找不到一个比他更能干的人。

奥赛罗 手帕！

苔丝狄蒙娜 请您还是跟我谈谈卡西奥的事情吧。

奥赛罗 手帕！

苔丝狄蒙娜 他一向受您的眷爱，跟着您同甘共苦，历尽艰辛——

⑤ in sooth 事实上

奥赛罗 手帕！

苔丝狄蒙娜 凭良心说，您也太不该。

· 171 ·

ACT III

Othello. **Zounds**①!

Exit Othello.

Emilia. Is not this man jealous?

Desde. I ne'er saw this before.
Sure, there's some wonder in this handkerchief;
I am most unhappy in the loss of it.

Emilia. 'Tis not a year or two shows us a man.
They are all but stomachs and we all but food;
They eat us hungerly, and when they are full
They **belch**② us. Look you, Cassio and my husband.

Enter Cassio and Iago.

Iago. There is no other way; 'tis she must do 't.
And lo the happiness: go and importune her.

Desde. How now, good Cassio! What's the news with you?

Cassio. Madam, my former suit. I do beseech you
That by your virtuous means, I may again
Exist, and be a member of his love,
Whom I with all the office of my heart
Entirely honor, I would not be delay'd.
If my offense, be of such mortal kind
That nor my service past nor present sorrows,
Nor purposed merit in futurity,
Can **ransom**③ me into his love again,
But to know so must be my benefit;
So shall I clothe me in a forced content
And shut myself up in some other course
To Fortune's alms.

Desde. Alas, thrice-gentle Cassio.
My **advocation**④ is not now in tune;
My lord is not my lord, nor should I know him,

① zounds [zaundz] *int.* [古语]（用以表示愤怒、惊讶、失望等）咄，哎，哎呀

② belch [beltʃ] *v.* 嗳气

③ ransom ['rænsəm] *v.* 赎回

④ advocation [ædvə'keiʃən] *n.* 支持，辩护

奥赛罗 去！（下）

埃米莉亚 这个人在嫉妒吗？

苔丝狄蒙娜 我从来没有看见过他这样子。这手帕一定有些不可思议的魔力；我真倒霉把它丢了。

埃米莉亚 好的男人一两年里头也难得碰见一个。男人是一只胃，我们是一块肉；他们贪馋地把我们吞下去，吃饱了，就把我们呕出来。您瞧！卡西奥跟我的丈夫来啦。

伊阿古及卡西奥上。

伊阿古 没有别的法子，只好央求她出力。瞧！好运气！去求求她吧。

苔丝狄蒙娜 啊，好卡西奥！您有什么见教？

卡西奥 夫人，我还是要向您重提我原来的请求，希望您发挥鼎力，让我重新做人，能够在我所尊敬的主帅麾下再邀恩眷。我不能这样延宕下去了。假如我果然罪大恶极，无论过去的微劳，现在的悔恨，或是将来立功自赎的决心，都不能博取他的矜怜宽谅，那么我也希望得到一个明白的答复，我就死心塌地向别处去乞讨命运的布施了。

苔丝狄蒙娜 唉，善良的卡西奥！我的话已经变成刺耳的烦渎了；我的丈夫已经不是我的丈夫，要是他的面貌也像他的脾气一样改变，我简直要不认识他

ACT III

       Were he in favor as in humor alter'd.
       So help me every spirit **sanctified**①,
       As I have spoken for you all my best
       And stood within the blank of his displeasure
       For my free speech. You must **awhile**② be patient.
       What I can do I will; and more I will
       Than for myself, I dare. Let that suffice you.

Iago. Is my lord angry?

Emilia. He went hence but now,
       And certainly in strange unquietness.

Iago. Can he be angry? I have seen the cannon,
       When it hath blown his ranks into the air,
       And like the devil from his very arm
       Puff'd his own brother. And can he be angry?
       Something of moment then. I will go meet him.
       There's matter in 't indeed, if he be angry.

Desde. I prithee do so.

Exit Iago.

       Something sure of state,
       Either from Venice, or some **unhatch'd**③ practice
       Made demonstrable here in Cyprus to him,
       Hath puddled his clear spirit; and in such cases,
       Men's natures **wrangle with**④ inferior things,
       Though great ones are their object. 'tis even so;
       For let our finger ache, and it indues
       Our other healthful members, even to that sense
       Of pain. Nay, we must think men are not gods,
       Nor of them look for such observancy
       As fits the bridal. **Beshrew**⑤ me much, Emilia,
       I was unhandsome warrior as I am,

① sanctified ['sæŋktifaid] *a.* 神圣化的；圣洁的

② awhile [ə'wail] *ad.* 一小会儿；暂时

了。愿神灵保佑我！我已经尽力替您说话；为了我的言辞的戆拙，我已经遭到他的憎恶。您必须暂时忍耐；只要是我力量所及的事，我都愿意为您一试；请您相信我，倘然那是我自己的事情，我也不会这样热心的。

伊阿古　主帅发怒了吗？

埃米莉亚　他刚才从这儿走开，他的神气暴躁异常。

伊阿古　他会发怒吗？我曾经看见大炮冲散他的队伍，像魔鬼一样把他的兄弟从他身边轰掉，他仍旧不动声色。他也会发怒吗？那么一定出了什么重大的事情了。我要去看看他。他要是发怒，一定有些缘故。

③ unhatched [ʌn'hætʃt] *a.* 未孵化的；没实现的

④ wrangle with 与……争吵

苔丝狄蒙娜　请你就去吧。（伊阿古下）一定是什么国家大事，或是他在塞浦路斯这儿发现了威尼斯那边有什么秘密的阴谋，扰乱了他的清明的神志；人们在这种情形之下，往往会为了一些小事而生气，虽然实际激怒他们的却是其他更大的原因。正是这样，我们一个指头疼痛的时候，全身都会觉得难受。我们不能把男人当作完美的天神，也不能希望他们永远像新婚之夜那样殷勤体贴。埃米莉亚，我真该死，会在心里抱怨他的无情；现在我才觉悟我是错怪他了。

⑤ beshrew [bi'ʃru:] *v.* [古语] 诅咒 [主要用于温和的诅咒]

ACT III

    Arraigning① his unkindness with my soul;
    But now I find I had suborn'd the witness,
    And he's indicted falsely.
Emilia. Pray heaven it be state matters, as you think,
    And no conception nor no jealous toy,
    Concerning you.
Desde. Alas the day, I never gave him cause.
Emilia. But jealous souls will not be answer'd so;
    They are not ever jealous for the cause,
    But jealous for they are jealous. It is a monster
    Begot upon itself, born on itself.
Desde. Heaven keep that monster from Othello's mind.
Emilia. Lady, amen.
Desde. I will go seek him. Cassio, walk hereabout.
    If I do find him fit, I'll move your suit,
    And seek to effect it **to my uttermost**②.
Cassio. I humbly thank your ladyship.
  Exeunt Desdemona and Emilia.
  Enter Bianca.
Bianca. Save you, friend Cassio.
Cassio. What make you from home?
    How is it with you, my most fair Bianca?
    I' faith, sweet love, I was coming to your house.
Bianca. And I was going to your lodging, Cassio.
    What, keep a week away? Seven days and nights?
    Eight score eight hours? And lovers' absent hours,
    More tedious than the dial eight score times?
    Oh weary reckoning.
Cassio. Pardon me, Bianca.
    I have this while with leaden thoughts been press'd;

① arraign [əˈrein] v. 责难

② to the uttermost 到极致

埃米莉亚　谢天谢地，但愿果然像您所想的，是为了些国家的事情，不是因为对您起了疑心。

苔丝狄蒙娜　唉！我从来没有给过他一些可以使他怀疑的理由。

埃米莉亚　可是多疑的人是不会因此而满足的；他们往往不是因为有了什么理由而嫉妒，只是为了嫉妒而嫉妒，那是一个凭空而来、自生自长的怪物。

苔丝狄蒙娜　愿上天保佑奥赛罗，不要让这怪物钻进他的心里！

埃米莉亚　阿门，夫人。

苔丝狄蒙娜　我去找他去。卡西奥，您在这儿走走，要是我看见他可以说话，我会向他提起您的请求，尽力给您转圜就是了。

卡西奥　多谢夫人。（苔丝狄蒙娜、埃米莉亚下）
　　　比安卡上。

比安卡　你好，卡西奥朋友！

卡西奥　你怎么不在家里？你好，我的最娇美的比安卡？不骗你，亲爱的，我正要到你家里来呢。

比安卡　我也是要到你的尊寓去的，卡西奥。怎么！一个星期不来看我？七天七夜？一百六十八个小时？在相思里挨过的时辰，比时钟是要慢上八十倍的；啊，这一笔算不清的糊涂账！

卡西奥　对不起，比安卡，这几天来我实在心事太重，改日加倍补报你就是了。亲爱的比安卡，（以苔丝狄蒙娜手帕授比安卡）替我把这手帕上的花样描下来。

ACT III

    But I shall in a more **continuate**① time
    Strike off② this score of absence. Sweet Bianca,
    Take me this work out.
Bianca. Oh Cassio, whence came this?
    This is some token from a newer friend.
    To the felt absence now I feel a cause.
    Is 't come to this? Well, well.
Cassio. Go to, woman!
    Throw your vile guesses in the Devil's teeth,
    From whence you have them. You are jealous now,
    That this is from some mistress, some **remembrance**③.
    No, **by my faith**④, Bianca.
Bianca. Why, whose is it?
Cassio. I know not, sweet. I found it in my chamber.
    I like the work well. Ere it be demanded
    As like enough it will, I'ld have it copied.
    Take it, and do 't; and leave me for this time.
Bianca. Leave you? wherefore?
Cassio. I do attend here on the general;
    And think it no addition, nor my wish,
    To have him see me woman'd.
Bianca. Why, I pray you?
Cassio. Not that I love you not.
Bianca. But that you do not love me.
    I pray you, bring me on the way a little,
    And say, if I shall see you soon at night?
Cassio. 'tis but a little way that I can bring you,
    For I **attend**⑤ here, but I'll see you soon.
Bianca. 'Tis very good; I must be circumstanced.
    Exeunt.

① continuate [kən'tinjuit]
  a. [废语] 继续的，不间断的

② srike off（从名单中）划掉；除名

③ remembrance [ri'membrəns]
  n. 纪念物

④ by my faith 我担保！说真的！实在！

⑤ attend [ə'tend] *v.* 等候

比安卡　啊，卡西奥！这是什么地方来的？这一定是哪个新相好送给你的礼物；我现在明白你不来看我的缘故了。有这等事吗？好，好。

卡西奥　得啦，女人！把你这种瞎疑心丢还给魔鬼吧。你在吃醋了，你以为这是什么情人送给我的纪念品；不，凭着我的良心发誓，比安卡。

比安卡　那么这是谁的？

卡西奥　我不知道，爱人；我在寝室里找到它。那花样我很喜欢，我想乘失主没有来问我讨还以前，把它描了下来。请你拿去给我描一描。现在请你暂时离开我。

比安卡　离开你！为什么？

卡西奥　我在这儿等候主帅到来；让他看见我有女人陪着，恐怕不大方便。

比安卡　为什么？我倒要请问。

卡西奥　不是因为我不爱你。

比安卡　只是因为你并不爱我。请你陪我稍微走一段路，告诉我今天晚上你来不来看我。

卡西奥　我只能陪你稍走几步，因为我在这儿等人；可是我就会来看你的。

比安卡　那很好；我也不能勉强你。（各下）

· 179 ·

ACT IV

第四幕

Scene I. Cyprus. Before the castle.

Enter Othello and Iago.

Iago.   Will you think so?

Othello.   Think so, Iago?

Iago.   What, to kiss in private?

Othello.   An **unauthorized**① kiss?

Iago.   Or to be naked with her friend in bed,

　　　　An hour or more, not meaning any harm?

Othello.   Naked in bed, Iago and not mean harm!

　　　　It is **hypocrisy**② against the devil.

　　　　They that mean virtuously, and yet do so,

　　　　The devil their virtue tempts, and they tempt heaven.

Iago.   If they do nothing, 'tis a **venial**③ **slip**④.

　　　　But if I give my wife a handkerchief —

Othello.   What then?

Iago.   Why then, 'tis hers, my lord and being hers,

　　　　She may, I think, bestow 't on any man.

Othello.   She is **protectress**⑤ of her honor too.

　　　　May she give that?

Iago.   Her honor is an essence that's not seen;

第一场　塞浦路斯　城堡前

① unauthorized [ʌn'ɔ:θəraizd] a. 未经授权的；未经许可的；未经批准的

② hypocrisy [hi'pɔkrisi] n. 假装，虚伪

③ venial ['vi:niəl] a.（过失等）可以原谅的

④ slip [slip] n. 过错

⑤ protectress [prəu'tektris] n. 女保护者

　　　　　　　　奥赛罗及伊阿古上。

伊阿古　您愿意这样想吗？
奥赛罗　怎样想，伊阿古？
伊阿古　什么！背着人接吻？
奥赛罗　这样的接吻是为礼法所不许的。
伊阿古　脱光了衣服，和她的朋友睡在一床，经过一个多小时，却一点不起邪念？
奥赛罗　伊阿古，脱光衣服睡在床上，还会不起邪念！这明明是对魔鬼的假意矜持；他们的本心是规矩的，可偏是做出了这种勾当；魔鬼欺骗了这两个规规矩矩的人，而他们就去欺骗上天。
伊阿古　要是他们不及于乱，那还不过是一个小小的过失；可是假如我把一方手帕给了我的妻子——
奥赛罗　给了她便怎样？
伊阿古　啊，主帅，那时候它就是她的东西了；既然是她的东西，我想她可以把它送给无论什么人的。
奥赛罗　她的贞操也是她自己的东西，她也可以把它送给无论什么人吗？
伊阿古　她的贞操是一种不可捉摸的品质；世上有几个

· 183 ·

ACT IV

They have it very oft that have it not.

But for the handkerchief.

Othello. By heaven, I would most gladly have forgot it.

Thou said'st. Oh, it comes o'er my memory,

As doth the **raven**① o'er the **infected**② house,

Boding to all, he had my handkerchief.

Iago. Ay, what of that?

Othello. That's not so good now.

Iago. What, if I had, said I had seen him do you wrong?

Or heard him say, as knaves be such abroad,

Who having by their own importunate suit,

Or voluntary **dotage**③ of some mistress,

Convinced or supplied them, cannot choose

But they must **blab**④.

Othello. Hath he said anything?

Iago. He hath, my lord; but be you well assured,

No more than he'll unswear.

Othello. What hath he said?

Iago. Faith, that he did: I know not what he did.

Othello. What? What?

Iago. Lie.

Othello. With her?

Iago. With her, on her, what you will.

Othello. Lie with her? lie on her? We say lie on her, when they **belie**⑤ her. Lie with her! 'Zounds, that's **fulsome**⑥: handkerchief; confessions; handkerchief. To confess and be hanged for his labor. First, to be hanged, and then to confess. I tremble at it. Nature would not invest herself in such shadowing passion, without some instruction. It is not words that shakes me thus. **Pish**⑦! Noses, ears, and lips. Is 't possible? Confess? Handkerchief? O devil!

真正贞洁的贞洁妇人？可是讲到那方手帕——

奥赛罗　天啊，我但愿忘记那句话！你说——啊！它笼罩着我的记忆，就像预兆不祥的乌鸦①在一座染疫②的屋顶上回旋一样——你说我的手帕在他的手里。

伊阿古　是的，在他手里便怎么样？

奥赛罗　那可不大好。

伊阿古　什么！要是我说我看见他干那对您不住的事？或是听见他说——世上尽多那种家伙，他们靠着死命地追求征服了一个女人，或者得到什么情妇的自动的垂青③，就禁不住到处向人吹嘘④——

奥赛罗　他说过什么话吗？

伊阿古　说过的，主帅；可是您放心吧，他说过的话，他都可以发誓否认的。

奥赛罗　他说过什么？

伊阿古　他说，他曾经——我不知道他曾经干些什么事。

奥赛罗　什么？什么？

伊阿古　跟她睡——

奥赛罗　在一床？

伊阿古　睡在一床，睡在她的身上！随您怎么说吧。

奥赛罗　跟她睡在一床！睡在她的身上！说睡在她身上岂不是诽谤⑤她。该死！岂有此理！手帕——口供——手帕！叫他招供了，再把他吊死。先把他吊起来，然后叫他招供。我一想起就气得发抖。人们总是有了某种感应，阴暗的情绪才会笼罩他的心灵；一两句空洞的话是不能给我这样大的震动的。呸⑦！磨鼻子，咬耳朵，吮嘴唇。会有这样的事吗？口供——手帕！——啊，魔鬼！（晕倒）

---

① raven ['reivən] n.【鸟类】渡鸦

② infected [in'fektid] a.（伤口等）受感染的;（地方等）受污染的

③ dotage [dəutidʒ] n. 溺爱，宠爱

④ blab [blæb] v. 泄密，胡说

⑤ belie [bi'lai] v. 诋毁，对……进行诽谤

⑥ fulsome ['fulsʌm] a.（尤指因过分虚假、伪善等而）令人作呕的，令人厌恶的

⑦ pish [piʃ] int. 呸（表示轻蔑或厌恶）

ACT IV

*Falls in a **trance**①.*

Iago. Work on,

My medicine, work! Thus **credulous**② fools are caught,

And many worthy and chaste dames even thus,

All guiltless, meet reproach. What, hoa? My lord!

My lord, I say: Othello!

Enter Cassio.

How now, Cassio?

Cassio. What's the matter?

Iago. My lord is fall'n into an **epilepsy**③.

This is his second fit; he had one yesterday.

Cassio. Rub him about the temples.

Iago. No forbear;

The **lethargy**④ must have his quiet course.

If not, he foams at mouth, and by and by

Breaks out to savage madness. Look, he stirs.

Do you withdraw yourself a little while,

He will recover straight. When he is gone,

I would on great occasion speak with you.

Exit Cassio.

How is it general? Have you not hurt your head?

Othello. Dost thou mock me?

Iago. I mock you? Not, by heaven.

Would you would bear your fortune like a man.

Othello. A **horned**⑤ man's a monster and a beast.

Iago. There's many a beast then in a populous city,

And many a civil monster.

Othello. Did he confess it?

Iago. Good sir, be a man;

Think every bearded fellow that's but yoked

① trance [trɑ:ns] *n.* 昏迷

② credulous ['kredjuləs] *a.* 轻信的

③ epilepsy ['epilepsi] *n.* 癫痫，羊痫风

④ lethargy ['leθədʒi] *n.* 昏睡；嗜睡症

⑤ horned [hɔ:nd] *a.* [古语] 妻子与他人通奸的，戴着"绿帽子"的

伊阿古 显出你的效力来吧，我的妙药，显出你的效力来吧！轻信的愚人是这样落进了圈套；许多贞洁贤淑的娘儿们，都是这样蒙上了不白之冤。喂，主帅！主帅！奥赛罗！

卡西奥上。

伊阿古 啊，卡西奥！

卡西奥 怎么一回事？

伊阿古 咱们大帅发起癫痫来了。这是他第二次发作；昨天他也发过一次。

卡西奥 在他太阳穴上摩擦摩擦。

伊阿古 不，不行；他这种昏迷状态，必须保持安静；要不然的话，他就要嘴里冒出白沫，慢慢地会发起疯狂来的。瞧！他在动了。你暂时走开一下，他就会恢复原状的。等他走了以后，我还有要紧的话跟你说。（卡西奥下）怎么啦，主帅？您没有摔痛您的头吗？

奥赛罗 你在讥笑我吗？

伊阿古 我讥笑您！不，没有这样的事！我愿您像一个大丈夫似的忍受命运的拨弄。

奥赛罗 顶上绿头巾，还算一个人吗？

伊阿古 在一座热闹的城市里，这种不算人的人多着呢。

奥赛罗 他自己公然承认了吗？

伊阿古 主帅，您看开一点吧；您只要想一想，哪一个有家室的须眉男子，没有遭到跟您同样命运的可

ACT IV

> May draw with you. There's millions now alive,
> That nightly lie in those unproper beds,
> Which they dare swear peculiar. Your case is better.
> Oh, 'tis the spite of hell, the **fiend's**① arch-mock,
> To lip a wanton in a secure couch,
> And to suppose her chaste! No, let me know,
> And knowing what I am, I know what she shall be.

Othello. Oh, thou art wise; 'tis certain.

Iago. Stand you awhile apart,
> Confine yourself but in a patient list.
> Whilst you were here o'erwhelmed with your grief
> A passion most unsuiting such a man,
> Cassio came hither. I shifted him away,
> And laid good 'scuse upon your **ecstasy**②;
> Bad him anon return and here speak with me,
> The which he promised. Do but **encave**③ yourself,
> And mark the **fleers**④, the **gibes**⑤, and notable scorns,
> That dwell in every region of his face;
> For I will make him tell the tale **anew**⑥,
> Where, how, how oft, how long ago, and when
> He hath, and is again to cope your wife.
> I say, but mark his gesture. Marry, patience,
> Or I shall say you are all in all in spleen,
> And nothing of a man.

Othello. Dost thou hear, Iago?
> I will be found most cunning in my patience;
> But dost thou hear most bloody?

Iago. That's not **amiss**⑦;
> But yet keep time in all. Will you withdraw?
> *Othello hides himself.*

① fiend [fi:nd] *n.* 魔鬼，恶魔

② ecstasy ['ekstəsi] *n.* [古语] 昏厥

③ encave [en'keiv] *v.* 把……藏于洞穴中

④ fleer [fli:ə; fliə] *n.* 嘲笑，冷笑

⑤ gibe [dʒaib] *n.* 嘲笑（话）

⑥ anew [ə'nju:] *ad.* 再一次，重新

⑦ amiss [ə'mis] *a.* 错误的

能；世上不知有多少男人，他们的卧榻上容留过无数的生张熟魏，他们自己还满以为这是一块私人的禁地哩；您的情形还不算顶坏。啊！这是最刻毒的恶作剧，魔鬼的最大的玩笑，让一个男人安安心心地搂着一个荡妇亲嘴，还以为她是一个三贞九烈的女人！不，我要睁开眼先看清我自己是个什么东西，我也就看准了该事。

奥赛罗　啊！你是个聪明人；你说得一点不错。

伊阿古　现在请您暂时站在一旁，竭力耐住您的怒气。刚才您恼得昏过去的时候，卡西奥曾经到这儿来过；我告诉他您不省人事是因为一时不适，把他打发走了，叫他过一会儿再来跟我谈谈；他已经答应我了。您只要找一处所在躲一躲，就可以看见他满脸得意忘形、冷嘲热讽的神气；因为我要叫他从头叙述他历次跟尊夫人相会的情形，还要问他重温好梦的时间和地点。您留心看看他那副表情吧。可是不要气恼；否则我就要说您一味意气用事，一点没有大丈夫的气概啦。

奥赛罗　告诉你吧，伊阿古，我会很巧妙地不动声色；可是，你听着，我也会包藏一颗最可怕的杀心。

伊阿古　那很好；可是什么事都要看准时机。您走远一步吧。（奥赛罗退后）现在我要向卡西奥谈起比安

ACT IV

        Now will I question Cassio of Bianca,
        A housewife that by selling her desires
        Buys herself bread and clothes. It is a creature
        That dotes on Cassio, as 'tis the **strumpet's**[①] plague
        To beguile many, and be beguiled by one.
        He, when he hears of her, cannot refrain
        From the excess of laughter. Here he comes.
        Enter Cassio.
        As he shall smile, Othello shall go mad;
        And his unbookish jealousy must conserve
        Poor Cassio's smiles, gestures, and light behaviours
        Quite in the wrong. How do you now, lieutenant?

Cassio.   The worser that you give me the addition,
        Whose want even kills me.

Iago.   Ply Desdemona well, and you are sure on 't.
        Now, if this suit lay in Bianco's power,
        How quickly should you speed?

Cassio.   Alas, poor **caitiff**[②]!

Othello.   Look, how he laughs already!

Iago.   I never knew a woman love man so.

Cassio.   Alas, poor rogue, I think, i'faith, she loves me.

Othello.   Now he denies it faintly and laughs it out.

Iago.   Do you hear, Cassio?

Othello.   Now he importunes him
        To tell it o'er: go to, well said, well said.

Iago.   She gives it out, that you shall marry her.
        Do you intend it?

Cassio.   Ha, ha, ha!

Othello.   Do you triumph, Roman? Do you triumph?

Cassio.   I marry. What? A customer! I prithee bear some charity to my wit; do

① strumpet ['strʌmpit] n. 妓女，娼妓；荡妇

② caitiff ['keitif] n. [古语] 卑鄙小人

卡，一个靠着出卖风情维持生活的雌儿；她热恋着卡西奥；这也是娼妓们的报应，往往她们迷惑了多少的男子，结果却被一个男人迷昏了心。他一听见她的名字，就会忍不住捧腹大笑。他来了。

　　　　卡西奥重上。

伊阿古　他一笑起来，奥赛罗就会发疯；可怜的卡西奥的嬉笑的神情和轻狂的举止，在他那充满着无知的嫉妒的心头，一定可以引起严重的误会。——您好，副将？

卡西奥　我因为丢掉了这个头衔，正在懊恼得要死，你却还要这样称呼我。

伊阿古　在苔丝狄蒙娜跟前多说几句央求的话，包你原官起用。（低声）要是这件事情换在比安卡手里，早就不成问题了。

卡西奥　唉，可怜虫！

奥赛罗　（旁白）瞧！他已经在笑起来啦！

伊阿古　我从来不知道一个女人会这样爱一个男人。

卡西奥　唉，小东西！我看她倒是真的爱我。

奥赛罗　（旁白）现在他在含糊否认，想把这事情用一笑搪塞过去。

伊阿古　你听见吗，卡西奥？

奥赛罗　（旁白）现在他在要求他宣布经过情形啦。说下去，很好，很好。

伊阿古　她向人家说你将要跟她结婚；你有这个意思吗？

卡西奥　哈哈哈！

奥赛罗　（旁白）你这样得意吗，好家伙？你这样得意吗？

卡西奥　我跟她结婚！什么？一个卖淫妇？对不起，你

ACT IV

not think it so unwholesome. Ha, ha, ha!

Othello. So, so, so, so. They laugh that win.

Iago. Faith, the cry goes that you shall marry her.

Cassio. Prithee, say true.

Iago. I am a very villain else.

Othello. Have you scored me? Well.

Cassio. This is the monkey's own giving out.
   She is persuaded I will marry her
   Out of her own love and flattery, not out of my promise.

Othello. Iago **beckons**① me; now he begins the story.

Cassio. She was here even now; she haunts me in every place. I was the other day talking on the sea bank with certain Venetians, and **thither**② comes the **bauble**③, and, by this hand, she falls me thus about my neck.

Othello. Crying, "O dear Cassio", as it were; his gesture imports it.

Cassio. So hangs and **lolls**④, and weeps upon me; so **hales**⑤ and pulls me. Ha, ha, ha!

Othello. Now he tells how she **plucked**⑥ him to my chamber. Oh, I see that nose of yours, but not that dog, I shall throw it to.

Cassio. Well, I must leave her company.

Iago. Before me! Look where she comes.

Cassio. 'Tis such another fitchew: marry, a perfumed one?

Enter Bianca.

What do you mean by this haunting of me?

Bianca. Let the devil and his dam haunt you! What did you mean by that same handkerchief, you gave me even now? I was a fine fool to take it. I must take out the work? A likely piece of work that you should find it in your

① beckon ['bekən] v.（以招手、点头）表示招呼
② thither ['ðiðə;θi-] ad. 那里；向那里，到那里
③ bauble ['bɔːbl] n. 华而不实的东西，花哨的小玩意儿
④ loll [lɔl] v. 懒洋洋地倚靠（或躺）着
⑤ hale[heil] v. 用力拉，使劲拖
⑥ pluck [plʌk] v. 拉，扯，撕

不要这样看轻我，我还不至于糊涂到这等地步哩。哈哈哈！

奥赛罗 （旁白）好，好，好，好。得胜的人才会笑逐颜开。

伊阿古 不骗你，人家都在说你将要跟她结婚。

卡西奥 对不起，别说笑话啦。

伊阿古 我要是骗了你，我就是个大大的混蛋。

卡西奥 一派胡说！她自己一厢情愿，相信我会跟她结婚；我可没有答应她。

奥赛罗 （旁白）伊阿古在向我打招呼；现在他开始讲他的故事啦。

卡西奥 她刚才还在这儿；她到处缠着我。前天我正在海边跟几个威尼斯人谈话，那傻东西就来啦；不瞒你说，她这样攀住我的颈项——

奥赛罗 （旁白）叫一声"啊，亲爱的卡西奥！"我可以从他的表情之间猜得出来。

卡西奥 她这样拉住我的衣服，靠在我的怀里，哭个不停，还这样把我拖来拖去，哈哈哈！

奥赛罗 （旁白）现在他在讲她怎样把他拖到我的寝室里去啦。啊！我看见你的鼻子，可是不知道应该把它丢给哪一条狗吃。

卡西奥 好，我只好离开她。

伊阿古 啊！瞧，她来了。

卡西奥 好一头抹香粉的臭猫！

比安卡上。

卡西奥 你这样到处盯着我不放，是什么意思呀？

比安卡 让魔鬼跟他的老娘盯着你吧！你刚才给我的那方手帕算是什么意思？我是个大傻瓜，才会把它收了下来。叫我描下那花样！真好看的花样，你在你的寝室里找到它，却不知道谁把它丢在那边！这一

chamber, and not know who left it there. This is some minx's token, and I must take out the work? There, give it your hobby-horse. Wheresoever you had it, I'll take out no work on 't.

Cassio. How now, my sweet Bianca? How now? How now?

Othello. By heaven, that should be my handkerchief.

Bianca. If you'll come to supper tonight, you may; an you will not, come when you are next prepared for.

Exit.

Iago. After her, after her.

Cassio. Faith I must; she'll rail i' the street else.

Iago. Will you sup there?

Cassio. Faith I intend so.

Iago. Well, I may chance to see you, for I would very fain speak with you.

Cassio. Prithee come; will you?

Iago. Go to; say no more.

Exit Cassio.

Othello. [*Advancing.*] How shall I murther him, Iago.

Iago. Did you perceive how he laughed at his vice?

Othello. Oh, Iago!

Iago. And did you see the handkerchief?

Othello. Was that mine?

Iago. Yours by this hand. And to see how he prizes the foolish woman your wife! She gave it him, and he hath given it his whore.

Othello. I would have him nine years a killing. A fine woman, a fair woman, a sweet woman!

Iago. Nay, you must forget that.

Othello. Ay, let her rot and perish, and be damned tonight, for she shall not live. No, my heart is turned to stone; I strike it, and it hurts my hand. Oh, the world hath not a sweeter creature. She might lie by an Emperor's

定是哪一个贱丫头送给你的东西，却叫我描下它的花样来！拿去，还给你那个相好吧；随你从什么地方得到这方手帕，我可不高兴描下它的花样。

卡西奥 怎么，我的亲爱的比安卡！怎么！怎么！

奥赛罗 （旁白）天啊，那该是我的手帕哩！

比安卡 今天晚上你要是愿意来吃饭，尽管来吧；要是不愿意来，等你下回有兴致的时候再来吧。（下）

伊阿古 追上去，追上去。

卡西奥 真的，我必须追上去，否则她会沿街骂人的。

伊阿古 你预备到她家里去吃饭吗？

卡西奥 是的，我想去。

伊阿古 好，也许我会再碰见你；因为我很想跟你谈谈。

卡西奥 请你一定来吧。

伊阿古 得啦，别多说啦。（卡西奥下）

奥赛罗 （趋前）伊阿古，我应该怎样杀死他？

伊阿古 您看见他一听到人家提起他的丑事，就笑得多么高兴吗？

奥赛罗 啊，伊阿古！

伊阿古 您还看见那方手帕吗？

奥赛罗 那就是我的吗？

伊阿古 我可以举手起誓，那是您的。瞧他多么看得起您那位痴心的太太！她把手帕送给他，他却拿去给了他的娼妇。

奥赛罗 我要用九年的时间慢慢地磨死她。一个高雅的女人！一个美貌的女人！一个温柔的女人！

伊阿古 不，您必须忘掉那些。

奥赛罗 嗯，让她今夜腐烂，死亡，堕入地狱吧，因为她不能再活在世上。不，我的心已经变成铁石了；我打它，反而打痛了我的手。啊！世上没有一个比她更可爱的东西；她可以睡在一个皇帝的身边，命

ACT IV

side, and command him tasks.

Iago. Nay, that's not your way.

Othello. Hang her, I do but say what she is. So delicate with her needle, an admirable musician. Oh, she will sing the savageness out of a bear. Of so high and plenteous wit and invention!

Iago. She's the worse for all this.

Othello. Oh, a thousand, a thousand times.

And then, of so gentle a condition!

Iago. Ay too gentle.

Othello. Nay that's certain. But yet the pity of it, Iago:

Oh Iago, the pity of it, Iago!

Iago. If you are so fond over her iniquity, give her patent to offend, for if it touch not you, it comes near nobody.

Othello. I will chop her into messes. Cuckold me?

Iago. Oh, 'tis foul in her.

Othello. With mine officer?

Iago. That's fouler.

Othello. Get me some poison, Iago, this night. I'll not expostulate with her, lest her body and beauty unprovide my mind again. This night, Iago.

Iago. Do it not with poison, strangle her in her bed, even the bed she hath contaminated.

Othello. Good, good, the justice of it pleases, very good.

Iago. And for Cassio, let me be his undertaker.

You shall hear more by midnight.

Othello. Excellent good.

A trumpet within.

What trumpet is that same?

Iago. I warrant something from Venice, sure. 'Tis Lodovico

令他干无论什么事。

伊阿古　您素来不是这个样子的。

奥赛罗　让她死吧！我不过说她是怎么样的一个人。她的针线活儿是这样精妙！一个出色的音乐家！啊，她唱起歌来，可以驯服一头野熊的心！她的心思才智，又是这样敏慧多能！

伊阿古　唯其这样多才多艺，干出这种丑事来，才格外叫人气恼。

奥赛罗　啊！一千倍，一千倍的可恼！而且她的性格又是这样温柔！

伊阿古　嗯，太温柔了。

奥赛罗　对啦，一点不错。可是，伊阿古，可惜！啊！伊阿古！伊阿古！太可惜啦！

伊阿古　要是您对于一个失节之妇，还是这样恋恋不舍，那么索性放任吧；因为既然您自己也不以为意，当然更不干别人的事。

奥赛罗　我要把她剁成一堆肉酱。叫我当一个王八！

伊阿古　啊，她太不顾羞耻啦！

奥赛罗　跟我的部将通奸！

伊阿古　那尤其可恶。

奥赛罗　给我弄些毒药来，伊阿古；今天晚上。我不想跟她多费唇舌，免得她的肉体和美貌再打动了我的心，今天晚上，伊阿古。

伊阿古　不要用毒药，在她床上扼死她，就在那被她玷污了的床上。

奥赛罗　好，好；那是一个大快人心的处置，很好。

伊阿古　至于卡西奥，让我去取他的命吧；您在午夜前后，一定可以听到消息。

奥赛罗　好极了。（内喇叭声）那是什么喇叭的声音？

伊阿古　一定是从威尼斯来了什么人。——是洛多维科

ACT IV

        Come from the Duke. And, see your wife is with him.
        Enter Lodovico, Desdemona and Attendants.

Lodo.   God save the worthy general.

Othello.   With all my heart, sir.

Lodo.   The Duke and Senators of Venice greet you.
        Gives him a letter.

Othello.   I kiss the instrument of their pleasures.
        Opens the letter and reads.

Desde.   And what's the news, good cousin Lodovico?

Iago.   I am very glad to see you, signior;
        Welcome to Cyprus.

Lodo.   I thank you. How does lieutenant Cassio?

Iago.   Lives, sir.

Desde.   Cousin, there's fall'n between him and my lord
        An unkind breech; but you shall make all well.

Othello.   Are you sure of that?

Desde.   My lord?

Othello.   [*Reads.*] This fail you not to do, as you will —

Lodo.   He did not call; he's busy in the paper.
        Is there division 'twixt my lord and Cassio?

Desde.   A most unhappy one. I would do much
        To **atone**① them, for the love I bear to Cassio.

Othello.   Fire and **brimstone**②!

Desde.   My lord?

Othello.   Are you wise?

Desde.   What, is he angry?

Lodo.   May be the letter moved him;
        For as I think, they do command him home,
        Deputing Cassio in his government.

Desde.   By my **troth**③, I am glad on 't.

奉公爵之命到这儿来了；瞧，您那位太太也跟他在一起。

洛多维科、苔丝狄蒙娜及侍从等上。

洛多维科 　上帝保佑您，尊贵的将军！

奥赛罗 　祝福您，大人。

洛多维科 　公爵和威尼斯的元老们问候您安好。（以信交奥赛罗）

奥赛罗 　我敬吻他们的恩命。（拆信阅读）

苔丝狄蒙娜 　洛多维科大哥，威尼斯有什么消息？

伊阿古 　我很高兴看见您，大人；欢迎您到塞浦路斯来！

洛多维科 　谢谢。卡西奥副将好吗？

伊阿古 　他还健在，大人。

苔丝狄蒙娜 　大哥，他跟我的丈夫闹了点儿别扭；可是您可以使他们言归于好。

奥赛罗 　你有把握吗？

苔丝狄蒙娜 　您怎么说，我的主？

奥赛罗 　（读信）"务必照办为要，不得有误——"

洛多维科 　他没有回答；他正在忙着读信。将军跟卡西奥果然有了意见吗？

苔丝狄蒙娜 　有了很不幸的意见；为了我对卡西奥所抱的好感，我很愿意尽力调解他们。

奥赛罗 　该死！

苔丝狄蒙娜 　你怎么说，我的主？

奥赛罗 　你聪明吗？

苔丝狄蒙娜 　什么！他生气了吗？

洛多维科 　也许这封信激动了他；因为照我猜想起来，他们是要召他回国，叫卡西奥代理他的职务。

苔丝狄蒙娜 　真的吗？那好极了。

① atone [ə'təun] *v.* [废语] 使和解，使和好

② brimstone ['brimstəun] *n.* 硫黄

③ troth ['trəuθ] *n.* 诺言

ACT IV

Othello. Indeed?

Desde. My lord?

Othello. I am glad to see you mad.

Desde. Why, sweet Othello?

Othello. Devil!

Strikes her.

Desde. I have not deserved this.

Lodo. My lord, this would not be believed in Venice,

Though I should swear I saw 't. 'Tis very much.

Make her amends①; she weeps.

Othello. Oh devil, devil:

If that the earth could teem with woman's tears,

Each drop she falls would prove a crocodile.

Out of my sight.

Desde. [*Going.*] I will not stay to offend you.

Lodo. Truly obedient lady.

I do beseech your lordship, call her back.

Othello. Mistress.

Desde. My lord.

Othello. What would you with her, sir?

Lodo. Who I, my lord?

Othello. Ay, you did wish that I would make her turn.

Sir, she can turn and turn, and yet go on,

And turn again; and she can weep, sir, weep;

And she's obedient, as you say obedient,

Very obedient. Proceed you in your tears.

Concerning this, sir, Oh well-**painted**② passion!

I am commanded home. Get you away;

I'll send for you **anon**③. Sir, I obey the **mandate**④,

And will return to Venice. Hence, avaunt!

① make amends 赔偿（损失）；补偿（过失）

② painted ['peintid] *a.* 假装的，虚饰的

③ anon [ə'nɒn] *ad.* [古语] 不久

④ mandate ['mændeit] *n.* 命令；指令

奥赛罗 当真！

苔丝狄蒙娜 您怎么说，我的主？

奥赛罗 你要是发了疯，我才高兴。

苔丝狄蒙娜 为什么，亲爱的奥赛罗？

奥赛罗 魔鬼！（击苔丝狄蒙娜）

苔丝狄蒙娜 我没有错处，您不该这样对待我。

洛多维科 将军，我要是把这回事情告诉威尼斯人，即使发誓说我亲眼看见，他们也一定不会相信我。这太过分了；向她赔罪吧，她在哭了。

奥赛罗 啊，魔鬼！魔鬼！要是妇人的眼泪有孳生化育的力量，她的每一滴泪都会变成一条鳄鱼。走开，不要让我看见你！

苔丝狄蒙娜 我不愿留在这儿害您生气。（欲去）

洛多维科 真是一位顺从的夫人。将军，请您叫她回来吧。

奥赛罗 夫人！

苔丝狄蒙娜 我的主？

奥赛罗 大人，您要跟她说些什么话？

洛多维科 谁？我吗，将军？

奥赛罗 嗯，您要我叫她转来，现在她转过来了。她会转来转去，走一步路回一个身；她还会哭，大人，她还会哭；她是非常顺从的，正像您所说，非常顺从。尽管流你的眼泪吧。大人，这信上的意思——好一股装腔作势的劲儿！——是要叫我回去——你去吧，等会儿我再叫人来唤你——大人，我服从他们的命令，不日就可以束装上路，回到威尼斯去——去！滚开！（苔丝狄蒙娜下）卡西奥可以接替我的位置。今天晚上，大人，我还要请您赏光便饭。欢迎您到塞浦路斯来！——山羊和猴子！（下）

ACT IV

Exit Desdemona.

Cassio shall have my place. And sir, tonight,

I do entreat that we may **sup**① together.

You are welcome, sir, to Cyprus. Goats and monkeys!

Exit.

Lodo. Is this the noble Moor, whom our full senate

Call all in all sufficient? Is this the nature

Whom passion could not shake? Whose solid virtue

The shot of accident nor dart of chance

Could neither graze nor pierce?

Iago. He is much changed.

Lodo. Are his wits safe? Is he not light of brain?

Iago. He's that he is. I may not breathe my censure

What he might be: if what he might, he is not,

I would to heaven he were.

Lodo. What, strike his wife?

Iago. Faith that was not so well; yet would I knew

That stroke would prove the worst.

Lodo. Is it his **use**②?

Or did the letters work upon his blood,

And new create this fault?

Iago. **Alas**③, alas!

It is not honesty in me to speak

What I have seen and known. You shall observe him,

And his own courses will denote him so,

That I may save my speech. Do but go after,

And mark how he continues.

Lodo. I am sorry that I am deceived in him.

Exeunt.

① sup [sʌp] v. 吃晚饭

② use [ju:z] n. 习惯；惯例

③ alas [əˈlæs] int. 哎呀

洛多维科　这就是为我们整个元老院所同声赞叹，称为全才全德的那位英勇的摩尔人吗？这就是那喜怒之情不能把它震撼的高贵的天性吗？那命运的箭矢不能把它擦伤穿破的坚定的德操吗？

伊阿古　他已经大大变了样子啦。

洛多维科　他的头脑没有毛病吗？他的精神是不是有点错乱？

伊阿古　他就是他那个样子；我实在不敢说他还会变成怎么一个样子；如果他不是像他所应该的那样，那么但愿他也不至于这个样子！

洛多维科　什么！打他的妻子！

伊阿古　真的，那可不大好；可是我但愿知道他对她没有比这更暴虐的行为！

洛多维科　他一向都是这样的吗？还是因为信上的话激怒了他，才会有这种以前所没有的过失？

伊阿古　唉！唉！按着我的地位，我实在不便把我所看见所知道的一切说出口来。您不妨留心注意他，他自己的行动就可以说明一切，用不着我多说了。请您跟上去，看他还会做出什么花样来。

洛多维科　他竟是这样一个人，真使我大失所望啊。（同下）

Scene II. A room in the castle.

Enter Othello and Emilia.

Othello.   You have seen nothing, then?

Emilia.   Nor ever heard, nor ever did suspect.

Othello.   Yes, you have seen Cassio, and she together.

Emilia.   But then I saw no harm, and then I heard
　　　　　Each syllable that breath made up between them.

Othello.   What? Did they never whisper?

Emilia.   Never, my lord.

Othello.   Nor send you out o' the way?

Emilia.   Never.

Othello.   To fetch her fan, her gloves, her mask, nor nothing?

Emilia.   Never my lord.

Othello.   That's strange.

Emilia.   I durst, my lord, to **wager**① she is honest,
　　　　　Lay down my soul at stake. If you think other,
　　　　　Remove your thought; it doth abuse your bosom.
　　　　　If any wretch have put this in your head,
　　　　　Let heaven **requite**② it with the **serpent's**③ curse,
　　　　　For if she be not honest, chaste, and true,

第二场 城堡中的一室

奥赛罗及埃米莉亚上。

奥赛罗 那么你没有看见什么吗?

埃米莉亚 没有看见,没有听见,也没有疑心到。

奥赛罗 你不是看见卡西奥跟她在一起吗?

埃米莉亚 可是我不知道那有什么不对,而且我听见他们两人所说的每一个字。

奥赛罗 什么!他们从来不曾低声耳语吗?

埃米莉亚 从来没有,将军。

奥赛罗 也不曾打发你走开吗?

埃米莉亚 没有。

奥赛罗 没有叫你去替她拿扇子,手套,脸罩,或是什么东西吗?

埃米莉亚 没有,将军。

奥赛罗 那可奇怪了。

埃米莉亚 将军,我敢用我的灵魂打赌她是贞洁的。要是您疑心她有非礼的行为,赶快除掉这种思想吧,因为那是您心理上的一个污点。要是哪一个混蛋把这种思想放进您的脑袋里,让上天罚他变成一条蛇,受永远的诅咒!假如她不是贞洁、贤淑而忠诚

---

① wager ['weidʒə] *v.* 打赌

② requite [ri'kwait] *v.* 报答;回报

③ serpent ['sə:pənt] *n.* 蛇(尤指大蛇或毒蛇)

ACT IV

>　　　There's no man happy; the purest of their wives
>　　　Is foul as slander.

Othello.　Bid her come hither; go.
Exit Emilia.
　　　She says enough; yet she's a simple bawd
　　　That cannot say as much. This is a subtle whore,
　　　A closet lock and key of **villainous**① secrets.
　　　And yet she'll kneel and pray; I have seen her do 't.
Enter Desdemona with Emilia.

Desde.　My lord, what is your will?

Othello.　Pray you chuck, come hither.

Desde.　What is your pleasure?

Othello.　Let me see your eyes;
　　　Look in my face.

Desde.　What horrible fancy's this?

Othello.　Some of your function, mistress,
　　　Leave **procreants**② alone and shut the door;
　　　Cough, or cry hem, if anybody come.
　　　Your mystery, your mystery; nay dispatch.
Exit Emilia.

Desde.　Upon my knees, what doth your speech import?
　　　I understand a fury in your words,
　　　But not the words.

Othello.　Why? what art thou?

Desde.　Your Wife, my lord, your true and loyal wife.

Othello.　Come swear it, damn thyself;
　　　Lest being like one of heaven, the devils themselves
　　　Should fear to seize thee. Therefore be double-damn'd;
　　　Swear thou art honest.

Desde.　Heaven doth truly know it.

的，那么世上没有一个幸福的男人了；最纯洁的妻子，也会变成最丑恶的淫妇。

奥赛罗 叫她到这儿来；去。（埃米莉亚下）她的话说得很动听；可是这种拉惯皮条的人，都是天生的利嘴。这是一个狡猾的淫妇，一肚子千刁万恶，当着人却会跪下来向天祈祷；我看见过她这一种手段。

① villainous ['vilənəs] *a.* 邪恶的

埃米莉亚偕苔丝狄蒙娜重上。

苔丝狄蒙娜 我的主，您有什么吩咐？

奥赛罗 过来，乖乖。

苔丝狄蒙娜 您要我怎么样？

奥赛罗 让我看看你的眼睛；瞧着我的脸。

苔丝狄蒙娜 这是什么古怪的念头？

奥赛罗 （向埃米莉亚）你去干你的事吧，女士；把门关了，让我们两人在这儿谈谈心。要是有人来了，你就在门口咳嗽一声。干你的贵营生去吧；快，快！（埃米莉亚下）

② procreant ['prəukriənt] *n.* 夫妻

苔丝狄蒙娜 我跪在您的面前，请您告诉我您这些话是什么意思？我知道您在生气，可是我不懂您的话。

奥赛罗 嘿，你是什么人？

苔丝狄蒙娜 我的主，我是您的妻子，您的忠心不二的妻子。

奥赛罗 来，发一个誓，让你自己死后下地狱吧；因为你的外表太像一个天使了，倘不是在不贞之上，再加一重伪誓的罪名，也许魔鬼们会不敢抓你下去的；所以发誓说你是贞洁的吧。

苔丝狄蒙娜 天知道我是贞洁的。

Othello. Heaven truly knows that thou art false as hell.
Desde. To whom, my lord? With whom? How am I false?
Othello. Ah Desdemona! Away! away! away!
Desde. Alas the heavy day! Why do you weep?
  Am I the motive of these tears, my lord?
  If haply you my father do suspect
  An instrument of this your calling back,
  Lay not your blame on me. If you have lost him,
  I have lost him too.
Othello. Had it pleased heaven,
  To try me with affliction, had they rain'd
  All kinds of **sores**① and shames on my bare head,
  Steep'd me in poverty to the very lips,
  Given to **captivity**② me and my utmost hopes,
  I should have found in some place of my soul
  A drop of patience; but alas, to make me
  A fixed figure for the time of scorn,
  To point his slow **unmoving**③ finger at.
  Yet could I bear that too, well, very well;
  But there, where I have **garner'd up**④ my heart,
  Where either I must live or bear no life;
  The fountain from the which my current runs,
  Or else dries up; to be discarded thence,
  Or keep it as a **cistern**⑤ for foul toads
  To knot and gender in. Turn thy complexion there,
  Patience, thou young and rose-lipp'd **cherubin**⑥,
  Ay, there, look grim as hell!
Desde. I hope my noble lord esteems me honest.
Othello. Oh, ay, as summer flies are in the **shambles**⑦,
  That quicken even with blowing. Oh thou weed,

奥赛罗 天知道你是像地狱一样淫邪的。

苔丝狄蒙娜 我的主,我对谁干了欺心的事?我跟哪一个人有不端的行为?我怎么是淫邪的?

奥赛罗 啊,苔丝狄蒙娜!去!去!去!

苔丝狄蒙娜 唉,不幸的日子!——您为什么哭?您的眼泪是为我而流的吗,我的主?要是您疑心这次奉召回国,是我的父亲的主意,请您不要怪我;您固然失去他的好感,我也已经失去他的慈爱了。

奥赛罗 要是上天的意思,要让我受尽种种的折磨;要是他用诸般的痛苦和耻辱降在我的毫无防卫的头上,把我浸没在贫困的泥沼里,剥夺我的一切自由和希望,我也可以在我的灵魂的一隅之中,找到一滴忍耐的甘露。可是唉!在这尖酸刻薄的世上,做一个被人戳指笑骂的目标,那还可以容忍;可是我的心灵失去了归宿,我的生命失去了寄托,我的活力的源泉干涸了,变成蛤蟆繁育生息的污池!忍耐,你朱唇韶颜的天婴啊,转变你的脸色,让它化成地狱般的狰狞吧!

① sore [sɔ:] *n.* 伤心,精神痛苦

② captivity [kæp'tivəti] *n.* 关押,监禁

③ unmoving [ʌn'mu:viŋ] *a.* 无动于衷的,冷淡的

④ gather up 收集起

⑤ cistern ['sistən] *n.* 水塘

⑥ cherubin ['tʃerəbin] *n.* 智天使(天堂乐园的守护者)

⑦ shambles ['ʃæmblz] *n.* 屠宰场

苔丝狄蒙娜 我希望我在我的尊贵的夫主眼中,是一个贤良贞洁的妻子。

奥赛罗 啊,是的,就像夏天的肉铺里的苍蝇一样贞洁,飞来飞去撒它的卵子。你这野草闲花啊!你的颜色

ACT IV

        Who art so lovely fair and smell'st so sweet,

        That the sense aches at thee, would thou hadst ne'er been born.

Desde.   Alas, what ignorant sin have I committed?

Othello.   Was this fair paper? This most goodly book,

        Made to write whore upon? What committed?

        Committed? Oh, thou public commoner,

        I should make very forges of my cheeks,

        That would to **cinders**① burn up modesty,

        Did I but speak thy deeds. What committed?

        Heaven stops the nose at it, and the moon winks;

        The bawdy wind, that kisses all it meets,

        Is hush'd within the hollow mine of earth,

        And will not hear it. What committed?

        Impudent② strumpet!

Desde.   By heaven, you do me wrong.

Othello.   Are not you a strumpet?

Desde.   No, as I am a Christian.

        If to preserve this vessel for my lord,

        From any other foul **unlawful**③ touch

        Be not to be a strumpet, I am none.

Othello.   What, not a whore?

Desde.   No, as I shall be saved.

Othello.   Is 't possible?

Desde.   Oh, heaven forgive us.

Othello.   I cry you mercy then;

        I took you for that cunning whore of Venice

        That married with Othello. [*Raises his voice.*] You mistress,

        That have the office opposite to Saint Peter,

        And keep the gate of hell,

        Enter Emilia.

　　　　是这样娇美，你的香气是这样芬芳，人家看见你嗅到你就会心疼；但愿世上从来不曾有过你！

苔丝狄蒙娜　唉！我究竟犯了什么连我自己也不知道的罪恶呢？

奥赛罗　这一张皎洁的白纸，这一本美丽的书册，是要让人家写上"娼妓"两个字的吗？犯了什么罪恶！啊，你这人尽可夫的娼妇！我只要一说起你所干的事，我的两颊就会变成两座熔炉，把廉耻烧为灰烬。犯了什么罪恶！天神见了它要掩鼻而过；月亮看见了要羞得闭上眼睛；碰见什么都要亲吻淫荡的风，也静悄悄地躲在岩窟里面，不愿听见人家提起它的名字。犯了什么罪恶！不要脸的娼妇！

苔丝狄蒙娜　天啊，您不该这样侮辱我！

奥赛罗　你不是一个娼妇吗？

苔丝狄蒙娜　不，我发誓我不是，否则我就不是一个基督徒。要是为我的主保持这一个清白的身子，不让淫邪的手把它污毁，要是这样的行为可以使我免去娼妇的恶名，那么我就不是娼妇。

奥赛罗　什么！你不是一个娼妇吗？

苔丝狄蒙娜　不，否则我死后没有得救的希望。

奥赛罗　真的吗？

苔丝狄蒙娜　啊！上天饶恕我们！

奥赛罗　那么我真是多多冒昧了；我还以为你就是那个嫁给奥赛罗的威尼斯狡猾的娼妇哩。——喂，你这位刚刚和圣彼得[1]干着相反的差使的，看守地狱门户的奶奶！

　　　　埃米莉亚重上。

① cinder ['sində] n. 灰烬

② impudent ['impjudənt] a. 厚颜无耻的；冒失的

③ unlawful [ʌn'lɔ:ful] a. 不道德的

---

1 圣彼得（St. Peter），耶稣的十二门徒之一，传说他掌天堂门户的钥匙。

ACT IV

>   You, you, ay, you!
>   We have done our course; there's money for your pains.
>   I pray you, turn the key, and keep our **counsel**①.
>   *Exit.*

Emilia. Alas, what does this gentleman conceive?
>   How do you, madam? How do you, my good lady?

Desde. Faith, half asleep.

Emilia. Good madam, what's the matter with my lord?

Desde. With who?

Emilia. Why, with my lord, madam.

Desde. Who is thy lord?

Emilia. He that is yours, sweet lady.

Desde. I have none. Do not talk to me, Emilia;
>   I cannot weep, nor answer have I none
>   But what should go by water. Prithee tonight
>   Lay on my bed my wedding sheets. Remember,
>   And call thy husband hither.

Emilia. Here's a change indeed.
>   *Exit.*

Desde. 'Tis meet I should be used so, very meet.
>   How have I been behaved, that he might stick
>   The small'st opinion on my least **misuse**②?
>   *Enter Emilia with Iago.*

Iago. What is your pleasure, madam? How is 't with you?

Desde. I cannot tell. Those that do teach young babes
>   Do it with gentle means and easy tasks.
>   He might have chid me so, for in good faith,
>   I am a child to chiding.

Iago. What's the matter, lady?

Emilia. Alas Iago, my lord hath so bewhored her,

① counsel ['kaunsəl] n. [废语] 秘密

奥赛罗 你，你，对了，你！我们的谈话已经完毕。这几个钱是给你作为酬劳的；请你开了门上的锁，不要泄露我们的秘密。（下）

埃米莉亚 唉！这位老爷究竟在转些什么念头呀？您怎么啦，夫人？您怎么啦，我的好夫人？

苔丝狄蒙娜 我是在半醒半睡之中。

埃米莉亚 好夫人，我的主到底有些什么心事？

苔丝狄蒙娜 谁？

埃米莉亚 我的主呀，夫人。

苔丝狄蒙娜 谁是你的主？

埃米莉亚 我的主就是你的丈夫，好夫人。

苔丝狄蒙娜 我没有丈夫。不要对我说话，埃米莉亚；我不能哭，我没有话可以回答你，除了我的眼泪。请你今夜把我结婚的被褥铺在我的床上，记好了；再去替我叫你的丈夫来。

埃米莉亚 真是变了，变了！（下）

苔丝狄蒙娜 我应该受到这样的待遇，全然是应该的。我究竟有些什么不检的行为——哪怕只是一丁点儿——才会引起他的猜疑呢？

　　　　埃米莉亚率伊阿古重上。

伊阿古 夫人，您有什么吩咐？您怎么啦？

苔丝狄蒙娜 我不知道。小孩子做了错事，做父亲的总是用温和的态度，轻微的责罚教训他们；他也应该这样责备我，因为我是一个娇养惯了的孩子，不惯受人家责备的。

伊阿古 怎么一回事，夫人？

埃米莉亚 唉！伊阿古，将军口口声声骂她娼妇，用那

② misuse [mis'ju:z; mis'ju:s] n. 错用，误用

ACT IV

        Thrown such despite and heavy terms upon her,
        That true hearts cannot bear it.
Desde.   Am I that name, Iago?
Iago.   What name, fair lady?
Desde.   Such as she says my lord did say I was.
Emilia.   He call'd her whore; a beggar in his drink
        Could not have laid such terms upon his **callet**①.
Iago.   Why did he so?
Desde.   I do not know; I am sure I am none such.
Iago.   Do not weep, do not weep. Alas the day!
Emilia.   Hath she **forsook**② so many noble matches?
        Her father and her country and her friends?
        To be call'd whore? Would it not make one weep?
Desde.   It is my wretched fortune.
Iago.   Beshrew him for 't:
        How comes this trick upon him?
Desde.   Nay, heaven doth know.
Emilia.   I will be hang'd, if some eternal villain,
        Some busy and **insinuating**③ rogue,
        Some cogging, **cozening**④ slave, to get some office,
        Have not devised this slander; I'll be hang'd else.
Iago.   Fie, there is no such man; it is impossible.
Desde.   If any such there be, heaven pardon him.
Emilia.   A **halter**⑤ pardon him! And hell gnaw his bones!
        Why should he call her whore? Who keeps her company?
        What place? What time? What form? What likelihood?
        The Moor's abused by some most villainous knave,
        Some base notorious knave, some scurvy fellow.
        Oh heaven, that such companions thou'ldst unfold,
        And put in every honest hand a whip

样难堪的名字加在她的身上,稍有人心的人,谁听见了都不能忍受。

苔丝狄蒙娜 我应该得到那样一个称呼吗,伊阿古?

伊阿古 什么称呼,好夫人?

苔丝狄蒙娜 就像她说我的主称呼我的那种名字。

埃米莉亚 他叫她娼妇;一个喝醉了酒的叫花子,也不会把这种名字加在他的姘妇身上。

伊阿古 为什么他要这样?

苔丝狄蒙娜 我不知道;我相信我不是那样的女人。

伊阿古 不要哭,不要哭。唉!

埃米莉亚 多少名门贵族向她求婚,她都拒绝了;她抛下了老父,离乡背井,远别亲友,结果却只讨他骂一声娼妇吗?这还不叫人伤心吗?

苔丝狄蒙娜 都是我自己命薄。

伊阿古 他太岂有此理了!他怎么会起这种心思的?

苔丝狄蒙娜 天才知道。

埃米莉亚 我可以打赌,一定有一个万劫不复的恶人,一个爱管闲事、鬼讨好的家伙,一个说假话骗人的奴才,因为要想钻求差使,造出这样的谣言来;要是我的话说得不对,我愿意让人家把我吊死。

伊阿古 呸!哪里有这样的人?一定不会的。

苔丝狄蒙娜 要是果然有这样的人,愿上天宽恕他!

埃米莉亚 宽恕他!一条绳子箍住他的颈项,地狱里的恶鬼咬碎他的骨头!他为什么叫她娼妇?谁跟她在一起?什么所在?什么时候?什么方式?什么根据?这摩尔人一定是上了不知哪一个千刁万恶的坏人的当,一个下流的大混蛋,一个卑鄙的家伙;天啊!愿你揭破这种家伙的嘴脸,让每一个老

① callet ['kælit] *n.* 荡妇;妓女

② forsake [fə'seik] *v.* 放弃

③ insinuating [in'sinjueitiŋ] *a.* 讨好的;巴结的

④ cozen ['kʌzən] *v.* 欺骗

⑤ halter ['hɔːltə] *n.* 绞索;绞刑

ACT IV

    To lash the rascals naked through the world,
    Even from the east to the west!
Iago. Speak within door.
Emilia. Oh fie upon them! Some such squire he was
    That turn'd your wit the seamy side without,
    And made you to suspect me with the Moor.
Iago. You are a fool; go to.
Desde. Alas Iago,
    What shall I do to win my lord again?
    Good friend, go to him, for by this light of heaven,
    I know not how I lost him. Here I kneel:
    If e'er my will did trespass 'gainst his love,
    Either in discourse of thought or actual deed,
    Or that mine eyes, mine ears, or any sense,
    Delighted them or any other form,
    Or that I do not yet, and ever did,
    And ever will, though he do shake me off
    To beggarly divorcement, love him dearly,
    Comfort forswear me. Unkindness may do much,
    And his unkindness may defeat my life,
    But never taint my love. I cannot say whore.
    It doth abhor me now I speak the word;
    To do the act, that might the addition earn
    Not the world's mass of vanity could make me.
Iago. I pray you be content; 'tis but his humour.
    The business of the state does him offense,
    And he does chide with you.
Desde. If 'twere no other.
Iago. 'Tis but so, I **warrant**[①].
    Hark, how these instruments summon to supper:

实人的手里都拿一根鞭子,把这些混蛋们脱光了衣服抽一顿,从东方一直抽到西方!

伊阿古　别嚷得给外边都听见了。

埃米莉亚　哼,可恶的东西!前回弄昏了你的头,使你疑心我跟这摩尔人有暧昧的,也就是这种家伙。

伊阿古　好了,好了;你是个傻瓜。

苔丝狄蒙娜　好伊阿古啊,我应当怎样重新取得我的丈夫的欢心呢?好朋友,替我向他解释解释;因为凭着天上的太阳起誓,我实在不知道我怎么会失去他的宠爱。我对天下跪,要是在思想上行动上,我曾经有意背弃他的爱情;要是我的眼睛,我的耳朵,或是我的任何感觉,曾经对别人发生爱悦;要是我在过去、现在和将来,不是那样始终深深地爱着他,即使他把我弃如敝屣,也不因此而改变我对他的忠诚;要是我果然有那样的过失,愿我终身不能享受快乐的日子!无情可以给人重大的打击;他的无情也许会摧残我的生命,可是永不能毁坏我的爱情。我不愿提起"娼妇"两个字,一说到它就会使我心生憎恶,更不用说亲自去干那博得这种丑名的勾当了;整个世界的荣华也不能诱动我。

伊阿古　请您宽心,这不过是他一时的心绪恶劣,在国事方面受了点刺激,所以跟您怄起气来啦。

苔丝狄蒙娜　要是没有别的原因——

伊阿古　只是为了这个原因,我可以保证。(喇叭声)听!喇叭在吹晚餐的信号了;威尼斯的使者在等候

---

① warrant ['wɔrənt] v. 担保

ACT IV

The messengers of Venice stay the meat.
Go in, and weep not; all things shall be well.
Exeunt Desdemona and Emilia.
Enter Roderigo.
How now, Roderigo?

Rod. I do not find that thou dealest justly with me.

Iago. What in the contrary?

Rod. Every day thou daffest me with some device, Iago, and rather, as it seems to me now, keepest from me all conveniency, than suppliest me with the least advantage of hope. I will indeed no longer endure it; nor am I yet persuaded to put up in peace, what already I have foolishly suffered.

Iago. Will you hear me, Roderigo?

Rod. Faith, I have heard too much, for your words and performances are no kin together.

Iago. You charge me most unjustly.

Rod. With nought but truth. I have wasted myself out of my means. The jewels you have had from me to deliver to Desdemona, would half have corrupted a **votarist**[①]. You have told me she hath received them, and returned me expectations and comforts of sudden respect and acquaintance; but I find none.

Iago. Well, go to, very well.

Rod. Very well! Go to! I cannot go to, man nor 'tis not very well. By this hand, I say it is very scurvy, and begin to find myself **fopped**[②] in it.

Iago. Very well.

Rod. I tell you 'tis not very well. I will make myself known to Desdemona. If she will return me my jewels, I will give over my suit and repent my unlawful **solicitation**[③]; if not, assure yourself I will seek satisfaction of you.

Iago. You have said now.

进餐。进去，不要哭：一切都会圆满解决的。（苔丝狄蒙娜、埃米莉亚下）

罗德利哥上。

伊阿古　啊，罗德利哥！

罗德利哥　我看你全然在欺骗我。

伊阿古　我怎么欺骗你？

罗德利哥　伊阿古，你每天在我面前捣鬼，把我支吾过去；照我现在看来，你非但不给我开一线方便之门，反而使我的希望一天一天地微薄下去。我实在忍不住了。为了自己的愚蠢，我已经吃了不少的苦头，这一笔账我也不能就此善罢甘休。

伊阿古　您愿意听我说吗，罗德利哥？

罗德利哥　哼，我已经听得太多了；你的话和行动是不相符合的。

伊阿古　你太冤枉人啦。

罗德利哥　我一点没有冤枉你。我的钱都花光啦。你从我手里拿去送给苔丝狄蒙娜的珠宝，即使一个圣徒也会被它诱惑的；你对我说她已经收下了，告诉我不久就可以得到喜讯，可是到现在还不见一点动静。

伊阿古　好，算了；很好。

罗德利哥　很好！算了！我不能就此算了，朋友；这事情也不很好。我举手起誓，这种手段太卑鄙了；我开始觉得我自己受了骗了。

伊阿古　很好。

罗德利哥　我告诉你这事情不很好。我要亲自去见苔丝狄蒙娜，要是她肯把我的珠宝还我，我愿意死了这片心，忏悔我这种非礼的追求；要不然的话，你留心点儿吧，我一定要跟你算账。

伊阿古　你现在话说完了吧？

① votarist ['vəutərist] n.（宗教等的）信徒

② fop [fɔp] v.［废语］愚弄，欺骗

③ solicitation [səlisi'teiʃən] n 引诱

Rod. Ay, and said nothing but what I protest intendment of doing.

Iago. Why, now I see there's **mettle**① in thee; and even from this instant do build on thee a better opinion than ever before. Give me thy hand, Roderigo. Thou hast taken against me a most just exception; but yet, I protest I have dealt most directly in thy affair.

Rod. It hath not appeared.

Iago. I grant indeed it hath not appeared, and your suspicion is not without wit and judgement. But Roderigo, if thou hast that in thee indeed, which I have greater reason to believe now than ever, I mean purpose, courage, and **valor**②, this night show it. If thou the next night following enjoy not Desdemona, take me from this world with treachery, and devise engines for my life.

Rod. Well, what is it? Is it within reason and compass?

Iago. Sir, there is especial commission come from Venice to depute Cassio in Othello's place.

Rod. Is that true? Why then Othello and Desdemona return again to Venice.

Iago. Oh, no; he goes into **Mauritania**③, and takes away with him the fair Desdemona, unless his abode be lingered here by some accident; wherein none can be so determinate as the removing of Cassio.

Rod. How do you mean, removing of him?

Iago. Why, by making him uncapable of Othello's place; knocking out his brains.

Rod. And that you would have me to do?

Iago. Ay, if you dare do yourself a profit and a right. He sups tonight with a **harlotry**④, and thither will I go to him. He knows not yet of his honorable fortune. If you will watch his going thence, which his will fashion to fall out between twelve and one, you may take him at your pleasure; I will be near to second your attempt, and he shall fall between us. Come, stand not amazed at it, but go along with me; I will show you such a necessity in his death that you shall think yourself bound to put it on him. It is now

① mettle ['metl] *n.* 勇气

② valor ['vælə] *n.* 英勇

③ Mauritania [mɔri'teiniə] *n.* 毛里塔尼亚（西非国家）

④ harlotry ['hɑːlətri] *n.* 娼妓

罗德利哥　嗯，我的话都是说过就做的。

伊阿古　好，现在我才知道你是一个有骨气的人；从这一刻起，你已经使我比从前加倍看重你了。把你的手给我，罗德利哥。你责备我的话，都非常有理；可是我还要声明一句，我替你干这件事情，的的确确是尽忠竭力，不敢昧一分良心的。

罗德利哥　那还没有事实的证明。

伊阿古　我承认还没有事实的证明，你的疑心不是没有理由的。可是，罗德利哥，要是你果然有决心，有勇气，有胆量——我现在相信你一定有的——今晚你就可以表现出来；要是明天夜里你不能享用苔丝狄蒙娜，你可以用无论什么恶毒的手段，阴险的计谋，取去我的生命。

罗德利哥　好，你要我怎么干？是说得通做得到的事吗？

伊阿古　老兄，威尼斯已经派了专使来，叫卡西奥代替奥赛罗的职位。

罗德利哥　真的吗？那么奥赛罗和苔丝狄蒙娜都要回到威尼斯去了。

伊阿古　啊，不，他要到毛里塔尼亚去，把那美丽的苔丝狄蒙娜一起带走，除非这儿出了什么事，使他耽搁下来。最好的办法是把卡西奥除掉。

罗德利哥　你说把他除掉是什么意思？

伊阿古　砸碎他的脑袋，让他不能担任奥赛罗的职位。

罗德利哥　那就是你要我去干的事吗？

伊阿古　嗯，要是你敢做一件对你自己有利益的事。他今晚在一个妓女家里吃饭，我也要到那儿去见他。现在他还没有知道他自己的幸运。我可以设法让他在十二点钟到一点钟之间从那儿出来，你只要留心在门口守候，就可以照你的意思把他处置；我就在

· 221 ·

ACT IV

high supper time, and the night grows to waste. About it.

Rod. I will hear further reason for this.

Iago. And you shall be satisfied.

Exeunt.

附近接应你，他在我们两人之间一定逃不了。来，不要发呆，跟我去；我可以告诉你为什么他的死是必要的，你听了就会知道这是你的一件无可推辞的行动。现在正是晚餐的时候，夜过去得很快，准备起来吧。

罗德利哥　我还要听一听你要叫我这样做的理由。

伊阿古　我一定可以向你解释明白。（同下）

Scene III. Another room in the castle.

Enter Othello, Lodovico, Desdemona, Emilia, and Attendants.

Lodo.　I do beseech you sir, trouble yourself no further.

Othello.　Oh pardon me; 'twill do me good to walk.

Lodo.　Madam, good night; I humbly thank your ladyship.

Desde.　Your honor is most welcome.

Othello.　Will you walk, sir?

　　Oh Desdemona!

Desde.　My lord?

Othello.　Get you to bed on the instant; I will be returned forthwith. Dismiss your attendant there; look it be done.

Desde.　I will, my lord.

Exeunt Othello, Lodovico and Attendants.

Emilia.　How goes it now? He looks gentler than he did.

Desde.　He says he will return **incontinent**①.

　　He hath commanded me to go to bed,

　　And bade me to dismiss you.

Emilia.　Dismiss me?

Desde.　It was his bidding; therefore good Emilia,

　　Give me my nightly wearing, and adieu.

　　We must not now displease him.

第三场　城堡中的另一室

奥赛罗、洛多维科、苔丝狄蒙娜、埃米莉亚及侍从等上。

洛多维科　将军请留步吧。

奥赛罗　啊，没有关系；散散步对于我也是很好的。

洛多维科　夫人，晚安；谢谢您的盛情。

苔丝狄蒙娜　大驾光临，我们是十分欢迎的。

奥赛罗　请吧，大人。啊！苔丝狄蒙娜——

苔丝狄蒙娜　我的主？

奥赛罗　你快去睡吧；我马上就回来的。把你的侍女们打发开了，不要忘记。

苔丝狄蒙娜　是，我的主。（奥赛罗、洛多维科及侍从等下）

埃米莉亚　怎么？他现在的脸色温和得多啦。

苔丝狄蒙娜　他说他就会回来的；他叫我去睡；还叫我把你遣开。

埃米莉亚　把我遣开！

苔丝狄蒙娜　这是他的吩咐；所以，好埃米莉亚，把我的睡衣给我，你去吧，我们现在不能再惹他生气了。

① incontinent [in'kɔntinənt] *ad.* 立即，即刻

Emilia. I, would you had never seen him!

Desde. So would not I. My love doth so approve him,
That even his stubbornness, his checks, his frowns,
Prithee, unpin me, have grace and favor in them.

Emilia. I have laid those sheets you bade me on the bed.

Desde. All's one. Good faith, how foolish are our minds!
If I do die before thee, prithee, **shroud**① me
In one of those same sheets.

Emilia. Come, come, you talk.

Desde. My mother had a maid call'd Barbary;
She was in love, and he she loved proved mad
And did forsake her. She had a song of willow;
An old thing 'twas, but it express'd her fortune,
And she died singing it. That song tonight
Will not go from my mind; I have much to do
But to go hang my head all at one side
And sing it like poor Barbary. Prithee, dispatch.

Emilia. Shall I go fetch your night-gown?

Desde. No, unpin me here.
This Lodovico is a proper man.

Emilia. A very handsome man.

Desde. He speaks well.

Emilia. I know a lady in Venice would have walked barefoot to Palestine for a touch of his **nether**② lip.

Desde. The poor soul sat sighing by a **sycamore tree**③,
Sing all a green willow;
Her hand on her bosom, her head on her knee,
Sing willow, willow, willow.
The fresh streams ran by her, and murmur'd her moans,
Sing willow, willow, willow.

① shroud [ʃraud] v. 用裹尸布裹，给……穿上寿衣

② nether ['neðə] a. 下的，下方的

③ sycamore tree 枫树

埃米莉亚 我希望您当初并不和他相识！

苔丝狄蒙娜 我却不希望这样；我是那么喜欢他，即使他的固执，他的呵斥，他的怒容——请你替我取下衣上的扣针——在我看来也是可爱的。

埃米莉亚 我已经照您的吩咐，把那些被褥铺好了。

苔丝狄蒙娜 很好。天哪！我们的思想是多么傻！要是我比你先死，请你就把那些被褥做我的殓衾。

埃米莉亚 得啦得啦，您在说呆话。

苔丝狄蒙娜 我的母亲有一个侍女名叫巴巴拉，她跟人家有了恋爱；她的爱人发了疯，把她丢了。她有一支《杨柳歌》，那是一支古老的曲调，可是正好说中了她的命运；她到死的时候，嘴里还在唱着它。那支歌今天晚上老是萦回在我的脑际；我的烦乱的心绪，使我禁不住侧下我的头，学着可怜的巴巴拉的样子把它歌唱。请你赶快点儿。

埃米莉亚 我要不要就去把您的睡衣拿来？

苔丝狄蒙娜 不，先替我取下这儿的扣针，这个洛多维科是一个俊美的男子。

埃米莉亚 一个很漂亮的人。

苔丝狄蒙娜 他的谈吐很好。

埃米莉亚 我知道威尼斯有一个女郎，愿意赤了脚步行到巴勒斯坦，为了希望碰一碰他的下唇。

苔丝狄蒙娜 （唱）

可怜的她坐在枫树下啜泣，

歌唱那青青杨柳；

她手抚着胸膛，她低头靠膝，

唱杨柳，杨柳，杨柳。

清澈的流水吐出她的呻吟，

唱杨柳，杨柳，杨柳；

她的热泪溶化了顽石的心——

ACT IV

  Her salt tears fell from her, and soften'd the stones,
  Lay be these.
  Sing willow, willow, willow.
  Prithee hie thee; he'll come anon.
  Sing all a green willow must be my **garland**①.
  Let nobody blame him; his scorn I approve.
  Nay, that's not next. Hark, who is 't that knocks?
Emilia. It's the wind.
Desde. I call'd my love false love; but what said he then?
  Sing willow, willow, willow.
  If I court moe women, you'll couch with moe men.
  So get thee gone; good night. Mine eyes do itch;
  Doth that bode weeping?
Emilia. 'Tis neither here nor there.
Desde. I have heard it said so. O, these men, these men!
  Dost thou in conscience think, tell me Emilia,
  That there be women do abuse their husbands
  In such gross kind?
Emilia. There be some such, no question.
Desde. Wouldst thou do such a deed for all the world?
Emilia. Why, would not you?
Desde. No, by this heavenly light.
Emilia. Nor I neither by this heavenly light; I might do 't as well i' the dark.
Desde. Wouldst thou do such a deed for all the world?
Emilia. The world's a huge thing; it is a great price
  For a small vice.
Desde. In troth, I think thou wouldst not.
Emilia. In troth, I think I should, and undo 't when I had done. Marry, I would not do such a thing for a joint ring, nor for measures of **lawn**②, nor for gowns, **petticoats**③, nor caps, nor any petty exhibition; but, for the whole

　　　　把这些放在一旁。——（唱）

　　　　　　唱杨柳，杨柳，杨柳。

　　　　快一点，他就要来了。——（唱）

　　　　　　青青的柳枝编成一个翠环；

　　　　　　不要怪他，我甘心受他的笑骂——

　　　　不，下面一句不是这样的。听！谁在打门？

埃米莉亚　是风哩。

苔丝狄蒙娜　（唱）

　　　　　　我叫情哥负心郎，他又怎讲？

　　　　　　唱杨柳，杨柳，杨柳。

　　　　　　我见异思迁，由你另换情郎。

　　　　你去吧；晚安。我的眼睛在跳，那是哭泣的预兆吗？

埃米莉亚　没有这样的事。

苔丝狄蒙娜　我听见人家这样说。啊，这些男人！这些男人！凭您的良心说，埃米莉亚，你想世上有没有背着丈夫干这种坏事的女人？

埃米莉亚　怎么没有？

苔丝狄蒙娜　你愿意为了整个世界而干这种事吗？

埃米莉亚　难道您不愿意吗？

苔丝狄蒙娜　不，我对着光明起誓。

埃米莉亚　不，对着光天化日，我也不敢这种事；要干也得暗地里干。

苔丝狄蒙娜　难道你愿意为了整个世界而干这种事吗？

埃米莉亚　世界是一个大东西；用一件小小的坏事换得这样大的代价是值得的。

苔丝狄蒙娜　真的，我想你不会。

埃米莉亚　真的，我想我会干；等做完之后，再想法补救。当然，为了一枚对合的戒指，几丈细麻布，或是几件衣服，几件裙子，一两顶帽子，以及诸如

① garland ['ɡɑːlənd] n. 花环

② lawn [lɔːn] n.（素色或印花的）上等细麻

③ petticoat ['petikəut] n. 衬裙

world: why, who would not make her husband a cuckold to make him a monarch? I should venture **purgatory**① for 't.

Desde.   Beshrew me, if I would do such a wrong
For the whole world.

Emilia.   Why, the wrong is but a wrong i' the world; and having the world for your labor, 'tis a wrong in your own world, and you might quickly make it right.

Desde.   I do not think there is any such woman.

Emilia.   Yes, a dozen, and as many to the vantage as would store the world they played for.
But I do think it is their husbands' faults.
If wives do fall; say that they slack their duties,
And pour our treasures into foreign laps,
Or else break out in **peevish**② jealousies,
Throwing restraint upon us, or say they strike us,
Or scant our former having in despite,
Why we have galls, and though we have some grace,
Yet have we some revenge. Let husbands know,
Their wives have sense like them; they see and smell,
And have their palates both for sweet and sour,
As husbands have. What is it that they do,
When they change us for others? Is it sport?
I think it is. And doth affection breed it?
I think it doth. Is 't frailty that thus errs?
It is so too. And have not we affections,
Desires for sport, and frailty, as men have?
Then let them use us well; else let them know,
The ills we do, their ills instruct us so.

Desde.   Good night, good night. Heaven me such uses send,
Not to pick bad from bad, but by bad mend.
Exeunt.

① purgatory ['pə:gətəri] n. 炼狱

② peevish ['pi:viʃ] a. 易怒的

此类的小玩意儿而叫我干这种事，我当然不愿意；可是为了整个的世界，谁不愿意出卖自己的贞操，让她的丈夫做一个皇帝呢？我就是因此而下炼狱，也是甘心的。

苔丝狄蒙娜 我要是为了整个的世界，会干出这种丧心的事来，一定不得好死。

埃米莉亚 世间的是非本来没有定准；您因为干了一件错事而得到整个的世界，在您自己的世界里，您还不能把是非颠倒过来吗？

苔丝狄蒙娜 我想世上不会有那样的女人的。

埃米莉亚 愿意做这种赌博的女人多着呢。照我想来，妻子的堕落总是丈夫的过失；要是他们疏忽了自己的责任，把我们所珍爱的东西浪掷在外人的怀里，或是无缘无故吃起醋来，约束我们的行动的自由，或是殴打我们，削减我们的花粉钱，我们也是有脾气的，虽然生就温柔的天性，到了一个时候也是会复仇的。让做丈夫的人们知道，他们的妻子也和他们有同样的感觉：她们的眼睛也能辨别美恶，她们的鼻子也能辨别香臭，她们的舌头也能辨别甜酸，正像她们的丈夫们一样。他们厌弃了我们，别寻新欢，是为了什么缘故呢？是逢场作戏吗？我想是的。是因为爱情的驱使吗？我想也是的。还是因为喜新厌旧的人之常情呢？那也是一个理由。那么难道我们就不会对别人发生爱情，难道我们就没有逢场作戏的欲望，难道我们就不会喜新厌旧，跟男人们一样吗？所以让他们好好地对待我们吧；否则我们要让他们知道，我们所干的坏事都是出于他们的指教。

苔丝狄蒙娜 晚安，晚安！愿上天监视我们的言行；我不愿以恶为师，我只愿鉴非自警！（各下）

ACT V

第五幕

Scene I. Cyprus. A street.

Enter Iago and Roderigo.

Iago.   Here, stand behind this bulk; straight will he come.
　　　　Wear thy good **rapier**① bare, and put it home.
　　　　Quick, quick, fear nothing, I'll be at thy elbow.
　　　　It makes us, or it mars us; think on that,
　　　　And fix most firm thy resolution.
Rod.   Be near at hand, I may **miscarry**② in 't.
Iago.   Here, at thy hand, be bold, and take thy stand.
　　　　Retires.
Rod.   I have no great devotion to the deed;
　　　　And yet he hath given me satisfying reasons.
　　　　'Tis but a man gone. Forth my sword; he dies.
Iago.   I have rubb'd this young **quat**③ almost to the sense,
　　　　And he grows angry. Now, whether he kill Cassio,
　　　　Or Cassio him, or each do kill the other,
　　　　Every way makes my gain. Live Roderigo,
　　　　He calls me to a **restitution**④ large
　　　　Of gold and jewels that I bobb'd from him,
　　　　As gifts to Desdemona;

第一场　塞浦路斯　街道

① rapier ['reipiə] *n.* （窄长的）双刃剑

② miscarry [mis'kæri] *v.* （计划、方案等）失败，受挫

③ quat ['kwɔt] *n.* 皮疹

④ restitution [resti'tju:ʃən] *n.* 归还；偿还

伊阿古及罗德利哥上。

伊阿古　来，站在这堵破屋后面；他就会来的。把你的宝剑拔出鞘来，看准要害刺过去。快，快，不要怕；我就在你旁边。成功失败，在此一举，你得下定决心。

罗德利哥　不要走开，也许我会失手。

伊阿古　我就在这儿，你的近旁。胆子放大些，站定了。（退后）

罗德利哥　我对于这件事情不是顶热心；可是他讲的理由十分充足。反正不过去掉一个人。出来，我的剑；他必须死！

伊阿古　我已经激动这小脓包的心，他居然动起怒来了。不管是他杀死卡西奥，还是卡西奥杀死他，或者两败俱伤，对于我都是有好处的。要是罗德利哥活在世上，他总有一天要问我讨还那许多我从他手里干没下来说是送给苔丝狄蒙娜的金银珠宝；这可断断不能。要是卡西奥活在世上，他那样风度翩翩，

235

ACT V

It must not be. If Cassio do remain,
He hath a daily beauty in his life
That makes me ugly; and besides, the Moor
May unfold me to him; there stand I in much peril.
No, he must die. Be 't so. I hear him coming.
Enter Cassio.

Rod. I know his **gait**①; 'tis he. Villain, thou diest!
Makes a pass at Cassio.

Cassio. That thrust had been mine enemy indeed,
But that my coat is better than thou know'st;
I will make proof of thine.
Stabs Roderigo.

Rod. Oh, I am slain.
Iago from behind wounds Cassio in the leg, and exit.

Cassio. I am **maim'd**② forever. Help, ho! Murther! Murther!
Enter Othello.

Othello. The voice of Cassio! Iago keeps his word.

Rod. O, villain that I am!

Othello. It is even so.

Cassio. Oh, help, hoa! Light! A surgeon!

Othello. 'Tis he. O brave Iago, honest and just!
That hast such noble sense of thy friend's wrong,
Thou teachest me. **Minion**③, your dear lies dead,
And your unblest fate hies. Strumpet, I come!
For of my heart those charms, thine eyes, are **blotted**④;
Thy bed lust-stain'd shall with lust's blood be spotted.
Exit Othello.
Enter Lodovico and Gratiano.

Cassio. What, hoa? No watch? No passage? Murther! Murther!

Gra. 'Tis some **mischance**⑤; the voice is very direful.

叫我每天都要在他的旁边相形见绌；而且那摩尔人万一向他当面质问起来，我的阴谋就会暴露，那时候我的地位就非常危险了。不，他非死不可。就这样吧，我听见他来了。

　　　　卡西奥上。

罗德利哥　我认识他的走路的姿势①；正是他。——恶人，你给我死吧！（挺剑刺卡西奥）

卡西奥　幸亏我穿着一身好甲，否则那一剑一定会致我的死命。让我也来试一试你的甲牢不牢吧。（拔剑刺伤罗德利哥）

罗德利哥　啊，我死了！（伊阿古自后刺伤卡西奥腿，下）

卡西奥　我从此终身残废②了！救命啊！杀了人啦！杀了人啦！（倒地）

　　　　奥赛罗自远处上。

奥赛罗　卡西奥的声音。伊阿古果然没有失信。

罗德利哥　啊，我真是个恶人。

奥赛罗　一点不错。

卡西奥　啊，救命哪！拿火来！找一个医生！

奥赛罗　正是他。勇敢正直的伊阿古呀，你这样奋不顾身，为你的朋友复仇雪耻，真是难得！你给我一个教训了。贱人③，你心爱的人已经死在这儿，你的末日就在眼前；娼妇，我来了！从我的心头抹去你的媚眼的魔力；让淫邪的血溅洒你那被淫邪玷④污了的枕席。（下）

　　　　洛多维科及格拉蒂亚诺自远处上。

卡西奥　喂！怎么！没有巡夜的逻卒？没有过路的行人？杀了人啦！杀人啦！

格拉蒂亚诺　出了什么乱子啦？这叫声很是凄惨。

① gait [geit] n. 步态，步法

② maim [meim] v. 使负重伤；使残废

③ minion ['minjən] n. 奴才

④ blot [blɔt] v. 涂污，玷污

⑤ mischance [mis'tʃɑːns; -'tʃæns] n. 厄运，坏运气，不幸

ACT V

Cassio. Oh, help!

Lodo. Hark.

Rod. Oh wretched villain!

Lodo. Two or three groan, it is a heavy night.
    These may be counterfeits, let's think 't unsafe
    To come in to the cry without more help.

Rod. Nobody come? Then shall I bleed to death.

Lodo. Hark!

Enter Iago, with a light.

Gra. Here's one comes in his shirt, with light and weapons.

Iago. Who's there? Whose noise is this that cries on murther?

Lodo. We do not know.

Iago. Did not you hear a cry?

Cassio. Here, here: for heaven's sake, help me.

Iago. What's the matter?

Gra. This is Othello's ancient, as I take it.

Lodo. The same indeed; a very valiant fellow.

Iago. What are you here that cry so grievously?

Cassio. Iago? Oh I am spoil'd, undone by villains!
    Give me some help.

Iago. O me, lieutenant! What villains have done this?

Cassio. I think that one of them is hereabout,
    And cannot make away.

Iago. Oh treacherous villains!
    [*To Lodovico and Gratiano.*] What are you there? Come in and give some help.

Rod. O, help me here!

Cassio. That's one of them.

Iago. O murtherous slave! O villain!
    Stabs Roderigo.

卡西奥 救命啊!

洛多维科 听!

罗德利哥 啊,该死的恶人!

洛多维科 两三个人在那儿呻吟。这是一个很阴沉的黑夜;也许他们是故意假装出来的,我们人手孤单,冒冒失失过去,恐怕不大安全。

罗德利哥 没有人来吗?那么我要流血而死了!

洛多维科 听!

　　　　　　伊阿古持火炬重上。

格拉蒂亚诺 有一个人穿着衬衫,一手拿火,一手举着武器来了。

伊阿古 那边是谁?什么人在那儿喊杀人?

洛多维科 我们不知道。

伊阿古 你们听见一个呼声吗?

卡西奥 这儿,这儿!看在上天的面上,救救我!

伊阿古 怎么一回事?

格拉蒂亚诺 这个人好像是奥赛罗麾下的旗官。

洛多维科 正是;一个很勇敢的汉子。

伊阿古 你是什么人,在这儿叫喊得这样凄惨?

卡西奥 伊阿古吗?啊,我被恶人算计,害得我不能做人啦!救救我!

伊阿古 哎哟,副将!这是什么恶人干的事?

卡西奥 我想有一个暴徒还在这儿;他逃不了。

伊阿古 啊,可恶的奸贼!(向洛多维科、格拉蒂亚诺)你们是什么人?过来帮帮忙。

罗德利哥 啊,救救我!我在这儿。

卡西奥 他就是恶党中的一人。

伊阿古 好一个杀人的凶徒!啊,恶人!(刺罗德利哥)

Rod. O damn'd Iago! O **inhuman**① dog!

Iago. Kill men i' the dark? Where be these bloody thieves?
How silent is this town! Hoa! Murther! Murther!
What may you be? Are you of good or evil?

Lodo. As you shall prove us, praise us.

Iago. Signior Lodovico?

Lodo. He sir.

Iago. I cry you mercy. Here's Cassio hurt by villains.

Gra. Cassio?

Iago. How is 't brother?

Cassio. My leg is cut in two.

Iago. Marry, heaven forbid:
Light gentlemen; I'll bind it with my shirt.
Enter Bianca.

Bianca. What is the matter, ho? Who is 't that cried?

Iago. Who is 't that cried?

Bianca. Oh my dear Cassio, my sweet Cassio! Oh Cassio, Cassio, Cassio!

Iago. O notable strumpet. Cassio, may you suspect
Who they should be that have thus **mangled**② you?

Cassio. No.

Gra. I am sorry to find you thus; I have been to seek you.

Iago. Lend me a **garter**③. So. Oh, for a chair,
To bear him easily hence!

Bianca. Alas, he faints! Oh Cassio, Cassio, Cassio!

Iago. Gentlemen all, I do suspect this trash
To be a party in this injury.
Patience awhile, good Cassio. Come, come!
Lend me a light. Know we this face or no?

① inhuman [in'hju:mən] a. 无人性的

罗德利哥 啊，万恶的伊阿古！没有人心的狗！

伊阿古 在暗地里杀人！这些凶恶的贼党都在哪儿？这地方多么寂静！喂！杀了人啦！杀了人啦！你们是什么人？是好人还是坏人？

洛多维科 请你自己判断我们吧。

伊阿古 洛多维科大人吗？

洛多维科 正是。

伊阿古 恕我失礼了。这儿是卡西奥，被恶人们刺伤，倒在地上。

格拉蒂亚诺 卡西奥！

伊阿古 怎么样，兄弟？

卡西奥 我的腿断了。

伊阿古 哎哟，罪过罪过！两位先生，请替我照火；我要用我的衫子把它包扎起来。

比安卡上。

比安卡 喂，什么事？谁在这儿叫喊？

伊阿古 谁在这儿叫喊！

比安卡 哎哟，我的亲爱的卡西奥！我的温柔的卡西奥！啊，卡西奥！卡西奥！卡西奥！

② mangle ['mæŋgl] v. 将（皮肉）撕裂，乱砍

伊阿古 哼，你这声名狼藉的娼妇！卡西奥，照你猜想起来，向你下这样毒手的大概是什么人？

格拉蒂亚诺 我正要来找你，谁料你会遭逢这样的祸事，真是恼人！

③ garter ['gɑ:tə] n.（吊）袜带

伊阿古 借给我一条吊袜带。好。啊，要是有一张椅子，让他舒舒服服躺在上面，把他抬去才好！

比安卡 哎哟，他晕过去了！啊；卡西奥！卡西奥！卡西奥！

伊阿古 两位先生，我很疑心这个贱人也是那些凶徒们的同党。——忍耐点儿，好卡西奥。——来，来，借我一个火。我们认不认识这一张面孔？哎哟！是

· 241 ·

ACT V

Alas, my friend and my dear countryman
Roderigo? No, yes, sure. Yes, 'tis Roderigo.

Gra. What, of Venice?

Iago. Even he, sir. Did you know him?

Gra. Know him? Ay.

Iago. Signior Gratiano? I cry you gentle pardon;
These bloody accidents must excuse my manners,
That so neglected you.

Gra. I am glad to see you.

Iago. How do you, Cassio? Oh, a chair, a chair!

Gra. Roderigo?

Iago. He, he, 'tis he.

Enter some with a chair.

O, that's well said: the chair.
Some good man bear him carefully from hence;
I'll fetch the general's surgeon. For you, mistress,
Save you your labor. He that lies slain here, Cassio,
Was my dear friend; what **malice**① was between you?

Cassio. None in the world; nor do I know the man.

Iago. What, look you pale? Oh, bear him out o' the air.

Cassio and Roderigo are borne off.

Stay you, good gentlemen. Look you pale, mistress?
Do you perceive the **gastness**② of her eye?
Nay, if you stare, we shall hear more anon.
Behold her well; I pray you, look upon her.
Do you see gentlemen? Nay, guiltiness will speak,
Though tongues were out of use.

Enter Emilia.

Emilia. Alas, what's the matter? What's the matter, husband?

Iago. Cassio hath here been set on in the dark

· 242 ·

我的同国好友罗德利哥吗？不。唉，果然是他！天哪！罗德利哥！

格拉蒂亚诺 什么！威尼斯的罗德利哥吗？

伊阿古 正是他，先生。你认识他吗？

格拉蒂亚诺 认识他！我怎么不认识他？

伊阿古 格拉蒂亚诺先生吗？请您原谅，这些流血的惨剧，使我礼貌不周，失敬得很。

格拉蒂亚诺 哪儿的话；我很高兴看见您。

伊阿古 您怎么啦，卡西奥？啊，来一张椅子！来一张椅子！

格拉蒂亚诺 罗德利哥！

伊阿古 他，他，正是他。（众人携椅上）啊！很好；椅子。几个人把他小心抬走；我就去找军医官来。（向比安卡）你，女士，你也不用装腔作势啦。——卡西奥，死在这儿的这个人是我的好朋友。你们两人有什么仇恨？

卡西奥 一点没有；我根本不认识这个人。

伊阿古 （向比安卡）什么！你的脸色变白了吗？——啊！把他抬进屋子里去。（众人舁卡西奥、罗德利哥二人下）等一等，两位先生，女士，你脸色变白了吗？你们看见她眼睛里这一股惊慌的神气吗？哼，要是你这样睁大了眼睛，我们还要等着听一些新鲜的话哩。留心瞧着她；你们瞧，你们看见了吗，两位先生？哼，犯了罪的人，即使舌头僵住了，也会不打自招的。

    埃米莉亚上。

埃米莉亚 唉！出了什么事啦？出了什么事啦，丈夫？

伊阿古 卡西奥在这儿黑暗之中，被罗德利哥和几个在

① malice ['mælis] *n.* 恶意，怨恨，敌意

② gastness ['gæstnis] *n.* [废语] 恐怖；恐惧

ACT V

    By Roderigo, and fellows that are 'scaped;

    He's almost slain, and Roderigo quite dead.

Emilia. Alas, good gentleman: alas good Cassio.

Iago. This is the fruit of whoring. Prithee, Emilia,

    Go know of Cassio where he supp'd tonight.

    What, do you shake at that?

Bianca. He supp'd at my house; but I therefore shake not.

Iago. O, did he so? I charge you go with me.

Emilia. Fie, fie upon thee, strumpet!

Bianca. I am no strumpet, but of life as honest,

    As you that thus abuse me.

Emilia. As I? Foh! Fie upon thee!

Iago. Kind gentlemen, let's go see poor Cassio dress'd.

    Come, mistress, you must tell's another tale.

    Emilia, run you to the **citadel**[①],

    And tell my lord and lady, what hath happ'd:

    Will you go on afore? [*Aside.*] This is the night

    That either makes me or **fordoes**[②] me quite.

    Exeunt.

逃的同党袭击；他几乎送了性命，罗德利哥已经死了。

埃米莉亚 哎哟，好一位绅士！哎哟，好卡西奥！

伊阿古 这是他爱嫖的结果。埃米莉亚，你去问问卡西奥，他今天晚上在什么地方吃饭的。——什么！你听了这句话就发抖吗？

比安卡 他在我家里吃饭；可是我并没有因此而发抖。

伊阿古 噢，他在你家里吃饭？你跟我走！

埃米莉亚 呸，呸，你这不要脸的娼妇！

比安卡 我不是娼妇；我跟你一样清白。

埃米莉亚 跟我一样清白！呸！呸！不要脸！

伊阿古 两位好先生，让我们去帮助帮助可怜的卡西奥，替他把伤口扎好。来，奶奶，您必须对我们讲老实话。埃米莉亚，你快奔到城堡里去，告诉将军和夫人这儿发生了什么事。你们先请吧。（旁白）今夜是我的命运所寄，倘不能青云直上，就要一败涂地。（同下）

① citadel ['sitədəl] *n.* 城堡

② fordo [fɔː'duː] *v.* ［古语］摧毁，毁掉

Scene II. A bedchamber in the castle.

Desdemona in bed asleep; a light burning. Enter Othello.

Othello.   It is the cause, it is the cause, my soul.
　　　　Let me not name it to you, you chaste stars,
　　　　It is the cause. Yet I'll not shed her blood,
　　　　Nor scar that whiter skin of hers than snow
　　　　And smooth as monumental **alabaster**①.
　　　　Yet she must die, else she'll betray more men.
　　　　Put out the light, and then put out the light.
　　　　If I quench thee, thou flaming minister,
　　　　I can again thy former light restore,
　　　　Should I repent me. But once put out thy light,
　　　　Thou cunning'st pattern of **excelling**② nature,
　　　　I know not where is that Promethean heat
　　　　That can thy light **relume**③. When I have pluck'd the rose,
　　　　I cannot give it vital growth again,
　　　　It must needs wither; I'll smell it on the tree. [*Kisses Desdemona.*]
　　　　Oh, **balmy**④ breath, that dost almost persuade
　　　　Justice to break her sword! One more, one more;

第二场　城堡中的卧室

苔丝狄蒙娜睡床上，一灯照耀室内，奥赛罗上。

奥赛罗　只是为了这一个原因，只是为了这一个原因，我的灵魂！纯洁的星星啊，让我不要向你们说出它的名字！只是为了这一个原因……可是我不愿溅她的血，也不愿毁伤她那比白雪更皎洁，比石膏更腻滑的肌肤。可是她不能不死，否则她将要陷害更多的男子。让我熄灭了这一盏灯，然后我就熄灭你的生命的火焰。融融的灯光啊，我把你吹熄以后，要是我心生后悔，仍旧可以把你重新点亮；可是你，造化最精美的形象啊，你的火焰一旦熄灭，我不知道什么地方有那天上的神火，能够燃起你的原来的光彩！我摘下了蔷薇，就不能再给它已失的生机，只好让它枯萎凋谢；当它还在枝头的时候，我要嗅一嗅它的芳香。（吻苔丝狄蒙娜）啊，甘美的气息！你几乎诱动公道的心，使他折断他的利剑

---

① alabaster [ˈæləbɑːstə] *n.* 雪花石膏

② excelling [ikˈsɛliŋ] *a.* 杰出，卓越

③ relume [riˈljuːm] *v.* 重新点燃

④ balmy [ˈbɑːmi] *a.* 芳香的

ACT V

  Be thus when thou art dead, and I will kill thee,
  And love thee after. One more, and this the last.
  So sweet was ne'er so fatal. I must weep,
  But they are cruel tears; this sorrow's heavenly,
  It strikes where it doth love. She wakes.

Desde. Who's there? Othello?

Othello. Ay, Desdemona.

Desde. Will you come to bed, my lord?

Othello. Have you pray'd tonight, Desdemona?

Desde. Ay, my lord.

Othello. If you bethink yourself of any crime
  Unreconciled as yet to heaven and grace,
  Solicit[①] for it straight.

Desde. Alas, my lord, what may you mean by that?

Othello. Well, do it, and be brief; I will walk by.
  I would not kill thy unprepared spirit.
  No, **heaven forfend**[②]! I would not kill thy soul.

Desde. Talk you of killing?

Othello. Ay, I do.

Desde. Then heaven have mercy on me.

Othello. Amen, with all my heart!

Desde. If you say so, I hope you will not kill me.

Othello. Hum!

Desde. And yet I fear you, for you are fatal then
  When your eyes roll so. Why I should fear I know not,
  Since guiltiness I know not; but yet I feel I fear.

Othello. Think on thy sins.

Desde. They are loves I bear to you.

Othello. Ay, and for that thou diest.

Desde. That death's unnatural that kills for loving.

了！再一个吻，再一个吻。愿你到死都是这样；我要杀死你，然后再爱你。再一个吻，这是最后的一吻了；这样销魂，却又是这样无比的惨痛！我必须哭泣，然而这些是无情的眼泪。这一阵阵悲伤是神圣的，因为它要惩罚的正是它最疼爱的。她醒来了。

苔丝狄蒙娜 谁？奥赛罗吗？

奥赛罗 嗯，苔丝狄蒙娜。

苔丝狄蒙娜 您要睡了吗，我的主？

奥赛罗 你今晚有没有祈祷过，苔丝狄蒙娜？

苔丝狄蒙娜 祈祷过了，我的主。

奥赛罗 要是你想到在你的一生之中，还有什么罪恶不曾为上帝所宽宥，赶快恳求他的恩赦吧。

苔丝狄蒙娜 哎哟！我的主，您这句话是什么意思？

奥赛罗 嘿，祈祷吧，干脆点儿；我就在一旁等着你。我不愿杀害你的没有准备的灵魂；不，上天禁止这种罪行！我不愿杀害你的灵魂。

苔丝狄蒙娜 您在说杀人的话吗？

奥赛罗 嗯，是的。

苔丝狄蒙娜 那么愿上天垂怜于我！

奥赛罗 阿门，但愿如此！

苔丝狄蒙娜 要是您这样说，我希望您不至于把我杀死。

奥赛罗 哼！

苔丝狄蒙娜 可是我怕您；因为您的眼珠这样滚转的时候，您总是要杀人的。我不知道我为什么害怕，因为我不知道我有什么罪，可是我觉得害怕。

奥赛罗 想想你的罪恶吧。

苔丝狄蒙娜 除非我对您的爱是罪恶，我不知道我有什么罪恶。

奥赛罗 好，你必须因此而死。

苔丝狄蒙娜 为了爱而被杀，那样的死是违反人情的。

① solicit [sə'lisit] v. 请求，恳求

② heaven forfend 上天不容

ACT V

　　　Alas, why gnaw you so your nether lip?

　　　Some bloody passion shakes your very frame.

　　　These are portents; but yet I hope, I hope,

　　　They do not point on me.

Othello. Peace, and be still!

Desde. I will so. What's the matter?

Othello. That handkerchief which I so loved and gave thee,

　　　Thou gavest to Cassio.

Desde. No, by my life and soul!

　　　Send for the man, and ask him.

Othello. Sweet soul, **take heed**①,

　　　Take heed of **perjury**②; thou are on thy deathbed.

Desde. Ay, but not yet to die.

Othello. Yes, presently:

　　　Therefore confess thee freely of thy sin,

　　　For to deny each article with oath

　　　Cannot remove nor choke the strong conception

　　　That I do groan withal. Thou art to die.

Desde. O, heaven have mercy on me.

Othello. I say, amen.

Desde. And have you mercy too. I never did

　　　Offend you in my life; never loved Cassio,

　　　But with such general warranty of heaven

　　　As I might love. I never gave him token.

Othello. By heaven, I saw my handkerchief in's hand.

　　　O, perjured woman! Thou dost stone my heart,

　　　And makest me call what I intend to do,

　　　A murther, which I thought a sacrifice.

　　　I saw the handkerchief.

Desde. He found it then;

唉！您为什么这样咬着您的下唇呢？一种饮血的欲念震撼您的全身，这便是它的征兆；可是我希望，我希望您的怒气不是对我而发。

奥赛罗 闭嘴，不要作声！

苔丝狄蒙娜 是；可是请您告诉我究竟为了什么事？

奥赛罗 你把我给你的那条我的心爱的手帕送给卡西奥。

苔丝狄蒙娜 不，凭着我的生命和灵魂起誓！您叫他来问好了。

奥赛罗 好人儿，留心不要发伪誓；你的死已经在眼前了。

苔丝狄蒙娜 不，我现在还不能死。

奥赛罗 你必须立刻死，所以赶快坦白招认你的罪恶吧；即使你发誓否认每一件事实，也不能除去那使我痛心的坚强的确信。你必须死。

苔丝狄蒙娜 那么愿上帝垂怜于我！

奥赛罗 阿门。

苔丝狄蒙娜 愿您也大发慈悲！我生平从不曾得罪过您，也从不曾用上天所不容的非分的爱情滥施在卡西奥的身上；我没有给过他什么东西。

奥赛罗 苍天在上，我亲眼看见我的手帕在他的手里。欺罔神明的妇人！你使我的心变成坚硬；我本来想把你作为献祭的牺牲，现在却被你激起我的屠夫的恶念来了。我明明看见那手帕的。

苔丝狄蒙娜 那么他在什么地方拾到的；我没有给他。

① take heed 小心，注意
② perjury ['pə:dʒəri] n. 假誓；伪证

ACT V

> I never gave it him. Send for him hither;
> Let him confess a truth.

Othello. He hath confess'd.

Desde. What, my lord?

Othello. That he hath used thee.

Desde. How? unlawfully?

Othello. Ay.

Desde. He will not say so.

Othello. No, his mouth is stopp'd;
> Honest Iago hath ta'en order for 't.

Desde. O, my fear interprets. What, is he dead?

Othello. Had all his hairs been lives, my great revenge
> Had stomach for them all.

Desde. Alas, he is betray'd, and I undone.

Othello. Out strumpet: weep'st thou for him to my face?

Desde. O, banish me, my lord, but kill me not!

Othello. Down, strumpet!

Desde. Kill me tomorrow; let me live tonight!

Othello. Nay, if you strive

Desde. But half an hour!

Othello. Being done, there is no pause.

Desde. But while I say one prayer!

Othello. It is too late.

> ***Smothers*[①] *her.***
> *Emilia calls at the door*

Emilia. My lord, my lord? What, hoa, My lord, my lord!

Othello. What noise is this? Not dead? not yet quite dead?
> I that am cruel am yet merciful;
> I would not have thee linger in thy pain.
> So, so.

叫他到这儿来,让他供认事实的真相。

奥赛罗　他已经承认了。

苔丝狄蒙娜　承认什么,我的主?

奥赛罗　承认他已经和你发生关系。

苔丝狄蒙娜　怎么?非法的关系吗?

奥赛罗　嗯。

苔丝狄蒙娜　他不会这样说的。

奥赛罗　是的,他的嘴已经闭住,正直的伊阿古已经把他解决了。

苔丝狄蒙娜　啊,我的恐惧叫我明白过来了!什么!他死了吗?

奥赛罗　即使他每一根头发里都有生命,我的复仇的怒火也会把它们一起吞下。

苔丝狄蒙娜　唉!他被人陷害,我的一生也从此断送了!

奥赛罗　不要脸的娼妇!你当着我的面为他哭泣吗?

苔丝狄蒙娜　啊,我的主,把我放逐,可是不要杀我!

奥赛罗　倒下,娼妇!

苔丝狄蒙娜　明天杀我,让我活过今天!

奥赛罗　不,要是你想挣扎——

苔丝狄蒙娜　给我半点钟的时间!

奥赛罗　已经决定了,没有挽回的余地。

苔丝狄蒙娜　可是让我做一次祷告吧!

奥赛罗　太迟了。(扼苔丝狄蒙娜的咽喉)

　　埃米莉亚敲门。

埃米莉亚　将军,将军!喂!将军,将军!

奥赛罗　这是什么声音?没有死吗?还没有完全死去吗?我虽然狠心,却还有几分慈悲;我不愿你多挨受一刻痛苦。好,好。(刺苔丝狄蒙娜)

① smother ['smʌðə] v. 使窒息

· 253 ·

ACT V

Emilia. [*Within.*] What hoa? My lord, my lord?

Othello. Who's there?

Emilia. Oh good my lord, I would speak a word with you.

Othello. Yes, 'tis Emilia. By and by. She's dead.

'Tis like she comes to speak of Cassio's death.

The noise was here. Ha, no more moving?

Still as the grave. Shall she come in? Were 't good?

I think she stirs again. No. What's best to do?

If she come in, she'll sure speak to my wife.

My wife! My wife! What wife? I have no wife.

Oh, **insupportable**[①]! Oh heavy hour!

Methinks[②] it should be now a huge eclipse

Of sun and moon, and that the **affrighted**[③] globe

Did yawn at alteration.

Emilia. I do beseech you

That I may speak with you. Good my lord!

Othello. I had forgot thee. Oh come in, Emilia.

Soft, by and by. Let me the curtains draw. [*Opens the door.*]

Where art thou?

Enter Emilia.

What's the matter with thee now?

Emilia. Oh, my good lord, yonder's foul murthers done.

Othello. What, now?

Emilia. But now, my lord.

Othello. It is the very error of the moon;

She comes more nearer earth than she was wont,

And makes men mad.

Emilia. Cassio, my lord, hath kill'd a young Venetian,

Call'd Roderigo.

Othello. Roderigo kill'd?

① insupportable [insəˈpɔːtəbl] *a.* 难以忍受的；不能容忍的

② methinks [miˈθiŋks] *v.* [无人称动词] 我想

③ affright [əˈfrait] *v.* 使害怕

埃米莉亚 （在内）喂！将军，将军！

奥赛罗 哪一个？

埃米莉亚 （在内）啊，将军！我要跟您说句话儿。

奥赛罗 是的，这是埃米莉亚。——等一等。——她死了。她多半要来说起卡西奥的死。外边已经听得见嘈杂的声音。吓！一动也不动了吗？像坟墓一样沉寂。要不要让她进来？妥当不妥当？我想她又在动了，不，怎么办呢？要是她进来，她一定要跟我的妻子说话。我的妻子！我的妻子！什么妻子？我没有妻子。啊，难堪！啊，不幸的时辰！我想现在日月应该晦暗不明，受惊的地球看见这种非常的灾变，也要吓得目瞪口呆。

埃米莉亚 将军！我恳求您让我跟您说句话儿。

奥赛罗 我忘记了。啊，进来，埃米莉亚。慢点儿，等一等。让我把帷幕拉下来，你在哪儿？（启锁开门）

埃米莉亚上。

奥赛罗 现在你可有什么事？

埃米莉亚 啊，好将军！那边出了杀人命案啦！

奥赛罗 什么！现在？

埃米莉亚 就是刚才，将军。

奥赛罗 那都是因为月亮走错了轨道，比平常更近地球，所以人们都发起疯来了。

埃米莉亚 将军，卡西奥杀死了一个名叫罗德利哥的威尼斯青年。

奥赛罗 罗德利哥被杀了！卡西奥也被杀了吗？

ACT V

And Cassio kill'd?

Emilia. No, Cassio is not kill'd.

Othello. Not Cassio kill'd? Then murther's **out of tune**①,

And sweet revenge grows harsh.

Desde. O falsely, falsely murther'd.

Emilia. Alas, what cry is that?

Othello. That? What?

Emilia. Out and alas! That was my lady's voice.

Help! Help, ho! Help! Oh lady, speak again,

Sweet Desdemona, Oh sweet mistress, speak.

Desde. A guiltless death I die.

Emilia. Oh who hath done this deed?

Desde. Nobody; I myself. Farewell;

Commend me to my kind lord. O, farewell!

Dies.

Othello. Why, how should she be murther'd?

Emilia. Alas, who knows?

Othello. You heard her say herself, it was not I.

Emilia. She said so; I must needs report the truth.

Othello. She's like a liar gone to burning hell;

'Twas I that kill'd her.

Emilia. Oh the more angel she,

And you the blacker devil!

Othello. She turn'd to folly, and she was a whore.

Emilia. Thou dost belie her, and thou art a devil.

Othello. She was false as water.

Emilia. Thou art rash as fire, to say

That she was false. Oh she was heavenly true.

Othello. Cassio did top her; ask thy husband else.

O, I were damn'd beneath all depth in hell,

① out of tune 走调

埃米莉亚 不,卡西奥没有死!

奥赛罗 卡西奥没有死!那么杀人认错了对象,痛快的复仇又有了变卦啦。

苔丝狄蒙娜 啊,死得好冤枉呀!

埃米莉亚 哎哟!那是什么呼声?

奥赛罗 哪!什么?

埃米莉亚 哎哟!那是夫人的声音。救命!救命啊!救命!啊,夫人,再说一声话儿!亲爱的苔丝狄蒙娜!啊,亲爱的夫人,说呀!

苔丝狄蒙娜 我是无罪而死的。

埃米莉亚 啊!这是谁干的事?

苔丝狄蒙娜 谁也没有干;是我自己。再会吧;替我向我的仁慈的夫君致意。啊,再会吧!(死)

奥赛罗 啊!她怎么会被人杀死的?

埃米莉亚 唉!谁知道?

奥赛罗 你听见她说是她自己,我没有杀死她。

埃米莉亚 她是这样说;我只好按照事实去报告。

奥赛罗 她到地狱的火焰里去,还不愿说一句真话。杀死她的是我。

埃米莉亚 啊,她多么的如同天使一般,你多么的是一个黑心的魔鬼!

奥赛罗 她干了无耻的事,她是个淫妇。

埃米莉亚 你冤枉她,你是个魔鬼。

奥赛罗 她像水一样轻浮。

埃米莉亚 你说她轻浮,你自己才像火一样粗暴。啊,她是圣洁而忠贞的!

奥赛罗 卡西奥和她通奸,不信你去问你的丈夫吧。啊,要是我采取这种极端的手段并没有正当的理由,死

ACT V

        But that I did proceed upon just grounds
        To this **extremity**①. Thy husband knew it all.

Emilia.   My husband?

Othello.   Thy husband.

Emilia.   That she was false to wedlock?

Othello.   Ay, with Cassio. Nay, had she been true,
        If heaven would make me such another world
        Of one entire and perfect **chrysolite**②,
        I'd not have sold her for it.

Emilia.   My husband?

Othello.   Ay, 'twas he that told me first.
        An honest man he is, and hates the **slime**③
        That sticks on filthy deeds.

Emilia.   My husband?

Othello.   What needs this **iteration**④, woman? I say thy husband.

Emilia.   Oh mistress, villainy hath made mocks with love!
        My husband say that she was false?

Othello.   He, woman;
        I say thy husband. Dost understand the word?
        My friend, thy husband, honest, honest Iago.

Emilia.   If he say so, may his pernicious soul
        Rot half a grain a day: he lies to the heart.
        She was too fond of her most filthy bargain.

Othello.   Hah?

Emilia.   Do thy worst;
        This deed of thine is no more worthy heaven
        Than thou wast worthy her.

Othello.   Peace, you were best.

Emilia.   Thou hast not half that power to do me harm,
        As I have to be hurt. O gull! O dolt!

① extremity [ik'stremiti] n. 激烈（或极端）措施

② chrysolite ['krisəulait] n. 贵橄榄石

③ slime [slaim] n. 烂泥

④ iteration [itə'reiʃən] n. 重复

后就要永远堕入地狱的底层！你的丈夫一切全都知道。

埃米莉亚 我的丈夫！

奥赛罗 你的丈夫。

埃米莉亚 他知道她不守贞节吗？

奥赛罗 嗯，他知道她跟卡西奥的暧昧。嘿，要是她是个贞洁的妇人，即使上帝为我用一颗完整的宝石另外造一个世界，我也不愿用她去交换。

埃米莉亚 我的丈夫！

奥赛罗 嗯，他最初告诉我这件事。他是个正人君子，他痛恨卑鄙龌龊的行为。

埃米莉亚 我的丈夫！

奥赛罗 妇人，为什么把这句话说了又说呢？我是说你的丈夫。

埃米莉亚 啊，夫人！你因为多情，受了奸人的愚弄了！我的丈夫说她不贞！

奥赛罗 正是他，妇人；我说你的丈夫；你懂得这句话吗？我的朋友，你的丈夫，正直的，正直的伊阿古。

埃米莉亚 要是他果然说了这样的话，愿他恶毒的灵魂每天一分一寸的糜烂！他全然胡说；她对她的最卑鄙的男人是太痴心了。

奥赛罗 吓！

埃米莉亚 随你把我怎么样吧。你配不上这样的好妻子，你这种行为是上天所不容的。

奥赛罗 还不闭嘴！

埃米莉亚 你没有半分力量可以伤害我，我也不能让人家把我欺侮。啊，笨蛋！傻瓜！泥土一样蠢的家

ACT V

           As ignorant as dirt! Thou hast done a deed
           I care not for thy sword; I'll make thee known,
           Though I lost twenty lives. Help! help, ho! help!
           The Moor hath kill'd my mistress! Murther, murther!

           Enter Montano, Gratiano, Iago and others.

Mont. What is the matter? How now, general?

Emilia. O, are you come, Iago? You have done well,
           That men must lay their murthers on your neck.

Gra. What is the matter?

Emilia. **Disprove**① this villain, if thou be'st a man.
           He says thou told'st him that his wife was false;
           I know thou didst not, thou'rt not such a villain.
           Speak, for my heart is full.

Iago. I told him what I thought, and told no more
           Than what he found himself was apt and true.

Emilia. But did you ever tell him she was false?

Iago. I did.

Emilia. You told a lie, an **odious**② damned lie;
           Upon my soul, a lie, a wicked lie.
           She false with Cassio? Did you say with Cassio?

Iago. With Cassio, mistress. Go to, charm your tongue.

Emilia. I will not charm my tongue; I am bound to speak.
           My mistress here lies murther'd in her bed.

All. O heavens forfend!

Emilia. And your reports have set the murther on.

Othello. Nay stare not, masters; it is true indeed.

Gra. 'Tis a strange truth.

Mont. O monstrous act!

Emilia. Villainy, villainy, villainy!
           I think upon 't, I think, I smell 't, O, villainy!

① disprove [dɪsˈpruːv] v. 证明（想法、信念或理论）为误

② odious [ˈəʊdɪəs] a. 可憎的

伙！你已经做了一件大大不该的事——我不怕你的剑；我要宣布你的罪恶，即使我将要因此而丧失二十条生命。救命！救命啊！救命！摩尔人杀死了夫人啦！杀了人啦！杀了人啦！

蒙塔诺、格拉蒂亚诺、伊阿古及余人等上。

蒙塔诺 什么事？怎么，将军！

埃米莉亚 啊！你来了吗？伊阿古？你做得好事，人家都把杀人的罪名架在你头上啦！

格拉蒂亚诺 什么事？

埃米莉亚 你倘是个汉子，赶快否认这恶人所说的话吧；他说你告诉他他的妻子不贞。我知道你不会说这种话，你还不会是这样一个恶人。说吧，我的心都要胀破了。

伊阿古 我不过把我自己的意思告诉他；我对他所说的话，已经由他自己证实了。

埃米莉亚 可是你有没有对他说她是不贞的？

伊阿古 我对他说过。

埃米莉亚 你说谎，一个可憎的、万恶不赦的谎！凭着我的灵魂起誓，一个谎，一个罪恶的谎！她跟卡西奥私通！你说她跟卡西奥私通吗？

伊阿古 跟卡西奥私通，太太。好了好了，收住你的舌头吧。

埃米莉亚 我不愿收住我的舌头；我必须说话。夫人在这床上给人谋杀了。

众人 啊，哪会有这样的事！

埃米莉亚 都是你造的谣言；引起这场血案。

奥赛罗 各位不必惊慌，这事情是真的。

ACT V

        I thought so then. I'll kill myself for grief.

        O villainy, villainy!

Iago.   What, are you mad? I charge you, get you home.

Emilia.   Good gentlemen, let me have leave to speak;

        'Tis proper I obey him, but not now.

        Perchance, Iago, I will ne'er go home.

        Othello falls on the bed.

Othello.   Oh, Oh, Oh.

Emilia.   Nay, lay thee down and roar;

        For thou hast kill'd the sweetest innocent,

        That e'er did lift up eye.

Othello.   [*Rises.*] Oh she was foul!

        I scaree did know you, uncle; there lies your niece,

        Whose breath indeed these hands have newly stopp'd.

        I know this act shows horrible and grim.

Gra.   Poor Desdemon: I am glad thy father's dead.

        Thy match was mortal to him, and pure grief

        Shore his old thread in twain; did he live now,

        This sight would make him do a desperate turn,

        Yea, curse his better angel from his side,

        And fall to **reprobation**[①].

Othello.   'Tis pitiful, but yet Iago knows

        That she with Cassio hath the act of shame

        A thousand times committed. Cassio confess'd it,

        And she did gratify his **amorous**[②] works

        With that **recognizance**[③] and pledge of love

        Which I first gave her. I saw it in his hand,

        It was a handkerchief, an antique token

        My father gave my mother.

Emilia.   Oh God! O, heavenly God!

格拉蒂亚诺　真有这样的事，那可奇了！

蒙塔诺　啊，骇人的行为！

埃米莉亚　诡计！诡计！诡计！我现在想起来了；啊，诡计！那时候我就有些怀疑；我要伤心死了！啊，诡计！诡计！

伊阿古　什么！你疯了吗？快给我回家去！

埃米莉亚　各位先生，让我有一个说话的机会。照理我应该服从他，可是现在却不能服从他。也许，伊阿古，我永远不再回家了。

奥赛罗　啊！啊！啊！（扑卧床上）

埃米莉亚　哼，你躺下来哭叫吧；因为你已经杀死一个世间最温柔纯洁的人。

奥赛罗　啊，她是淫污的！我简直不认识您啦，叔父。那边躺着您的侄女，她的呼吸刚才被我这双手扼断；我知道这行为在世人眼中看起来是惊人而残酷的。

格拉蒂亚诺　可怜的苔丝狄蒙娜！幸亏你父亲已经死了；你的婚事是他的致死的原因，悲伤摧折了他的衰老的生命。要是他现在还活着，看见这种惨状，一定会干出一些疯狂的事情来的；他会诅咒天地，赶走守护神，毁灭自己的灵魂。

奥赛罗　这诚然是一件伤心的事；可是伊阿古知道她曾经跟卡西奥干过许多回无耻的勾当，卡西奥自己也承认了。她还把我的定情礼物送给卡西奥，表示接受他的献媚。我看见它在他的手里；那是一方手帕，我的父亲给我的母亲的一件古老的纪念品。

埃米莉亚　天啊！天上的神明啊！

---

① reprobation [reprəuˈbeiʃən] n.【神学】摈弃

② amorous [ˈæmərəs] a. 多情的，求爱的

③ recognizance [riˈkɔgnizəns] n.［废语］符号；标志

Iago. 'Zounds! Hold your peace.

Emilia. 'Twill out, 'twill out. I peace?
No, I will speak as liberal as the north;
Let heaven and men and devils, let them all,
All, all, cry shame against me, yet I'll speak.

Iago. Be wise, and get you home.

Emilia. I will not.

Iago offers to stab Emilia.

Gra. Fie!
Your sword upon a woman.

Emilia. Oh thou dull Moor, That handkerchief thou speak'st of
I found by fortune and did give my husband,
For often with a solemn earnestness,
More than indeed belong'd to such a trifle,
He begg'd of me to steal it.

Iago. Villainous whore!

Emilia. She give it Cassio? No, alas, I found it,
And I did give 't my husband.

Iago. Filth, thou liest!

Emilia. By heaven, I do not, I do not gentlemen.
Oh murtherous **coxcomb**[①]! What should such a fool
Do with so good a wife?

Othello. Are there not stones in heaven,
But what serve for thunder? Precious villain.

The Moor runs at Iago. Iago kills his wife.

Gra. The woman falls; sure, he hath kill'd his wife.

Emilia. Ay, ay! O, lay me by my mistress' side.

Exit Iago.

Gra. He's gone, but his wife's kill'd.

Mont. 'Tis a notorious villain. Take you this weapon,

伊阿古　算了，闭住你的嘴！

埃米莉亚　事情总会暴露的，事情总会暴露的。闭住我的嘴？不，不，我要像北风一样自由地说话；让天神、世人和魔鬼全都把我嘲骂羞辱，我也要说我的话。

伊阿古　放明白一些，回家去吧。

埃米莉亚　我不愿回家。（伊阿古拔剑欲刺埃米莉亚）

格拉蒂亚诺　呸！你向一个妇人动武吗？

埃米莉亚　你这愚笨的摩尔人啊！你所说起的那方手帕，是我偶然拾到，把它给了我的丈夫的；虽然那只是一件小小的东西，他却几次三番恳求我替他偷了来。

伊阿古　长舌的淫妇！

埃米莉亚　她送给卡西奥！唉！不，是我拾到了，把它交给我的丈夫的。

伊阿古　贱人，你说谎！

埃米莉亚　苍天在上，我没有说谎；我没有说谎，各位先生。杀人的傻瓜啊！像你这样一个蠢材，怎么配得上这样好的一位妻子呢？

奥赛罗　天上没有石块，可以像雷霆一样打下来吗？好一个奸贼！（向伊阿古扑奔；伊阿古刺埃米莉亚逃下）

格拉蒂亚诺　这妇人倒下来了；他把他的妻子杀死了。

埃米莉亚　是，是；啊！把我放在夫人的身边吧！

格拉蒂亚诺　他走了，他的妻子给他杀了。

蒙塔诺　这是一个罪大恶极的凶徒。你拿着我从这摩尔

① coxcomb ['kɔksəum] n. （从前小丑戴的）鸡冠帽

Which I have here recover'd from the Moor.
Come, guard the door without; let him not pass,
But kill him rather. I'll after that same villain,
For 'tis a damned slave.
Exeunt all but Othello and Emilia.

Othello. I am not valiant neither,
But every **puny**① whipster gets my sword.
But why should honor outlive honesty?
Let it go all.

Emilia. What did thy song bode, lady?
Hark, canst thou hear me? I will play the swan,
And die in music: [*Sings.*] Willow, willow, willow.
Moor, she was chaste; she loved thee, cruel Moor;
So come my soul to bliss, as I speak true;
So speaking as I think, I die, I die. Dies.

Othello. I have another weapon in this chamber;
It is a sword of Spain, the ice-brook's temper—
Oh, here it is. Uncle, I must come forth.

Gra. [*Within.*] If thou attempt it, it will cost thee dear.
Thou hast no weapon, and **perforce**② must suffer.

Othello. Look in upon me then, and speak with me,
Or naked as I am, I will assault thee.
Enter Gratiano.

Gra. What is the matter?

Othello. Behold, I have a weapon;
A better never did itself sustain
Upon a soldier's thigh. I have seen the day,
That with this little arm and this good sword,
I have made my way through more impediments
Than twenty times your stop. But, Oh vain boast,

人手里夺下来的剑。来，在门外看守好了，别让他出去；他要是想逃走，尽管把他杀死。我要去追那恶人，那是一个不可宽恕的家伙。（蒙塔诺、葛莱西安诺下）

奥赛罗 我的勇气也离我而去了，每一个孱弱的懦夫都可以夺下我的剑来。可是奸恶既然战胜正直，哪里还会有荣誉存在呢？让一切都归于幻灭吧！

埃米莉亚 你的歌儿是一个谶兆吗？夫人？听，你听没听见我的声音？我要像天鹅一般在歌声里死去。（唱）

   杨柳，杨柳，杨柳……

摩尔人，她是贞洁的；她爱你，狠心的摩尔人。我说的是真话，愿我的灵魂享受天福；我的话是跟我的思想一致的。我死了，我死了。（死）

奥赛罗 我还有一柄剑在这屋子里，那是一柄用冰泉的水所浸炼的西班牙宝剑。啊，在这儿！叔父，我一定要出去。

格拉蒂亚诺 （在内）你要是敢试一试，就得付重大的代价；你没有武器，只好屈服。

奥赛罗 那么进来瞧瞧我吧，我有话对你说；否则我虽然没有武器，也只好不顾一切跟你拼一下了。

   格拉蒂亚诺重上。

格拉蒂亚诺 什么事？

奥赛罗 瞧！我有一柄剑；从来没有一个战士的身边佩带过比它更好的剑；凭着这一条小小的胳臂和这一柄利剑，我曾经冲破二十倍于你们这样人数的包围；可是，无聊的夸口啊！谁能主宰他自己的命运呢？现在我已经没有那样的本领了。虽然你看我拿着武器，可是不用害怕，这儿是我的旅途的终

① puny ['pju:ni] *a.* 小的；弱的

② perforce [pə'fɔ:s] *ad.* 必然地

ACT V

Who can control his fate? 'tis not so now.
Be not afraid, though you do see me weapon'd;
Here is my journey's end, here is my butt
And very sea-mark of my utmost sail.
Do you go back dismay'd? 'Tis a lost fear:
Man but a rush against Othello's breast,
And he retires. Where should Othello go?
Now, how dost thou look now? Oh ill-starr'd wench!
Pale as thy **smock**①! When we shall meet at compt,
This look of thine will hurl my soul from heaven,
And fiends will **snatch at**② it. Cold, cold, my girl?
Even like thy **chastity**③. O cursed, cursed slave!
Whip me, ye devils,
From the possession of this heavenly sight:
Blow me about in winds! Roast me in sulphur!
Wash me in steep-down gulfs of liquid fire!
Oh, Desdemon! Dead, Desdemon! Dead!

Enter Lodovico, Montano, Cassio carried in a chair, and Officers with Iago, prisoner.

Lodo. Where is this rash and most unfortunate man?

Othello. That's he that was Othello. Here I am.

Lodo. Where is that **viper**④? Bring the villain forth.

Othello. I look down towards his feet; but that's a **fable**⑤.
 If that thou be'st a devil, I cannot kill thee.

Lodo. Wrench his sword from him.

Iago. I bleed, sir, but not kill'd.

Othello. I am not sorry neither. I'ld have thee live,
 For in my sense, 'tis happiness to die.

Lodo. Oh, thou Othello, that wert once so good,
 Fall'n in the practice of a damned slave,

① smock [smɔk] n.（画家、营业员等穿的）罩衫
② snatch at 抓取
③ chastity ['tʃæstəti] n. 贞节

④ viper ['vaipə] n. 毒蛇
⑤ fable ['feibl] n. 传说

点，我的航程的最后的目标。你吓得退走了吗？这是不必要的惊恐；谁只要拿一根灯草向奥赛罗的胸前挺了过来，他也会向后退缩的。奥赛罗应该到什么地方去呢？——啊，让我再看看你的脸吧，薄命的女郎！像你的衬衣一样惨白！我们在天庭对簿的时候，你这一副脸色就可以把我的灵魂赶下天堂，让魔鬼把它抓去。你的全身冰冷，我的恋人！正像你的贞洁一样凛若寒霜。啊，该死的，该死的奴才！魔鬼啊，把我从这天仙一样美人的面前鞭逐出去吧！让狂风把我吹卷，硫黄把我熏烤，沸汤的深渊把我沉浸吧！啊，苔丝狄蒙娜！苔丝狄蒙娜！死了！啊！啊！啊！

　　　　　洛多维科、蒙塔诺、二侍从舁卡西奥卧椅中，警吏等押伊阿古同上。

洛多维科　　这鲁莽而不幸的人在哪儿？

奥赛罗　　那就是从前的奥赛罗；我在这儿。

洛多维科　　那条毒蛇呢？把这恶人带上来。

奥赛罗　　据说魔鬼的脚是分趾的，让我看看他的脚是不是这样。要是你真的是一个魔鬼，我也不能杀死你。
　　　　　（刺伤伊阿古）

洛多维科　　把他手里的剑夺下来。

伊阿古　　我不过流了点儿血，还没有给他杀死。

奥赛罗　　那也好，我要你留着活命；因为在我看来，死倒是一桩幸福。

洛多维科　　啊，奥赛罗！你本来是一个很好的汉子，却会中一个万恶的奸人的诡计，我们该说你什么呢？

ACT V

          What shall be said to thee.

Othello.   Why! any thing;
          An honorable murtherer, if you will,
          For nought did I in hate, but all in honor.

Lodo.   This wretch hath part confess'd his villainy.
          Did you and he consent in Cassio's death?

Othello.   Ay.

Cassio.   Dear general, I never gave you cause.

Othello.   I do believe it, and I ask your pardon.
          Will you, I pray, demand that demi-devil,
          Why he hath thus ensnared my soul and body?

Iago.   Demand me nothing; what you know, you know.
          From this time forth I never will speak word.

Lodo.   What, not to pray?

Gra.   Torments will ope your lips.

Othello.   Well, thou dost best.

Lodo.   Sir, you shall understand what hath befall'n,
          Which, as I think, you know not. Here is a letter
          Found in the pocket of the slain Roderigo,
          And here another. The one of them imports
          The death of Cassio to be undertook
          By Roderigo.

Othello.   O, villain!

Cassio.   Most **heathenish**[①] and most gross!

Lodo.   Now here's another **discontented**[②] paper,
          Found in his pocket too; and this, it seems,
          Roderigo meant to have sent this damned villain;
          But that, belike, Iago **in the interim**[③]
          Came in and satisfied him.

Othello.   O, thou pernicious caitiff!

奥赛罗　随便你们怎么说吧；要是你们愿意，不妨说我是一个正直的凶手，因为我所干的事，都是出于荣誉的观念，不是出于猜嫌的私恨。

洛多维科　这恶人已经承认了一部分他的奸谋；杀死卡西奥是你跟他同谋的吗？

奥赛罗　是的。

卡西奥　主帅，我从来不曾得罪过您。

奥赛罗　我相信你的话；请你原谅我吧。你们问一问那个顶着人头的恶魔，为什么他要这样陷害我的灵魂和肉体？

伊阿古　什么也不要问我；你们所知道的，你们已经知道了；从这一刻起，我不再说一句话。

洛多维科　什么？你也不要祈祷吗？

格拉蒂亚诺　酷刑可以逼你开口。

奥赛罗　你还是说吧。

洛多维科　将军，一切经过，你将会明白的，我相信你现在还一点也不知道。这是从已死的罗德利哥衣袋里搜到的一封信；这儿还有一封；其中一封信里说到杀死卡西奥的事情由罗德利哥动手执行。

奥赛罗　啊，奸贼！

卡西奥　野蛮残忍的阴谋！

洛多维科　这儿还有从他的衣袋里找到的一封充满怨言的信，看来好像是罗德利哥预备寄给这个万恶的奸人的；可是信还没有寄出，伊阿古就来给他满足了。

奥赛罗　啊，恶毒的奸贼！卡西奥，我的妻子的手帕怎

① heathenish ['hi:ðəniʃ] *a.* （似）异教徒的

② discontented [diskən'tentid] *a.* 不满的

③ in the interim 在其间

ACT V

        How came you, Cassio, by that handkerchief
        That was my wife's?

Cassio. I found it in my chamber;
        And he himself confess'd but even now,
        That there he dropp'd it for a special purpose,
        Which wrought to his desire.

Othello. O, fool! fool! fool!

Cassio. There is besides in Roderigo's letter,
        How he **upbraids**① Iago, that he made him
        Brave me upon the watch, whereon it came
        That I was cast. And even but now he spake
        After long seeming dead, Iago hurt him,
        Iago set him on.

Lodo. You must forsake this room, and go with us.
        Your power and your command is taken off,
        And Cassio rules in Cyprus. For this slave,
        If there be any cunning cruelty,
        That can torment him much and hold him long,
        It shall be his. You shall close prisoner rest,
        Till that the nature of your fault be known
        To the Venetian state. Come, bring away.

Othello. Soft you; a word or two before you go.
        I have done the state some service, and they know 't.
        No more of that. I pray you in your letters,
        When you shall these unlucky deeds relate,
        Speak of me as I am. Nothing **extenuate**②,
        Nor set down aught in malice. Then must you speak,
        Of one that loved not wisely but too well;
        Of one not easily jealous, but being wrought,
        Perplex'd③ in the extreme, of one whose hand,

么会到你手里的？

卡西奥　我在我的房间里找到它；他刚才已经亲口承认是他有意把它丢在那里，借此可以达到他自己的图谋。

奥赛罗　啊，傻瓜！傻瓜！傻瓜！

卡西奥　在罗德利哥的信里，他又埋怨伊阿古不该撺掇他在我值夜的时候向我寻事；我就是为了那一回事情而被撤职的。就在刚才，他从长时间的昏迷中醒了过来，还说起他一切都受伊阿古指使，结果却是伊阿古的剑伤了他的生命。

洛多维科　你必须离开这所屋子，跟我们去；你的军队和兵权必须全部交卸，让卡西奥主持塞浦路斯的军政重务。对于这一个家伙，我们将要用一切巧妙的酷刑加在他的身上，使他遍受种种的痛苦，而不至于立刻死去。我们还要把你严密监禁，等候威尼斯政府判决你的罪状。来，把他带下去。

奥赛罗　且慢，在你们未走以前，再听我说一两句话。我对于国家曾经立过相当的功绩，这是执政诸公所知道的；那些话现在也不用说了。当你们把这种不幸的事实报告他们的时候，请你们在公文上老老实实照我本来的样子叙述，不要徇情回护，也不要恶意构陷；你们应当说我是一个在恋爱上不智而过于深情的人；一个不容易发生嫉妒，可是一旦被人煽动以后，就会感到极度烦恼的人；一个像那愚蠢的印度人一般，把一颗比他整个部落所有的

---

① upbraid [ʌpˈbreid] v. 责备；谴责

② extenuate [ikˈstenjueit] v. （用偏袒的辩解或借口）减轻（或企图减轻）（罪行、过错等）严重性（或程度）

③ perplexed [pəˈplekst] a. 困惑的；茫然不知所措的

ACT V

          Like the base Indian, threw a pearl away
          Richer than all his tribe, of one whose subdued eyes,
          Albeit① unused to the melting mood,
          Drop tears as fast as the Arabian trees
          Their medicinal gum. Set you down this;
          And say besides, that in Aleppo once,
          Where a **malignant**② and a turban'd Turk
          Beat a Venetian and **traduced**③ the state,
          I took by the throat the **circumcised**④ dog,
          And **smote**⑤ him, thus.
          Stabs himself.

Lodo.   O bloody period.

Gra.   All that's spoke is marr'd.

Othello.   I kiss'd thee ere I kill'd thee. No way but this,
          Killing myself, to die upon a kiss.
          Falls on the bed and dies.

Cassio.   This did I fear, but thought he had no weapon;
          For he was great of heart.

Lodo.   [*To Iago.*] Oh Spartan dog,
          More fell than anguish, hunger, or the sea:
          Look on the tragic loading of this bed;
          This is thy work. The object poisons sight;
          Let it be hid. Gratiano, keep the house,
          And seize upon the fortunes of the Moor,
          For they succeed on you. To you, lord Governor,
          Remains the censure of this hellish villain,
          The time, the place, the torture. Oh inforce it:
          Myself will straight aboard, and to the state,
          This heavy act with heavy heart relate.
          Exeunt.

① albeit [ɔ:l'bi:it] conj. 尽管，即使
② malignant [mə'lignənt] a. 恶意的
③ traduce [trə'dju:s] v. 诋毁
④ circumcised ['sɜ:kəmsaizd] a. 受过割礼的
⑤ smite [smait] v. 打，重击

财产更贵重的珍珠随手抛弃的人；一个虽然不惯于流妇人之泪，可是当他被感情征服的时候，也会像涌流着胶液的阿拉伯胶树一般两眼泛滥的人。请你们把这些话记下，再补充一句说：在阿勒坡地方，曾经有一个裹着头巾、怀着敌意的土耳其人殴打一个威尼斯人，诽谤我们的国家，那时候我就一把抓住这受割礼的狗子的咽喉，就这样把他杀了。（以剑自刺）

洛多维科 啊，残酷的结局！

格拉蒂亚诺 一切说过的话，现在又要改变过来了。

奥赛罗 我在杀死你以前，曾经用一吻和你诀别；现在我自己的生命也在一吻里终结。（倒扑苔丝狄蒙娜身上，死）

卡西奥 我早就担心会有这样的事发生，可是我还以为他没有武器；他的心地是光明正大的。

洛多维科 （向伊阿古）你这比痛苦、饥饿和大海更凶暴的猛犬啊！瞧瞧这床上浴血的尸身吧；这是你干的好事。这样伤心惨目的景象，赶快把它遮盖起来吧。格拉蒂亚诺，请您接收这一座屋子；这摩尔人的全部家产，都应该归您继承。总督大人。怎么处置这一个恶魔般的奸徒，什么时候，什么地点，用怎样的刑法，都要请您全权办理，千万不要宽纵他！我现在就要上船回去禀明政府，用一颗悲哀的心报告这一段悲哀的事故。（同下）